ML

This book is to be returned on or before
the last date stamped below.

JUN. 18. 1982

-1. JUN 1984

12 2 JAN 1999 ◇

89/211
Due 21·12·89

1 0 JUN 1993

-2 4 MAY 1994-

LIBREX —

Oriental Architecture
in the West

Patrick Conner

Oriental Architecture in the West

with 154 illustrations
14 in colour

Thames and Hudson

For Anna

© 1979 Thames and Hudson Ltd, London

Filmset and printed in Great Britain by
BAS Printers Limited, Over Wallop, Hampshire

Contents

Preface

THIS BOOK is devoted to a group of architectural mongrels; many of them are delightful, but few have ever been entirely acceptable to conventional tastes. These buildings (or projected buildings) in Europe and North America are not faithful reproductions, but *interpretations* of oriental architecture – a very different matter – conceived between the last years of the seventeenth century and the middle of the nineteenth. It would be possible to venture into the twentieth century, to consider, for example, the influence of the Orient on the Bauhaus or on Frank Lloyd Wright, or perhaps to correlate the spread of oriental motifs in western cities with the rise in consumption of chow mein and Madras curry. But such topics as these lie beyond the scope of this study.

'Oriental' is a vague term, which usefully reflects the failure of many eighteenth-century Europeans to distinguish between the different civilizations of the East. Nevertheless it requires some definition. For present purposes it is taken to include Chinese, Japanese and Indian styles, and in some instances Turkish, but not Egyptian, whose influence requires a separate study, nor Moorish, although a case could be made for its inclusion.

Given these limitations, however, do the oriental pavilions and palaces of the West deserve a book to themselves? I believe they do, and primarily on their own merits – for the charm and grace of many of the small Chinese structures which decorated the parks of eighteenth-century Europe, and for the extravagant display of their nineteenth-century successors. Such buildings are still liable to be dismissed as 'gimcrack' or 'pseudo-oriental', just as the Gothic Revival was until quite recently considered to be 'in poor taste' and a little ridiculous. But their hybrid nature can also be seen as a potential source of novel and exciting design. The cross-breeding of Chinese with classical, of Chinese with Gothic, and even of Chinese with Indian, has produced a variety of unorthodox progeny, some of which are – perhaps unpredictably – most attractive.

Second, the circumstances surrounding their design are often of unusual interest. Anglo-oriental structures could claim neither the historical justification of Gothic architecture nor the prestige of Greek culture, and they have always been an easy prey to hostile critics. Even at the height of the vogue for chinoiserie in England it must have required a considerable measure of self-confidence, or disregard for conservative opinion, to erect a Chinese kiosk in one's garden. (Roman temples were likely to be more expensive, but less controversial.) In practice it seems that the choice of a Chinese or an Indian style was prompted either by some strong aesthetic preference or by a specific connection with the Far East.

Nevertheless there are discernible patterns in the popularity of both Chinese and Indian styles. The fluctuations of each were governed by several factors – the availability of well authenticated patterns, the public image of India or China at any particular time, and current attitudes to landscape gardening. The evolution of the landscape garden in England had a particularly decisive bearing on the European fashion for oriental pavilions, and it is the tradition of Anglo-oriental architecture which is the main subject of this book. Related developments in Europe and North America are considered in less detail; in defence of this policy it may be said that specialized studies of oriental architecture on the Continent have already been made, notably Eleanor von Erdberg's *Chinese Influence on European Garden Structures* (1936), which is most useful in its treatment of German architecture, and Osvald Sirén's *China and the Gardens of Europe* (1950), which contains the best documentation of Sweden and France. It is the ambition of the present volume to complement these works rather than to supersede them.

Many people have contributed to this project, but I would particularly like to thank Sir John Addis, Mr Allan Braham, Mr John Dinkel and Mr John Harris for reading the chapters relevant to their own specialized knowledge, and for making many valuable suggestions; also Dr Marcia Pointon for casting a sharp eye over the whole, and my wife Edwina for astute editorial advice. For their friendly hospitality I am grateful to Mrs Doreen Beaumont at Harristown, to Mr and Mrs Hegarty at Hope End, to Mr John Ladhams in Lisbon, and to Mrs Susanna Peake at Sezincote. I appreciate the assistance of the Royal Library at Windsor, the British Library, the British Architectural Library and Drawings Collection, the Bodleian Library, the National Gallery, the Library of the Royal Botanic Gardens at Kew, the Public Libraries of Chelsea and Gravesend, and the Record Offices of Bedfordshire, Leeds, Southampton, Staffordshire and Wiltshire; and of Brighton Reference Library, whose staff have been repeatedly helpful in every way. The editors of *Apollo* and *Country Life* have kindly allowed me to make use of material first published in article form.

I must also thank Mr Mark Bence-Jones; Mrs J. Bishop and Mrs J. Boston of the Holburne of Menstrie Museum at Bath; Mrs Jill Bryant; Mr George Clarke of Stowe School; Mr J. F. J. Collett-White, Assistant Archivist of Bedfordshire Record Office; Sir Francis Dashwood, Bt; Mr Michael Day of the Norfolk Museums Service; Mr Giles Eyre of Hartnoll & Eyre Ltd; Mr Brian Field, Senior Architect of the Department of the Environment (Historic Buildings branch); Mr Brian Knox; Mr S. H. E. Mansbridge; Mr John Morley, Director of the Royal Pavilion, Art Gallery and Museums, Brighton; the Pilgrimage Club of Natchez, Mississippi; Mr Ian Phillips; Mr John Redmill of Donald Insall and Partners; Mrs Pauline Rohatgi of the India Office Library; Mrs Susan Sloman; Mr F. B. Stitt, Archivist of the William Salt Library; Miss Dorothy Stroud; Mr W. T. C. Walker, Assistant County Architect of North Yorkshire; Weinreb Architectural Books; and Miss Joanne Wilkins, Curator of Knebworth House.

P.R.M.C.

Chapter One
The House of Pleasure: Medieval Interpretations

WHEN Coleridge dreamt of Kublai Khan, and awoke to record a fragment of his dream, he included a curiously inappropriate phrase in his second line:

In Xanadu did Kubla Khan
A stately pleasure-dome decree . . .

The jarring words are 'stately pleasure-dome'. Coleridge's contemporaries were well acquainted with oriental pleasure-buildings: in parks and gardens from Poland to Portugal, oriental pavilions were to be found, carefully situated within their landscaped surroundings. Such buildings were essentially *jeux d'esprit*; they could be extravagantly ornate, or light and insubstantial, but 'stately' they could not be. Coleridge had in fact borrowed the word (as he later acknowledged) from Purchas's abridgement of Marco Polo's *Travels*, which he had been reading when he fell asleep:

In Xaindu did Cublai Can build a stately pallace, encompassing sixteene mile of plaine ground with a wall, wherein are fertile meddowes, pleasant springs, delightfull streames, and all sorts of beasts of chase and game, and in the middest thereof a sumptuous house of pleasure which may be removed from place to place.[1]

So Kublai Khan's 'stately pallace' and the movable 'house of pleasure' were two distinct buildings, merged into one in Coleridge's drowsy imagination. But it was the oriental house of pleasure, not the oriental palace, which European architects and patrons had taken to heart. According to the canons of the landscape garden which prevailed in late eighteenth-century Europe, the grounds of a mansion should form a 'natural' variety of hills and groves, lakes and streams, with garden temples, bridges and pavilions, classical, gothic or oriental, deliberately positioned to surprise and delight the visitor. It is true that the immediate inspiration for such landscape gardens came largely from England, but China had for many years enjoyed

a high reputation in the arts of gardening and garden architecture. Even in the thirteenth century these aspects of Kublai Khan's civilization were of great interest to the visiting Venetian, Marco Polo.

Shang-tu (or Xaindu, or Xanadu) lies a hundred miles beyond the Great Wall to the north of Peking, and it was the most northerly point in Cathay that Marco Polo visited. The ruins of the city and palace still remain. Marco Polo's account of Shang-tu, which has been borrowed and abridged in travel volumes ever since, deals rather briefly with Kublai's palace, built 'of marble and other handsome stone', before turning to its adjoining park, with meadows, rivulets and animals:

In the centre of these grounds, where there is a beautiful grove of trees, he has built a royal pavilion, supported upon a colonnade of handsome pillars, gilt and varnished. Round each pillar a dragon, likewise gilt, entwines its tail, whilst its head sustains the projection of the roof, and its talons or claws are extended to the right and left along the entablature. The roof is of bamboo cane, likewise gilt, and so well varnished that no wet can injure it . . . The building is supported on every side (like a tent) by more than two hundred very strong silken cords, as otherwise, from the lightness of the materials, it would be liable to oversetting by the force of high winds. The whole is constructed with so much ingenuity of contrivance that all the parts may be taken asunder, removed, and again set up, at his majesty's pleasure.[2]

Here Kublai Khan resided in the summer months, but he spent his winters in the city of Kanbalu (Peking). The royal palace at Kanbalu, 'the most extensive that has ever yet been known', lay within three sets of walls. It was a single-storey colonnaded building on a raised pavement. Marco Polo also observed that its walls were richly gilt and painted; the exterior of its roof was coloured in red, green, azure and violet; and the beautiful chambers were 'so admirably disposed that it seems impossible to suggest any improvement to the system of their arrangement'. It was a splendid palace, duly praised by the Italian visitor, but he was no less impressed by a subsidiary feature. In the palace grounds the Khan had set up an artificial mountain of earth, about a mile in circuit, and created lakes and a stream from the resulting excavations. The hill was planted with evergreen trees, and called the Green Mount. 'On its summit is erected an ornamental pavilion, which is likewise entirely green. The view of this altogether, – the mount itself, the trees, and the building, form a delightful and at the same time a wonderful scene.'[3] The Green Mount can be identified today as Coal Hill, a fertile artificial hill just to the north of the Forbidden City, although now it has five pavilions on its summit. On this hill in 1643 the last Ming Emperor chose to hang himself from the branches of a sophora tree; in the following century Catherine the Great of Russia is said to have used one of its pavilions as a model in building her palace at Tsarskoe Selo.

Marco Polo was not the first to bring back to the western world information about Tartary, which under the Great Khans extended over much of the Asian continent. In 1246 the Franciscan Johannes de Plano Carpini crossed Russia and reached the camp of Kuyuk Khan near Karakorum, carrying a letter from Pope Innocent IV. Although he died from the rigours of the journey, Carpini's report of the nomadic 'Mongals or Tartars' was the first of any reliability to reach the Christian world. It included the observation (as related in Richard Hakluyt's edition of 1598–1600) that 'their habitations bee rounde and cunningly made with wickers and staves in manner of a tent'.[4] William de Rubruquis, sent by Louis IX to Tartary in 1253, confirmed that the Tartars slept in houses set up on 'a round foundation of wickers artificially wrought and compacted together',[5] and decorated with coloured felt painted with scenes of vines, trees, birds and beasts. It was in the following decade that Kublai Khan established his residence at Kanbalu in Cathay proper, where the Polos entered his employ and spent some twenty years in the Far East before returning to Venice in 1295.

Marco Polo's vivid *Travels* was succeeded by the most informative of the early missionary reports, that of Odoric of Pordenone, who spent several years in India and Cathay in the 1320s.

On his return he dictated an account of his journeys which was widely circulated in manuscript and then in print. But Odoric's experiences became still better known to European readers through the plagiarizing pen of 'Sir John Mandeville', mistakenly described by Samuel Purchas, the Jacobean collector of travel-journals, as 'the greatest Asian traveller that ever the world had'.[6] Mandeville's *Travels* was probably written in the 1360s: the earliest surviving manuscript, in French, is dated 1371. It consists of a cleverly integrated amalgam of genuine travel accounts, many of them already gathered together in Vincent de Beauvais's encyclopaedic *Speculum Mundi*. The narrative is presented as the author's eyewitness account, and it is full of cunning modesty and earnest disclaimers which reinforce that effect.

Much of the first half of the *Travels* describes the Biblical sites of the Middle East, but the fictitious traveller then moved irregularly eastward, noticing Amazonia ('that is the land of Feminye') and the monopods of Aethiopia, the rich islands of Java, and all manner of tribes, from one-eyed giants to tongueless pygmies who hissed like adders. At last he reached Cathay, which he populated less densely with monstrous beings because his description of the cities of Cathay was taken directly from Odoric, with a few minor alterations to create an effect of authenticity. At Peking Odoric (and 'Mandeville') declared the pavilion on the Green Mount to be the most beautiful in existence. In the Imperial Palace itself Odoric counted fourteen pillars of gold, and observed that the walls were hung with red skins; in Mandeville the gold pillars number twenty-four, and the wall coverings are hides of panthers. A curiosity of the palace was its peacocks made of gold, which moved their wings and tail, 'either by diabolic art, or by some engine underground', Odoric supposed.[7] Mandeville claimed that the peacocks sang in addition, and that in all sciences and crafts the men of Cathay were more subtle than any others.

The *Travels* then took Mandeville to India, and to less reliable literary sources. He found 'Ind' to consist of several thousand islands ruled by the Christian emperor Prester John. Here were more exotic creatures, some wholly imaginary and others merely unfamiliar, such as the orafle, a spotted creature with a very long neck – 'and he may look over a great high house'. Houses did not themselves much occupy Mandeville's attention, apart from the palaces of kings and potentates, which he predictably found laden with gold and precious stones. But when he came to 'the Isles coasting to Prester John's land' Mandeville described a certain rich man's gardens in terms which again adumbrate the European pleasure-ground:

And in the mid place of one of his gardens is a little mountain, where there is a little meadow. And in that meadow is a little toothill [observatory] with towers and pinnacles, all of gold. And in that little toothill will he sit often-time, for to take the air and to disport him. For the place is made for nothing else, but only for his disport.[8]

For several centuries after its composition, Mandeville's *Travels* played a large part in determining the image of the Orient in European minds. It was much the most popular travel book of its time, and several hundred manuscript versions survive, in a dozen languages. Abridgements of the *Travels* were still common in the eighteenth century, and at least one chap-book contains woodcuts showing the exploits of a Mandeville in eighteenth-century costume. Only in the nineteenth century was it demonstrated that the author had never seen the lands he so vividly described.

Political unrest in China, culminating in the expulsion of the Mongols in 1368, halted communications with Europe, which was itself suffering from the effects of the Black Death and the Hundred Years' War. Under the succeeding Ming dynasty it was made illegal (until 1533) for Chinese merchants to trade with Europe, and little was added to Europeans' understanding of China for more than a hundred years. The greatest obstacle to trade, during this interval, was the continent of Africa. The first nation to get round it was Portugal, led by Vasco da Gama, and for most of the century that followed his discovery of the sea route to the East, European trade with India and China was dominated by that country. It is not surprising that Portugal can claim to have been the first European nation to adopt oriental elements into its architecture to any significant extent.

In 1492 Christopher Columbus had set out westwards for China, with a letter to the Great Khan; but he was distracted from his mission by the West Indies and trade relations between Western Europe and China were held up for nearly a decade. Vasco da Gama sailed eastwards five years later, rounded the Cape of Good Hope, and on 20 May 1498 came to Calicut on the Malabar coast of India. Other expeditions soon followed. By setting up a naval base at Goa in 1510 the Portuguese made their trading position secure; they made contact with Chinese merchants in India, and presently reached China itself, although their foothold at Macao was not achieved until 1557. India and its spices remained their prime object for the first half of the century – during which period a dramatic development occurred in Portuguese architecture, which it is tempting to ascribe to the recently established contacts with India.

Imagery of Far Eastern origin was not entirely new to Europe, for oriental creatures had figured in European ecclesiastical sculpture since Romanesque times. Cynocephalic Indians on the twelfth-century tympanum at Vézelay can still be seen, as may an elephant and a sciapod at Sens, a dragon at Poitiers, and many similar beasts and demons, derived in the first instance from illuminated manuscripts; with these we are not directly concerned. But in sixteenth-century Portugal the influence of the Far East may for the first time have been strong enough to affect whole systems of architectural detail in a series of major Portuguese buildings. However we are now entering upon a matter of mystery and controversy. For the architecture under debate is the Manueline style – which has no equivalent outside Portugal, no obvious antecedents, and very little documentary material which might help us to understand its purposes. It arrived, quite suddenly, in the early years of the sixteenth century, and lasted for one generation only. Even the nationality of its leading architect, Diogo Boytac, is not known, although one may guess from his name that he was French.

The *estilo Manoelino* cannot be mistaken: it is a riot of extravagant contortions and elaborate detail. It takes its name from the reign of Manoel I (1495–1521), 'The Fortunate', who presided over the rapid expansion of Portuguese trade in the Far East which followed Vasco da Gama's discovery of the sea route to India. In fact the development of the eastern trade coincided closely with the flowering of this very idiosyncratic form of decoration; and the first great Manueline structure, the Jerónimos church at Belém, Lisbon, was largely built immediately after the return of Vasco da Gama from Calicut in the summer of 1499. The double cloister at Jerónimos consists of broad, round-headed arches with flowing tendril-like tracery, which in the upper storey takes the form of a pair of

1

scalloped lights whose central mullion stops short of the top of the arch. In this cloister the Manueline motifs of carved plants, ropes and nautical apparatus made perhaps their first appearance, under the direction of Diogo Boytac. Towards the middle of the century João de Castilho added detail in a Renaissance idiom, including sculptured friezes above each set of arches; and in the finials which project upwards from the lower frieze, conspicuously Indian-looking figures gaze out of their niches.

It is difficult to resist the conclusion that the sudden introduction of such a lavish, intricate style was inspired by the example of Indian architecture. But Portugal was subject to several competing influences at this time, Moorish and Spanish in particular; one can only judge each building on its merits.

Another example is the Tower of Belém, which stands near the Jerónimos at the edge of the Tagus. This fortress was built between 1515 and 1519, by which time communication between India and Portugal was well established, and the tower has an undeniably Islamic aspect. Again the question arises: was this influence received from the Mughal architecture of India,

1 The cloisters at the Church of the Jerónimos, Lisbon

2 The Tower of Belém, Lisbon

or did it reach Belém by way of the coastal forts of Morocco? The architect was Francisco de Arruda, who had extensive experience in North African military architecture, and the corbelled parapet with its concave merlons is certainly Moorish, as are the little mullioned balconies. The ribbed cupolas which flank and surmount the tower are a more doubtful and tantalizing case.[9] Perhaps the only part of the building which is incontrovertibly Indian is the rhinoceros carved on the north-west outer wall, which must surely derive from the rhinoceros sent as a gift to King Manoel by the Sultan of Gujarat. It arrived in Lisbon to great acclaim in May 1515, and helped to dispel the tradition that the rhinoceros and the unicorn were one and the same.[10]

Many of the distinctive motifs of Manueline architecture clearly represent Portugal's prowess at sea. The twisted rope which forms the string-courses at the Tower of Belém reappears, thoroughly knotted, at the Convent of Christ at Tomar, whose nave buttresses are encrusted with coral shapes as if the building had been submerged for several centuries. The nave and chapter house were added to the already existing monastery buildings in about 1514, in recognition of the maritime achievements of the Knights of Christ, and their architect was Diogo de Arruda, brother of the architect of Belém Tower. The result is a thick conglomeration of symbolic external decoration, notably around the rectangular lower window of the chapter house, which has ropes, floats and chain, seaweed and coral, the face of a sailor beneath, the armillary spheres of Dom Manuel at each side above, and above all the square cross of the order. Possibly this window drew 'inspiration from India in its inconceivable elaboration both of form and surface', as has been suggested,[11] but the effect of the window is not quite that of an Indian temple's sculptured surface; it stands out rather as a huge achievement of arms, with its crest, wreath, mantling and charges appropriate to an order of navigators.

3 Window tracery in the
Claustro Real, Batalha

One further group of buildings in Portugal must be mentioned, although its ancestry is as disputable as the others: the monastery of Batalha. Much of the monastery was built at an earlier date, but its most spectacular detailing is Manueline, such as the closely carved tracery (attributed to Boytac) in the splendid *Claustro Real*. Each side has seven arches, whose tracery is alternately grille-like, with cusped perforations, and sinuously flowing. Both patterns seem to exclude more light than they admit, as is often the case in Moorish tracery; they cast a beautifully variegated shadow into the cloisters when the sun is not quite overhead. The plant forms in the stonework appear to be poppy and artichoke, but might possibly represent the Indian lotus.

The *Capelas Imperfeitas* near by are another matter – Manueline again, partly by Boytac, but the main doorway designed by Mateus Fernandes shortly before his death in 1515. It is

this entrance, with its swirling, multiform arches and dense carving left open to the sky, which is most often referred to as 'Indian'. Its architect shared his surname with the military architect Diogo Fernandes, who was working in India shortly beforehand, but apart from that most tenuous connection there is no documentary evidence to link the *Capelas* with the East. Once again the case is unproved. It is almost certain that Manueline architecture borrowed a few details from the temples of India; but to attribute to India the tortuous, writhing spirit of that style is to go beyond the evidence available. In any case Indian motifs did not reappear in European building for more than two hundred years. And when in the late seventeenth and early eighteenth centuries the curiosity of Europeans was again aroused by oriental architecture, they turned not to India but to the pavilions and pagodas of China.

14

Chapter Two

The Porcelain Pagoda and its Offspring

While the Manueline style developed and then declined, information about the Orient in general was beginning to flow more rapidly into Europe, by way of Portugal and Spain. The first detailed accounts of Chinese life arrived back in Lisbon in the 1520s, having been written in a Cantonese prison by two members of Portugal's first official embassy to China. Other reports followed, sent by Portuguese and Spanish missionaries in China, India, Indonesia and Japan, and several of these included interesting references to the temples and palaces they saw. It has been estimated that in Portugal between 1540 and 1600, more pages were printed on the subject of the Far East than on any other non-religious topic.[1]

Most of these reports were not translated or read outside Iberia, but Juan Gonzalez de Mendoza's *Historia . . . del gran Reyno de la China*, published in Rome in 1585, reached a much wider audience. Pope Gregory XIII had instructed this Spanish Augustinian to set down 'the things that are known about the kingdom of China', which Mendoza did, clearly and attractively, so that by 1600 his book had been reprinted forty-six times in seven European languages. Mendoza greatly admired Chinese buildings: 'In this kingdom in al places there be men excellent in architecture', who built 'mightie buildings and verie curious'. But he was untypical in attributing this splendour to the superiority of Chinese building materials. 'They have a kinde of white earth of which they make brickes, of so great hardness and strength, that for to breake them, you must have pickaxes, and use much strength.' The governors' houses had great gardens, wooded and watered; more puzzling is Mendoza's description of the houses themselves, 'verie gallant, and after the manner of Rome'. Inside they were 'as white as milke in such sort that it seemeth to bee burnished paper . . .'[2]

By the middle of the seventeenth century Europeans were well served with information

(and legend) about the Far East. The great collectors of travel literature – Giovanni Battista Ramusio in Italy, Richard Hakluyt in England, Levinus Hulsius in Germany – had made a large quantity of sources readily available to the general reader. The second edition of Hakluyt's *Principall Navigations . . . of the English Nation* contained extracts from Galeote Pereira and Luis Fróis on China and Japan, but to the student of the Orient the invaluable reference work was *Purchas his Pilgrimes* (1625), compiled in five large volumes by Hakluyt's successor Samuel Purchas. These volumes included abridgements not only of the early accounts of Marco Polo, 'Mandeville' and William de Rubruquis, but also of most of the major writings of travellers in the late sixteenth and early seventeenth centuries: Gaspar da Cruz, Bento de Goës and Matteo Ricci on China; Captain John Saris and Richard Cocks on Japan; William Finch, Sir Thomas Roe and Edward Terry on India; Gasparo Balbi, Cesare Fedrici, Jan van Linschoten and Ralph Fitch on south-east Asia. Those readers who were curious about oriental architecture might learn for the first time of the temples at Agra, or the 'very many faire houses' along the Ganges at Benares, or of the splendid temples in 'Pegu' (Burma). In the view of the English traveller Ralph Fitch, the Shwe Dagon pagoda at 'Degu' (Rangoon) was 'the fairest place, I suppose, that is in the world'.[3]

Purchas also included about a third of Fernão Mendes Pinto's *Peregrination*, whose descriptions of Chinese cities are derivative and unreliable, but most entertaining. Among the marvels of Nanking were its many prisons, butchers' shambles, and 'two thousand three hundred Pagodes or Temples, one thousand of which are Monasteries of Religious persons, richly built, with Towres of sixtie or seventie Bells of Metall and Iron, which make a noise horrible to heare'. And at Peking:

The streets are long and large, the houses faire, of one or two lofts, encompassed with Iron and Latten grates, and at the streets end are triumphall arches, closed at night.[4]

'Latten' (brass) is not to be confused with 'lattice', but it is significant that 'latten grates' or (in Henry Cogan's translation) 'lattin ballisters'[5] are frequently mentioned in Pinto's Chinese episode, and it was the characteristic patterning of grilles and railings which, above all other aspects of Chinese architecture, was to delight European imitators in the eighteenth century. Although the *Peregrination* had failed to find a publisher in its author's lifetime, it was widely circulated in the seventeenth century, with numerous editions in Portuguese, Spanish, English, French, German and Dutch. It was not taken as an accurate rendering of fact; nor, on the other hand, was it read solely as amusing fiction. Dorothy Osborne commented on the book in a letter to Sir William Temple:

... tis as diverting a book of the kinde as ever I read, and is as handsomely written. You must allow him the Priviledge of a Travellour and hee dos not abuse it, his lyes are as pleasant harmlesse on's as lyes can bee, and in noe great number considering the scope he has for them ...[6]

At this point a major advance was made in the European comprehension of China. Nearly all the publications mentioned thus far lacked illustrations of any kind other than maps; and in the matter of architecture especially, the most graphic description is no substitute for an engraved plate. In 1655 Father Alvarez Semedo's *History of That Great and Renowned Monarchy of China* was published in London – 'now put into English by a Person of quality, and illustrated with several MAPPS and FIGURES, to satisfie the curious, and advance the Trade of Great BRITAIN'. A prospective reader who saw these words on the title-page, and who realized that Semedo had spent twenty-two years in China, must have expected that at last he would be granted a glimpse of the Great Within. But the 'several mapps and figures' in fact amount to four plates: two maps, a portrait of a mandarin with his wife, and a portrait of the author. If only Semedo had been able to illustrate, for example, the great tower at Nanking:

A Tower divided into seaven stories of singular beauty for the workmanship thereof, it being full of figures, and wrought like Porcellane: an edifice, which might be ranked among the most famous of ancient Rome. The river cometh to kisse the feet of this City ...[7]

But the disappointed reader would not have had long to wait. The Dutch, anxious to extend their eastern trade, had taken a number of Portuguese bases without managing to obtain from China even those trading concessions which had been granted to Portugal. The president of the Dutch East India Company therefore sent a formal embassy to the Manchu emperor, whose dynasty had succeeded that of the Mings in the 1640s. The members of the embassy reached the Canton estuary in July 1655, and were eventually allowed to proceed to Peking, where they spent six weeks under close supervision before returning. In terms of trading advantages the embassy achieved practically nothing, but the resulting published account, written by the ambassador's steward Jan Nieuhof, was a most authoritative and revealing portrayal of China. It contained more than a hundred engravings, based on drawings made apparently by Nieuhof himself.

Nieuhof's *Embassy* appeared first (in Dutch) in 1665, and Latin, French and English editions followed quickly. For Ogilby's English translation of 1669, moreover, the original plates were copied by the skilled hands of Wenceslaus Hollar and Francis Place. Selections from both text and engravings were reproduced again and again in the travel collections which were published throughout the eighteenth century, and scenes from Nieuhof found their way on to furniture and all kinds of chinoiserie surface ornament. If any single work served as a standard source of information on China, it was this splendid illustrated volume.

Nieuhof's was also the first book to take more than a passing interest in Chinese architecture. He was not overawed:

This Empire is not altogether void of Architecture, although for neatness and polite curiosity, it is not to be compared with that in Europe; neither are their Edifices so costly nor durable, in regard they proportion their Houses to the shortness of Life, building, as they say, for themselves, and not for others ... in China they dig no Foundations at all, but lay the Stones even with the surface of the ground, upon which they build high and heavy Towers; and by this means they soon decay, and require daily reparations. Neither is this all, for the Houses in China are for the most part built of Wood, or rest upon Wooden Pillars; yet they are covered with Tyles, as in Europe, and are contrived commodiously within, though not beautiful to the eye without ...[8]

Nieuhof's remarks on the impermanence of

4 The 'Porcelain Pagoda' at Nanking, engraving from Nieuhof, *An Embassy . . . to China*, 1669

Chinese domestic buildings were well justified, and the same could now be said of chinoiserie pavilions in Europe, also generally wooden, which were liable to decay in a few decades – especially if they stood on wooden stilts in a lake or a river. But the temples and palaces of China did occupy the Dutchman's attention, and his engravings, most of which were topographical and based on drawings made on location, showed a great variety of triumphal arches, pagodas, fortifications, and townships. The second part of the book, 'A General Description of the Empire of China', devoted short chapters to each of several types of building, such as arches, towers, bridges and idol-temples. The latter includes a print 'taken with great exactness' of a rectangular temple, showing internal columns and a tiled concave roof, adorned with fabulous animals, and supported on cantilevered brackets. Just inside can be seen a large and threatening statue, 'most dreadful to behold, being a horned Devil, in a most terrible and frightful shape, with a wide Mouth, and Hands like the Claws of a Griffon, in such a posture as it would have seized those that entered'. In another temple Nieuhof saw Hell 'curiously Painted to the Life'.[9] Later

writers, particularly Sir William Chambers, were to make great play with the notion of China as a land of terrors.

The diadem of all China, as Nieuhof described it, was the former imperial seat of Nanking. Its principal tower was the so-called Porcelain Pagoda, which became through Nieuhof's engraving the Chinese building best known in Europe, and few returning travellers failed to mention its glazed and painted tiles or its crowning golden pineapple. Nieuhof perpetuated the myth that the tower was actually 'made of Purceline', although unlike Semedo he counted nine storeys above the broader ground-floor octagon.

The Imperial Palace at Peking is attractively portrayed, with its gilt or varnished woodwork and yellow-glazed pantile roofs reflecting the sun 'brighter than Gold'; another engraving shows the inner court of the palace thronged with life-guards, and the ambassadors waiting to kotow. The palace gardens, in which were 'delicate Summer-Houses, which the Emperor caused to be made for his Pleasure', impressed Nieuhof as they had impressed Marco Polo and Odoric. He also commented on the large sculptured rocks

5–7 'Cliffs made by Art' (above),
'Pagode by Sinkicien' (below),
'A Street in Nanking' (opposite)
Engravings from Nieuhof, *An Embassy . . . to China*, 1669

which for centuries had been an important
element in Chinese gardens: one example, forty
feet high and grotesquely shaped, is pictured
earlier in the book.

There is not any thing wherein the Chineses shew their
Ingenuity more, than in these Rocks or Artificial Hills,
which are so curiously wrought, that Art seems to
exceed Nature: These cliffs are made of a sort of Stone,
and sometimes of Marble, and so rarely adorned with
Trees and Flowers, that all that see them are surprized
with admiration ... These Artificial Mountains or
Cliffs are commonly contrived with Chambers and
Anti-chambers, for a defence against the scorching
heat in Summer, and to refresh and delight the Spirits;
for they commonly make their great entertainments in
these Grots, and the Learned seek to study in them
rather than any other place.[10]

This passage and the engraving must surely have
been the source of many of those extraordinary
rock formations which appear in eighteenth-
century garden designs and pattern-books. In a
similar way Nieuhof's illustrations of small
temples and pavilions were useful to European
designers and architects, perhaps more useful
than the grander pagodas and palaces. His neat,
three-storey 'Pagode by Sinkicien', and his
'Temple upon a high Hill',[11] approached by steps
up a riverside promontory, are the prototypes of
innumerable chinoiserie ceramic and textile
designs, and also of several pavilions actually
built in Europe. One of the most interesting views
depicts a street of shops in Nanking,[12] each of
whose occupants advertised his own trades by
attaching a pennant, a crescent or some other
symbol to a tall pole outside his premises. This
engraving bears a resemblance to one of A. C.
Pugin's illustrations of the corridor of the Royal
Pavilion at Brighton, in the first of its several
decorative schemes. The standards which the
Prince Regent installed in about 1818 may
simply have been scaled-down adaptations of
those tradesmen's signs depicted in Nieuhof's
volume 150 years before.

Hard on the heels of Nieuhof's work came two
compilations by Arnoldus Montanus, *Atlas
Japannensis* and *Atlas Chinensis*, both 'English'd'
by Ogilby (1670 and 1671) and 'Adorned with
above a hundred several sculptures'. These plates
tend to the sensational, showing violent scenes of
fire, murder, earthquake and volcanic eruption,
often with panicking crowds to heighten the
effect. From an architectural point of view the
exteriors depicted are less striking than
Nieuhof's, although there are terrifying interiors
of 'idol-temples' and their monstrous deities.

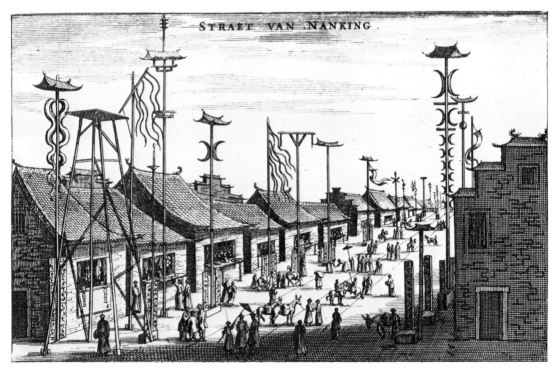

STRAET VAN NANKING.

8 The Trianon de Porcelaine, Versailles, engraving, *c.* 1675

Most of the pagodas in the *Atlas Japannensis* are square-sided and rather less exotic than their Chinese counterparts; the *Atlas Chinensis* shows a variant of the Porcelain Pagoda only distantly related to Nieuhof's engraving. The greatest travesty of this famous spectacle occurs in another elaborate and well illustrated publication, Athanasius Kircher's *China monumentis . . . illustrata* (1667), in which the tower must have been drawn solely from literary description. The result was a bleak pile of hexagonal chunks, built of brick unrelieved except by small rosettes and (on the upper four storeys) pairs of bells hung out like street-lamps at either side. On its summit was a seated Chinaman.

It is not surprising that the first recorded European structure to be built in a supposedly Chinese manner should have been inspired by this much-publicized Porcelain Pagoda at Nanking; nor is it surprising that the European version must have been quite dissimilar to its prototype. The Trianon de Porcelaine, built in the grounds of Versailles, was designed by Louis le Vau, commissioned by Louis XIV and intended for the pleasure of Mme de Montespan. Like the vast majority of the oriental pavilions which came after it, the Trianon de Porcelaine had a brief existence, from late in 1670 to 1687. But in other respects it was unlike its successors, and moreover

scarcely influenced them, for it was several decades before another mock-oriental structure appeared in Europe.

Although its inspiration was undoubtedly the 'Pagode de Porcelaine' described in the French edition of Nieuhof's *Embassy* of 1665, the Trianon owed more to literary description than to engraved or painted views. It comprised a group of single-storey buildings occupying three sides of a courtyard, with small lodges by the entrance on the fourth side, none of which was in the least oriental in outline. The principal building had a classical, pedimented entrance, the double-sloping mansard roofs were thoroughly *Louis Quatorze*, and the vases and statuary upon them were unmistakably baroque and European. But the great feature of the roofing was the blue-and-white patterned *faience* which covered it – a reasonable approximation to the porcelain which was said to face the famous pagoda at Nanking. According to the *Déscription sommaire* written by Jean François Félibien shortly after the Trianon was built, some of the furniture and interior decoration was in the Chinese manner, but the painting of the *faience* tiles on the roof sounds occidental:

On the entablature is a balustrade laden with a great number of vases, and the entire roof forms a kind of finial, whose lower part is decorated with young cupids, armed with bows and arrows, in pursuit of animals. Above these are numerous porcelain vases, arranged in rows up to the ridge of the roof, with various birds reproduced to the life. The pavilions beside the main block are ornamented in the same fashion, and help to fulfil the initial object: to construct what is both a little palace in an extraordinary style, and the perfect place to pass the time on a summer's day.[13]

The Trianon de Porcelaine was indeed a palace, sumptuous and formal in layout, in keeping with the splendid formal gardens of Versailles, and modelled – freely – on a celebrated structure with royal associations (in one Nieuhof's engravings the Nanking pagoda is shown as a background to the emperor of China). It was a unique building, whose 'extraordinary style' could be followed only in a very limited degree.

Soon after the Trianon de Porcelaine had been demolished, its *faience* panels no doubt suffering from the ill-effects of seventeen winters, the first coherent criticism of Chinese architecture was published by the French Jesuit Père Louis Le Comte, who had gone to China as a missionary thirty years after the Dutch embassy. Evidently the buildings of Peking could not compare with the Paris of Louis XIV: 'they are always pestered with mud or dirt', and moreover 'the houses are not proportionable, being neither well built nor high enough'. The only structure in Peking which Le Comte found remarkable was the Imperial Palace, over each of whose arches 'stands a large square Gothick building; the roof looks odd, but yet handsome; for the ends of the joices are continued beyond the wall in manner of a cornice, which at a distance looks very neat'. However, the dazzling effects of marble, gilding and porcelain were marred by 'the unpardonable faults they are guilty of':

The apartments are ill contrived, the ornaments irregular, there wants that uniformity in which consists the beauty and conveniency of our palaces. In a word, there is as it were, deformity in the whole, which renders it very unpleasing to foreigners, and must needs offend any one that has the least notion of true architecture.[14]

Le Comte conceded that the great pagoda at Nanking, 'vulgarly called the China tower', was the noblest edifice in the East, but he felt that even this had been overrated:

I confess that medley of beams, joists, rafters, and

pinions is a singularity which surprises us, because we must needs judge that such a work was not done without great expence; but to speak truth it proceeds only from the ignorance of their workmen, who never could find out that noble simplicity, in which consists both the strength and beauty of our buildings.[15]

Deterred by such sentiments as these, French architects were slow to follow the Trianon's lead,[16] although the early decades of the eighteenth century saw the establishment of many lacquered rooms and *Porzellankammer*. Perhaps next of kin to Le Vau's pavilion, but certainly not a close relation, was the small 'Pagodenburg' built in 1716–19 for the Elector Max Emanuel of Bavaria in his palace gardens at Nymphenburg. Max Emanuel's military alliance with France was proved a costly error at the battle of Blenheim; after this defeat of the French and Bavarian armies, Max Emanuel went into exile in Paris. But his artistic allegiance to France remained strong, and soon after his return to Bavaria he had a small pavilion, nominally in the style of a pagoda, built for him by his French-trained architect Josef Effner. The Pagodenburg was in reality an extended octagon with classical pilasters, 'Chinese' only in certain furnishings and in the blue-and-white tiles of its lower interior.

The oriental character of Augustus the Strong's Wasserpalais at Pillnitz, on the other hand, is evident in the double concave roofs and overhanging eaves, whose curving undersides are painted with Chinese scenes. The architects of this *indianisches Lustschloss* on the Elbe were Mathaes Pöppelmann and Zacharias Longuelune, who in the early 1720s created a series of pavilions which are now amalgamated. Pöppelmann was also primarily responsible for converting Augustus's *Holländisches Palais* at Dresden into a *Japanisches Palais*, a task which occupied the years between 1723 and 1730. The interior was to serve as a showpiece for the porcelain produced in Augustus's new factory of Meissen, which may have led to the choice of oriental features in the exterior: gently undulating roofs, and Chinese caryatids in the central courtyard.

These innovations followed closely on the publication of Fischer von Erlach's ambitious and exciting *Entwurf einer historischen Architektur* (1721), which reappeared as *A Plan of Civil and Historical Architecture* in 1730 and 1737. Fischer's engraved plates ranged from the seven wonders

9

9 The Wasserpalais at Pillnitz, East Germany

of the world to his own splendid Baroque projects (some of them fulfilled) for palaces and churches in the cities of Austria. Book III offered 'The Buildings of the Arabians, Turks, &c., together with some modern One's of the Persians, Siamese, Chinese & Japonese'. His illustrations of Middle Eastern mosques served as models for many of the 'Turkish' garden temples erected in Europe later in the century. But his Chinese views, although stimulating to the imagination of his readers, would seem less promising as models for imitation, since they consisted not of pavilions but of the great monuments drawn by seventeenth-century visitors – the Great Wall, the Imperial Palace of Peking, the Porcelain Pagoda and four spectacular bridges, including one supported by 'square Pillars of Stone of a frightful Height', and another described as 'the largest & most surprizing Bridge that is mention'd in History'.[17]

Nevertheless, if we allow ourselves to consider Fischer von Erlach's engravings as sources of design, it seems possible that the origin of the device of deep eaves curving up to meet a similarly concave roof, so conspicuously deployed at the Wasserpalais, lay in Fischer's reproduction of Nieuhof's view of the Porcelain Pagoda. This theme was repeated at Lunéville, where the architect Emmanuel Héré built a

'Kiosque, ou Bâtiment à la Turque' in 1738 for the Polish King Stanislaus Leszczynski, newly created Duc de Lorraine. The extraordinary central portions of the otherwise orthodox Kiosque comprised (in ascending order) an arcaded portico, concave eaves and roof, a balcony, and two concave roofs above. Shortly afterwards Héré added 'un Bâtiment Chinois nommé Le Trèfle', which, although arguably less Chinese than the 'Bâtiment à la Turque' near by, was much more original in plan, taking the shape of a three-leafed clover, as its title suggests. The outer perimeter formed a narrow and sinuous gallery, while a central salon gave on to bedrooms at each side. The principal roof was broad, nearly flat, and undulating, while a more conical roof capped the apparently inaccessible upper storey above the salon.

The Kiosque and Le Trèfle were but two of the Polish king's diversions at Lunéville. Héré's designs show a long expanse of rockworks incorporating a windmill, a watermill, a forge, a cave with resident hermit, and various kinds of rustic activity – a foretaste of the inventive *jardins anglo-chinois* which were to become fashionable in the last decades of the century. Engraved views of Héré's projects were published in a volume [18] which was to form a significant link in the tradition of exotic architecture in Europe; for

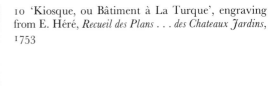

10 'Kiosque, ou Bâtiment à La Turque', engraving from E. Héré, *Recueil des Plans . . . des Chateaux Jardins*, 1753

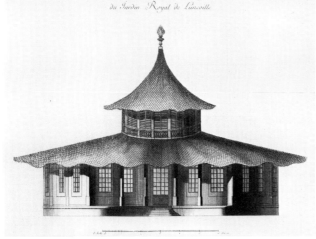

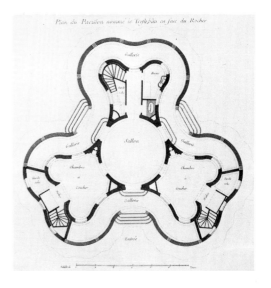

11 Le Trèfle, engraving from E. Héré, *Recueil . . .*, 1753

12 Plan of Le Trèfle, engraving from E. Héré, *Recueil . . .*, 1753

King Stanislaus sent a copy to Frederick the Great at Potsdam, and in the following year Frederick supplied a drawing of his own, based on Le Trèfle, to his architect Johann Gottfried Büring. By 1757 Büring had completed the delightful Chinese tea-house at Potsdam in the park of Sans Souci, where it is now used to exhibit Chinese and chinoiserie porcelain. The tea-house follows Héré's clover-leaf pattern, but at Sans Souci the central salon is larger in relation to its three vestibules than was that of Le Trèfle; the main roof is angled more steeply and ripples more gently. In place of the grilled lantern at Lunéville, Büring constructed an elegantly decorated drum with six oval windows to light the interior, and on the shallow cupola he placed a gilded Chinese figure holding a parasol. (This grotesque finial, which attracted some severe criticism,[19] may have been suggested by an 'Indian' house built by Clemens August, son of Max Emanuel of Bavaria, in the Pheasantry at Brühl on the Rhine, where several umbrella-carrying figures were stationed on the concave double roofs.) The gilt columns which support the lower roof take the form of palm-trunks opening out in luxuriant sprays of shoots as they meet the entablature. For several decades mock-Chinese figures had squatted above European doorways or leaned outward from pilasters. But at Sans Souci the life-size gilt Chinese figures were made to play an altogether more prominent role. They can be seen sitting round the bases of the palm-columns, playing musical instruments or engaging in animated conversation, while others stand nonchalantly between the windows of the three vestibules.

Thus Frederick the Great and his architect domesticated Héré's deliberately bizarre interpretation of oriental architecture. A Chinese kitchen and a four-storeyed Dragon House were added in the succeeding decades.

Both in England and on the continent of Europe, Chinese motifs in architecture seem to have been communicated largely through family connections. One of Frederick's sisters, the Margravine Wilhelmine von Bayreuth, had a Chinese kiosk erected over a grotto in the Bayreuth Hermitage gardens;[20] his brother Prince Henry erected a version of the Potsdam tea-house at Rheinsberg, where a sequence of Chinese pavilions followed;[21] and another sister of Frederick, Queen Lovisa Ulrika of Sweden, received a Chinese pavilion – Kina Slott, Drottningholm – for her birthday in 1753, a present accompanied by every Chinese ceremony her husband could devise.[22] This timber-built pavilion with transverse wings was set in place with great rapidity (overnight, according to tradition) and soon decayed; during the years 1763–69 a more permanent Chinese pavilion of stone and brick was built to the designs of Karl Frederick Adelcrantz. Drottningholm's Chinese House followed the repertoire of motifs established by its predecessors: lightly undulating double roofs, a vivid colour-scheme, and Chinese figures and dragons flanking the upper windows at the eaves. The plan of the new pleasure-house was inventive – a central block with wings curving out to meet a pair of rectangular outer rooms, and two more pairs of detached pavilions continuing the circuit. However, the proportions and the structural basis of the Chinese House were firmly European, and the overall effect is of a pleasantly playful but occidental rococo.

The Chinese pavilion at Drottningholm was the last in a succession of substantial royal pleasure-houses which were deemed Chinese or Japanese by virtue of a set of conventionalized features which no native of either country would have recognized as oriental. But well before the foundations of the second pavilion were laid in 1763, an alternative and more fruitful tradition of architectural chinoiserie had established itself in England. Sir William Chambers's *Designs of Chinese Buildings* (1757) was known to the designers of the Drottningholm pavilion, who adapted Chambers's engravings of costumed figures and interior wall-panels for two of the ground-floor rooms. But his illustrations of Chinese architectural elements, which although far from authentic were in many respects more oriental than the chinoiserie of Héré, Büring and Adelcrantz, had no observable impact on the architecture of the Swedish Queen's new pavilion. Indeed the English fashion that Chambers inherited was fundamentally different from theirs. Since the late 1730s small oriental pavilions had been appearing in English parks, very modest in size and characterized by fanciful latticework, sweeping rooflines and watery sites. In the last third of the eighteenth century the taste for such pavilions spread to the Continent, but it was no accident that this strain of oriental architecture did not cross the English Channel before that time. So strange a product required a suitable context in which to gain acceptance. And it was only in Britain that such a setting was evolved, in the form of the landscape garden.

13 The Chinese tea-house at Sans Souci, Potsdam, East Germany ▶

Chapter Three
China and the Landscape Garden

LANDSCAPE GARDENING is often considered as one of Britain's greatest contributions to the arts. The movement away from geometrical arrangements and straight lines towards an apparently 'natural' landscape occurred, in the first half of the eighteenth century, exclusively in Britain, and the peak of its development can still be admired in the gardens of Stowe and Stourhead. Later in the century this informal style of landscape gardening became fashionable throughout Europe, and its product became widely known as 'the Anglo-Chinese garden'.

But what had the Chinese to do with it? Very little, in the view of several writers then and now, and it is true that for the first quarter of the eighteenth century, when certain elements of the landscape garden were beginning to appear alongside the regular avenues and parterres, most gardeners (and garden owners) would have known no more about Chinese gardening than what was contained in a single paragraph written by an English diplomat who had never visited China. To them 'the Chinese manner' meant no more than studied irregularity. But as the century progressed, scattered pieces of evidence reached Europe in the form of engravings and literary descriptions, which tended to confirm the rumour that the new English fashion had a good deal in common with the traditional principles of Chinese gardening. By the last quarter of the century, when the continent of Europe adopted the landscape garden, the French were well justified in speaking of '*le jardin anglo-chinois*', particularly since their own essays in this genre tended to exaggerate the Chinese aspect and minimize the English. How much the English owed to the Chinese was still a matter for debate, but the similarity between the two was firmly established.

Today, of course, much more information is available about the methods and traditions of Chinese gardening, and it may be useful to summarize these from a twentieth-century standpoint.[1]

Firstly, architectural structures played as fundamental a role in Chinese gardening as in the landscaped parks of mid-eighteenth-century England. Their siting was of paramount importance: it was necessary both that they should harmonize with the surrounding scenery, and that the most satisfying views should be available from the pavilions themselves. In China as in England, the arts of landscape gardening and landscape painting were closely associated, and a walk in a Chinese garden was intended to reveal a succession of carefully composed scenes, as if a pictorial scroll were being gradually unwound. (Conversely, the fifth-century theorist Tsung Ping asserted that a well executed painting could serve the beholder in place of a ramble among gloomy and dangerous cliffs.)[2]

In China, however, many of these pavilions were designed not merely to be appreciated from the outside, or as temporary resting-places, but to be occupied by poets, artists and philosophers, who would contemplate the beauty and meaning of nature at their leisure. The 'study pavilion' was a recognized institution, and often pavilions were constructed for more specific activities, such as music, chess, or poetry. In one variety a canal was cut in the stone floor, and along it would be floated a small wine-cup in a saucer; each time the cup wound its way from one end of the canal to the other, a poet had to compose some appropriate lines, or else drain the cup. 'In this way innumerable poems were written, and one may imagine oneself in the land of the immortals', according to *Yuan Yeh*, the seventeenth-century treatise on gardening.[3]

The author of *Yuan Yeh* was no less sensitive to visual niceties of distance, texture and contrast than were the eighteenth-century Europeans who developed the principles of landscape gardening and the picturesque. But Chinese gardens were not intended to look like a fortuitously arranged piece of natural scenery. Rather, the elements of their gardens *alluded* to nature through symbolism and association. Paths should 'meander like playing cats', the trunk of a plum tree should look like an old man's body but give an impression of energy, and the pine represented silence and strength of character; the lotus, the peach tree and the peony all had a symbolical significance which could affect their role within the garden. The growth of the lotus, for example, was seen as an allegory of the progress of the human spirit. At the bottom of the lake the lotus emerges from the mud, which represents the material world; it then comes up through the water (the emotional middle region) to the free air above the surface (the world of the spirit), where 'it opens its perfect perianth to the sun, thus illustrating the flowering of the human spirit or Buddha-nature'.[4]

14 'Dreaming of Immortality in a Thatched Cottage', detail of painting by Chou Chen, 16th century

15 The Imperial Gardens at Jehol, engraving by Matteo Ripa, c. 1713

Effects of water were carefully contrived, and the imperial parks at Yuan-ming yuan, Jehol and the Sea Palaces all possessed a much greater proportion of water to land than their European counterparts. If water was not available, however, channels and cavities might be dug and filled with selected stones to represent rivers and pools. Artificial 'mountains' in the form of naturally sculptured rocks, symbolizing the creative force of nature, were greatly prized; by the start of the eighteenth century these rock-sculptures were familiar to Europeans through wallpaper, lacquer and porcelain designs.

Of all the imperial parks, the fortunes of the 'Old Summer Palace' at Yuan-ming yuan were most closely and curiously involved with Europe. Yuan-ming yuan (or 'round bright garden') was established by the Emperor K'ang Hsi at the beginning of the eighteenth century, but it was largely developed in the early part of the reign of Ch'ien Lung (1735–96) – at much the same time as Stowe and Stourhead in England, but unlike them laid out in accordance with a long and conservative tradition. Under Ch'ien Lung a great expanse of countryside was adorned with steep hills and broad lakes, together with groups of palatial halls and several hundred small temples and pavilions, most of them built on islands or lakeside promontories.

Through reports of missionaries and travellers, and through paintings and woodcuts commissioned by Ch'ien Lung from Chinese court artists in the 1740s, Yuan-ming yuan exerted more influence in Europe than did any other Chinese park. But it also contained a strong European element within its boundaries. In the years 1747–59 a series of marble and brick buildings was built there to the designs of Giuseppe Castiglione and his fellow Jesuits, in a European style best described as flamboyant Italianate baroque, but tending to rococo in its intricately carved columns and elaborate festoons. The dominant features were powerful curves, scrolls and cartouches, with Borrominesque oval ground-floor windows which may have reminded the Chinese of their own moon gateways. In front of these buildings the Jesuits laid out small formal gardens, including spectacular *jets d'eau* contrived by the mechanically minded Père Benoit. The least European aspect was the tiled roofing, which in combination with the statuesque stonework created a façade not wholly unlike that of Louis XIV's Trianon de Porcelaine.

In 1860 Yuan-ming yuan was sacked by British troops under Lord Elgin, who destroyed five palace complexes and all their subsidiary buildings. The Italianate buildings proved more resistant to fire than all but a few of the Chinese, and when Osvald Sirén visited the devastated site in 1922[5] he was able to photograph the volutes and pilasters as they lay in the dust – a double reminder to China of the strange ways of Europe.

As Lord Elgin's troops had effectively demonstrated, Chinese pavilions were not built to last. Their builders valued the permanence of ideas and traditions, but expected the material manifestations of them to come and go without regrets – a philosophy to which the threat of earthquakes may well have contributed. They were generally timber-framed and built on stone foundations; the roof was then supported by wooden posts. The outer walls were not load-bearing, and were often dispensed with altogether, leaving the building 'open'. The occupant could then achieve a closer communion with the natural surroundings, and, moreover, the pavilion would serve as a frame to the scenery behind instead of obscuring it. Alternatively the supporting columns might be linked by trellis-work or ornamental balustrades, in an infinite variety of wave or meander patterns, swastikas or cloud spirals. Many trellis patterns are represented in *Yuan Yeh* and in Chinese applied design, and some appear also in European chinoiserie.

Within this simple formula there was scope for decorative effect. The structure could be formed exclusively of straight lines; or, against the parallel verticals of the columns and the rigid right angles of the lattice-work, a sweeping curve of the roof could be brought dramatically into play. Pavilions might be rectangular, polygonal or circular, and they could be extended upwards by means of ever-diminishing storeys, or else sideways in the form of a colonnaded portico, conveying the visitor from one vantage-point to another. Long, exposed corridors of this kind are alien to Europe (although the remains of something similar can still be seen at Woburn); according to *Yuan Yeh*, however, no garden should be without one. 'They follow the rise and fall of the ground, sweep in curves and are sometimes visible, sometimes invisible.' Walls and even bridges could be expected to adopt a sinuous or zigzag course; as Sir William Temple rightly reported, much of the beauty of the Chinese garden lay in its calculated asymmetry.

The principle underlying all Chinese gardening – applicable to the great parks, to the much more numerous small town gardens, and to many of the individual components of these – was that a garden should serve as a microcosm of the external world. It was an enclosed space, inward-looking and self-sufficient, in which illusions of landscape were created with the aid of a wide range of traditional devices and conventional signs. By these means Chinese gardens retained a relationship to the natural world which was not to be found in the elaborate formal gardens of Europe in the seventeenth century, where geometry and symmetry were the ruling ideals. It is true that within Europe there were national differences: the grand avenues and broad lawns laid out by Le Nôtre could not be confused with the small-scale details of flowers and topiary favoured by the Dutch. But all were laid out to a rigid pattern, intersected by straight walks which cut the grounds into decorative plots. Their principal avenues were flanked by matching pairs of urns and statues, and their 'groves' were planted like orchards at regular intervals.

It was therefore likely that European travellers in the East should notice and remark on the Chinese art of gardening, although they were inevitably limited in their ability to interpret what they saw. Sir William Temple, diplomat and essayist, did not himself travel in the East, but he was eager to learn from those who had done so, and he was also a connoisseur of garden design. Dorothy Osborne, who recommended Pinto's *Peregrination* to Temple in 1654, soon became his wife, and her enthusiasm may have fostered the interest which her husband later displayed in travellers' accounts of the East. As Ambassador to The Hague in 1668 he was well placed to know Nieuhof's *Embassy* even before its translation into English, and his own description of Peking is based closely on that work. Temple's essay 'Of Heroick Virtue' (1690) praised the political organization of China and the wisdom of Confucius, drawing on Nieuhof, Kircher and Montanus. And in the same year he published his observations 'Upon the Gardens of Epicurus', which were considerably to influence the land-scape gardening and the garden architecture of the following century.

When Temple composed this essay in 1685 he was himself in retirement at his estate of Sheen, enjoying many of the pleasures which he attributed to Epicurus. 'Epicurus passed his life wholly in his Garden; there he studied, there he

Exercised, there he Taught his Philosophy . . .'[6] Temple's own tastes were not unconventional: the 'perfectest' garden he had ever seen was that of Moor Park in Hertfordshire, which was laid out in a regular fashion on a gently sloping hillside, with a broad gravel-walk flanked by laurels, and two fountains and eight statues in each of the four quarters of the parterre. The lower garden contained a grotto and fruit trees. On the other side of the house was a third garden, 'very Wild, Shady, and adorned with rough Rock-work and Fountains'. Such an ensemble, Temple believed, was best suited to the country and climate of Britain, but he qualified his belief as follows:

What I have said, of the best Forms of Gardens, is meant only of such as are in some Sort regular; for there may be other Forms wholly irregular, that may, for aught I know, have more Beauty than any of the others; but they must owe it to some extraordinary Dispositions of Nature in the Seat, or some great Race of Fancy or Judgment in the Contrivance, which may reduce many disagreeing Parts into some Figure which shall yet, upon the Whole, be very agreeable. Something of this I have seen in some Places, but heard more of it from others, who have lived much among the *Chineses*; a People, whose Way of Thinking seems to lie as wide of ours in *Europe*, as their Country does. Among us, the Beauty of Building and Planting is placed chiefly in some certain Proportions, Symmetries, or Uniformities; our Walks and our Trees ranged so, as to answer one another, and at exact Distances. The *Chineses* Scorn this Way of Planting, and say a Boy, that can tell an Hundred, may plant Walks of Trees in strait Lines, and over-against one another, and to what Length and Extent he pleases. But their greatest Reach of Imagination is employed in contriving Figures, where the Beauty shall be great, and strike the Eye, but without any Orders or Disposition of Parts, that shall be commonly or easily observ'd. And though we have hardly any Notion of this Sort of Beauty, yet they have a particular Word to express it; and, where they find it hit their Eye at first Sight, they say the *Sharawadgi* is fine or admirable, or any such Expression of Esteem. Any whoever observes the Work upon the best *Indian* Gowns, or the Painting upon their best Skreens or Purcellans, will find their Beauty is all of this Kind (that is) without Order. But I should hardly advise any of these Attempts in the Figure of Gardens among us; they are Adventures of too hard Achievement for any common hands; and tho' there may be more Honour if they succeed well, yet there is more Dishonour if they fail, and 'tis Twenty to One they will; whereas, in regular Figures, 'tis hard to make any great and remarkable Faults.

It is worth speculating a little on the source of this oft-quoted passage. Temple would have learnt from the writings of Nieuhof and his predecessors that the grander gardens of China included hillocks, twisting paths and rivulets, waterfalls, contorted rocks, lakes, bridges and scattered small buildings; but Temple went considerably beyond this, in claiming that all these sprang from a conscious philosophy of beauty, whose essence was a contrived irregularity or 'Sharawadgi'. Since this conception was entirely novel in seventeenth-century Europe – so that the passage quoted above has been called 'one of the most amazing in the English language'[7] – it would be interesting to know whether Temple had himself inferred this aesthetic of irregular beauty from travellers' accounts and Chinese prints and paintings, or whether (as seems more likely) he was convinced of it from conversation with returned travellers. Temple could have spoken with a native of China, named Mikelh Xin or Shen Fu-tsung, who was brought to Europe in 1684 by a Belgian Jesuit and visited London in 1687–88, just before the publication of Temple's essay. Mikelh Xin certainly met some of the leading figures in English society; Sir Godfrey Kneller painted his portrait for James II, which shows him clasping a crucifix with a slightly melancholy smile. But if Temple owed his information to a native of China, why should he attribute it to the less authoritative source of 'others, who have lived much among the Chineses'? Surely his informants were Europeans, as he clearly implies – either former missionaries or former ambassadors, whom Temple is likely to have met in the course of his diplomatic duties, and particularly during his three terms of service at The Hague, where he could easily have discussed Chinese gardening with a member of the Dutch expedition to China of 1655–57.[8]

The word 'sharawadgi' used by Temple is another puzzle, for it does not seem to correspond to any Chinese word in use then or now. One suggestion is that the term combines two Chinese terms, 'Saro' and 'Kwaichi', so that the whole means 'quality of being impressive or surprising through careless or unorderly grace'.[9] This is certainly what Temple had in mind (although whether any such word was ever used in China remains doubtful), and the term was adopted in the eighteenth century by writers who found it applicable to the developing landscape garden in England. Sometimes the term 'Sharawadgi' (and its several alternative spellings) was used simply

to mean the wildness of untutored nature: a traveller in 1713 compared the 'regular manner of greens and gravel-gardening' unfavourably with 'the sublime unconfinedness of nature' and 'the beautiful Scaravagie of noble grown Trees in a Wild Wood'.[10] More often, however, 'Sharawadgi' suggested not merely irregularity but deliberately organized irregularity – as Temple put it, a beautiful contrivance 'without any Order or Disposition of Parts, *that shall be commonly or easily observed*'. As the principle spread in Britain, buildings too were given artfully irregular profiles, but this practice did not extend to garden architecture in the Chinese style, which (like its prototype) remained purely symmetrical in the great majority of cases.

Temple's essay 'Upon the Gardens of Epicurus' has often been taken as the initial stimulus to the English landscape garden, but it is reasonable to imagine that the 'natural' garden would have flourished in much the same way if news of China had never crossed the Channel. It is true that Addison's influential promotion (in *The Spectator*)[11] of 'natural wildness' and irregular planting, in place of precise topiary and 'the little labyrinths of the most finished parterre', invoked the practice of the Chinese, drawing directly on Temple's essay. But Addison looked also to France and Italy, 'where we see a large extent of ground covered over with an agreeable mixture of garden and forest, which represents everywhere an artificial rudeness, much more charming than that neatness and elegancy which we meet with in those of our own country'. The landscape garden did not need to go to China for its model, since 'artificial rudeness' already existed in some degree, beside (and sometimes within) the grand formal layouts whose greatest draughtsman was André Le Nôtre. Even the smaller regular garden which Temple admired at Moor Park was balanced by a 'wild and shady' garden near by.

And it is a mistake to think that Addison simply paraphrased Temple's remarks; in fact he skilfully altered the image of Chinese gardening to make it more acceptable to his readers. In Temple's account the Chinese scorned the 'Proportions, Symmetries [and] Uniformities' which constituted beauty in the eyes of Europeans. Addison made the milder suggestion that the Chinese respected natural scenery, which they subtly amended. Temple had warned his compatriots against attempting anything so ambitious as the Chinese conception of beauty;

but for Addison it was the British gardeners who were the deviants, snipping at every plant and bush and forcing them into unnatural shapes and rows. Temple's pioneering remarks contained no guide to the *scale* of Chinese gardening, but Addison unjustifiably assumed that Chinese gardens were typically park-sized: '. . . why may not a whole estate be thrown into a kind of garden by frequent plantations?' he asked, and in the next paragraph claimed that the Chinese showed 'a genius in works of this nature'.

Addison's precepts were more forcefully phrased by Alexander Pope, who urged that an 'artful wildness' should replace symmetrical paths and groves. To some extent Pope put his own precepts into practice in his famous garden at Twickenham. Even before Pope bought his five acres in 1719, Stephen Switzer was beginning to break down the barriers between formalized enclosures and surrounding estate. At the Manor of Paston, he claimed, 'I have sprinkled the wood gently all over the Estate, and mix'd Lawns, Enclosures of Grass, and Corn Fields therewith, and this, as is the most essential Beauty of an Estate, so likewise it looks more rural . . .'[12]

In the following decades others followed Switzer's lead, concentrating their efforts increasingly on the park at the expense of the traditional inner garden. The landscape revolution was not necessarily sudden, for often the country was 'called in' to the garden by stages. Walls and fences were sunk into ditches to make boundaries less evident, and wooded banks and streams were incorporated only after careful doctoring, so that nature might appear (in Pope's words) neither 'overdressed' nor 'wholly bare'. Serpentine paths were introduced within the primary axes of the garden before they replaced the axial layout itself; and garden buildings, which initially served as terminal points to straight avenues, gradually came to be sited less conspicuously, so that they might be discovered one after another by the perambulating visitor. What we now recognize as fully fledged landscape gardens did not take shape until the 1730s. In 1734 a correspondent reported that 'a general alteration of some of the most considerable gardens in the kingdom is begun, after Mr. Kent's notion, viz. to lay them out, and to work without level or line'.

It has the appearance of beautiful nature, and without being told, one would imagine art had no part in the finishing, and is, according to what one hears of the Chinese, entirely after their models for works of this nature, where they never plant straight lines or make regular designs. The celebrated gardens of Claremount, Chiswick and Stowe are now full of labourers, to modernise the expensive works finished in them, even since everyone's memory.[13]

By this time there was additional evidence to justify the reference to China. Father Matteo Ripa, an Italian Jesuit, had travelled via London to China in 1708, and on reaching Peking was immediately put to painting 'landscapes with Chinese houses',[14] since the Emperor K'ang Hsi was not interested in pictures of figures. Soon afterwards he was asked to attempt an engraving of a landscape, and although Ripa's entire knowledge of the subject was based on a single lesson he had received in Rome, he managed to delight K'ang Hsi by producing the first copper engraving that the emperor had ever seen. After making progress in that art, and designing a rudimentary printing-press, Ripa was sent to the emperor's summer palace and gardens at Jehol, a hundred miles north-east of Peking, in order to execute thirty-six engravings of the imperial estate. *En route* Ripa fell from his horse, 'receiving frightful wounds', but thanks to the unorthodox methods used by a Tartar surgeon 'to set the brain, which he supposed had been misplaced', Ripa arrived at Jehol – the first European to do so – and carried out his task.

The engravings were made in the course of several summer visits, from originals by the court artist Shen-Yu, and several sets were distributed by the emperor to members of his family. After K'ang Hsi's death the small Jesuit population was placed in some difficulty, and Ripa returned home on an East Indiaman, docking in London on 7 September 1724. News of his arrival spread quickly: he had two audiences of three hours each with King George I, and in his conversation with the leading Londoners of the day the topic of Chinese gardening must have been raised on many occasions. When he sailed from London after a month's visit he left behind at least one set of his thirty-six engravings of Jehol; for an album of Ripa's views entered the Burlington Library, whence it passed into the Devonshire collection. This album, now in the British Library, still bears the 'Chiswick' bookplate – a most satisfying piece of testimony. At the time of Ripa's visit, the 3rd Earl of Burlington had already begun to collaborate with William Kent in the arrangement

The Reception of the Diplomatique & his Suite, at the Court of Pekin.

I

II

III

IV

VI

V

IX

X

XI

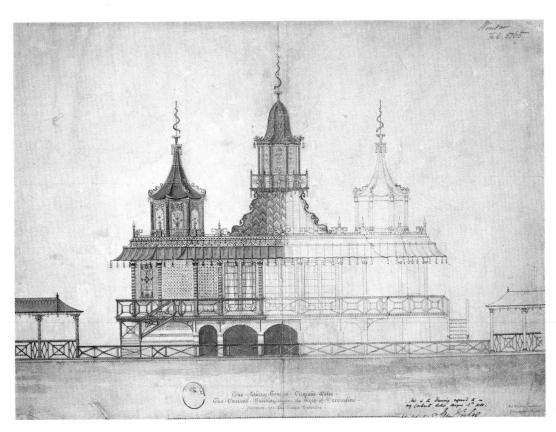

The ~ Kewny ~ Centre ~ Principal ~ Ruler ·
The ~ Central ~ Building in ~ the ~ Style ~ of ~ Decoration ·
Proposed ~ for ~ the ~ Public ~ Gardens ·

XII

XIII

of his garden at Chiswick, This included a measure of classically sanctioned irregularity, so that Ripa's authentic record of the huge and lavish imperial gardens must have arrived at a most opportune moment. Burlington and his associates cannot have failed to study the engravings and their manuscript titles which, written in Italian, are apparently in Ripa's own hand. As far as that influential group was concerned, Ripa's album would have superseded both the miscellaneous 'skreens' and exported paintings previously available, and the literary descriptions passed on and distorted since Sir William Temple's essay first appeared.

Ripa's own description of Chinese gardening was not published in English (as part of an abridgement of his memoirs) until 1844, and perhaps for this reason has been overlooked by historians of landscape gardening, but it does give an idea of what Ripa might have said on the subject during his month in England. The following passage refers particularly to K'ang Hsi's estate at Ch'ang-chun yuan.

This, as well as the other country residences which I have seen in China, is in a taste quite different from the European; for whereas we seek to exclude nature by art, levelling hills, drying up lakes, felling trees, bringing paths into a straight line, constructing fountains at great expense, and raising flowers in rows, the Chinese on the contrary, by means of art, endeavour to imitate nature. Thus in these gardens there are labyrinths of artificial hills, intersected with numerous paths and roads, some straight, and others undulating ... the lakes are interspersed with islets upon which small pleasure-houses are constructed, and which are reached by means of boats or bridges. To these houses, when fatigued by fishing, the Emperor retires accompanied by his ladies.[15]

It is a clear and pleasant image. But what would an Englishman of the 1720s have made of Ripa's engravings? It has been suggested that he would have interpreted them as confirming the pastoral ideas of Horace and Cicero; that he would have found 'the same virtues of simple rusticity in Claude's Virgilian renderings of the Roman Campagna and in Chinese landscapes', and that he would have seen in them the 'judicious wildness' which had been claimed to be typical of Chinese gardens.[16] But looking at the engravings today we may find that hard to believe, even if we allow for considerable changes of outlook over two and a half centuries. The 'gardens' portrayed by Ripa are vast and

mountainous, with lakes extending to the horizon, ranges of barren hump-backed hills, and a sprinkling of prickly-looking trees. There are some rapid streams, but these are not the domesticated brooks which were beginning to wind their gentle way around English gardens; nor was the park at Jehol a contrived 'wilderness' in the sense understood by Pope, Switzer and Kent. Temple's description had not prepared his readers for so menacing a landscape as this. And only the wealthiest and most dedicated sinophile could have attempted to reproduce the spectacular contrasts of Ripa's Jehol in the gently undulating terrain of the Home Counties of England.

On the other hand the architecture shown by Ripa is altogether less forbidding than the scenery. The buildings appear singly or in small groups, simply built, with either straight or slightly curving ridged roofs. Most are of one storey, but some are miniature pagodas of two or three stages. Light bridges form shallow arcs, covered walkways lead to lakeside belvederes, and open pavilions command views across the valleys. Several plates show patterns cut into walls, and in one a 'moon gateway' is formed by a circular hole in the latticework. In Ripa's own words, 'these summer-houses are built in different forms, but all in good taste, and very clean'.[17]

But however attractive to English eyes these pavilions may have been, Chinese structures did not spring up immediately in English parks. The impulse to variety took effect by stages, in architecture no less than in the design of the garden proper. Merely to set out a profusion of non-functional garden buildings was an innovation in the 1720s; since this development coincided with the renewed and powerful influence of Palladio on British architecture, the temples and casinos of 1715–40 were very largely in the classical manner. Rudolf Wittkower has argued compellingly that the landscape garden and the Palladian style encouraged by Burlington were twin sides of the same coin marked 'liberty' – that both expressed 'the blessings of a free commonwealth'.[18] But liberty is expressed in many ways, another of which is freedom of architectural style: so that in the 1740s both Gothic and Chinese styles emerged as acceptable alternatives to Palladianism in garden structures. By the 1760s it was considered positively desirable to include contrasting styles of pavilion to complement the variety of the parkland.

15, 16

42

16 The Imperial Gardens at Jehol, engraving by Matteo Ripa, *c.* 1713

Moreover Ripa's engravings may not have come immediately into Burlington's possession, and even if they did, some time may have elapsed before others were able to see them. As late as 1751 Joseph Spence wrote to the Rev. Robert Wheeler:

I have lately seen thirty-six prints of a vast garden belonging to the present Emperor of China: there is not one regular walk of trees in the whole ground, they seem to exceed our late best designers in the natural taste almost as far as those do the Dutch taste, brought over into England in King William's time.[19]

Spence took a keen interest in the customs of China, and it was he who first brought to English readers a detailed and enticing description of a Chinese park – this time the imperial estate of Yuan-ming yuan, which had not yet received its baroque additions. *A Particular Account of the Emperor of China's Gardens near Pekin* (1752) was translated by Spence (under the pseudonym of Sir Harry Beaumont) from a letter written in 1743 by the Jesuit lay-brother Jean-Denis Attiret, who had established himself as a portrait-painter at the Chinese court. The letter had already been published in France in 1749, but it had a greater significance in Britain, where both the landscape garden and the fashion for *chinoiserie* were in the ascendant; three more English editions followed in the 1760s. Attiret wrote with authority of the colonnaded pleasure-houses on 'raised hills', magnificent boats on the lakes, grottoes, flowering trees and menageries. The garden buildings were approached 'not by regular Stone Steps, but by a rough sort of Rock-work; formed as if there had been so many Steps produced there by Nature'. There were bridges which might be made of brick, stone or wood, and like the pathways they 'wind about and serpentize'. 'They are fenced in with Ballisters finely wrought, and adorned with Works in Relievo; but all of them varied from one another, both in their ornaments, and Design.' Small pavilions were often situated in the middle of the bridges, Attiret added, or they might be placed at each end.[20]

Attiret made the important distinction (later to be ignored by Coleridge) between the symmetry of the Chinese palace, and the Chinese pleasure-house where 'they rather chuse a beautiful Disorder, and a wandering as far as possible from all the Rules of Art'. The Jesuit must have anticipated a degree of resistance to this notion, for he took pains to demonstrate that the appreciation of architecture was a matter of habit. For this reason the Chinese did not admire European buildings, he wrote; he, on the other hand, had come to admire the architecture of China. It was clearly implied that others could do the same.

Chapter Four
Early 'Chinese Houses' in England, 1735–50

'Whose house is that,' (said I to some labourers on the London road) 'with the little
cupola on the top, and an enormous length of Chinese rails before it?' 'Squire
Shapely's the Londoner's . . .'

Richard Graves, *The Spiritual Quixote*

THE EARLIEST Chinese pavilion in England, so far as I can discover,[1] was built by 1738 at Stowe, near Buckingham. The park at Stowe already held the reputation it holds today as one of the finest in England. Seeley's *Description of the Garden of Lord Viscount Cobham at Stow*, first published in 1744, has claims to being the first guide-book to any country estate in Britain, but Stowe was a popular resort of tourists well before that. One visitor to the gardens in 1738 made the following observation:

In the middle of an old Pond (which is to be enlarged) is a house built on piles, after the manner of the Chinese, odd & Pretty enough, but as the form of their Building is so well known from Prints and other Descriptions, there is no Occasion to say more of it.[2]

In 1742 another anonymous tourist drew a neat map of the gardens locating the Chinese House, which he also described as 'An India House', close to 'The Temple of Worthy's' a little to the east of the river.[3] In August of that year *The Gentleman's Magazine* published the last instalment of 'The Triumph of Nature', a long poem which catalogued the delights of Stowe in heroic fashion:

> Eastward the spacious *pond* relieves the sight;
> In which of form *Chinese* a structure lies,
> Where all her wild grotesques display'd surprise;
> Within *Japan* her glittering treasure yields,
> And ships of amber sail on golden fields!
> In radiant clouds are silver turrets found,
> And mimic glories glitter all around.[4]

From the various descriptions of the Chinese House,[5] and from Seeley's engraving of 1750,[6] it is possible to make a fairly detailed reconstruction of this innovatory building. It was a simple rectangular hut, standing on wooden piles in a pond and connected to the shore by a bridge adorned with vases. Each side had a small lattice window (or 'Lettice'), and the exterior was painted 'in the Chinese taste' by Francisco Sleter

(alternatively spelt Slauter, Sletea or Sleats), who decorated a number of the rooms and buildings at Stowe. These paintings were preserved by a covering of canvas. The interior was 'quite wainscotted with Japan', in the words of the Marchioness Grey; 'a great many Screens have been cut to pieces (I fancy) to make it, but it is Fine & Pretty.' Inside was also 'a Chinese lady as if asleep, her hands covered by her gown'. In the pond swam two models of Chinese birds about the size of ducks, 'which move with the wind as if living' – counterparts, perhaps, to the mechanical peacocks which Friar Odoric saw at the imperial court of Peking. The most prominent feature was the curved roof, which had generous eaves and supported a pair of S-shaped dolphins.

The spectacle of the Chinese House together with the Shell Bridge near by and the unorthodox quadrant of the Temple of British Worthies would have served as a rococo curtain-raiser to the more serene delights of the Elysian Fields across the bridge. The architect of the Chinese House may perhaps have been the versatile William Kent, who according to tradition was involved in the design of the Elysian Fields, and who was certainly responsible for the Temple of British Worthies. The little hut on stilts does not fit easily into Kent's *oeuvre*, but another of Kent's buildings (now lost) was described as 'Chinese Gothic',[7] and one of his illustrations to Spenser's *The Faerie Queene* depicts 'a little Gondelay' bedecked in Chinese fashion, while the enticing lady in the boat holds an oriental parasol. A Chinese pavilion would not have been beyond Kent's resources.

At Stowe, as in many similar gardens, the exotic structures proved less durable than the classical. The visitor of the 1740s was able to admire the Egyptian pyramid and Dido's Cave, both by Vanbrugh, and the so-called Saxon Temple designed by Gibbs, none of which exist today; and the Chinese Temple was an early

17 The Chinese House at Stowe, Buckinghamshire, engraving by B. Seeley, 1750

casualty, removed no doubt in accordance with the purely classical tastes of Richard Grenville, whose uncle Lord Cobham had died in 1749.

'The Chinese House is taken away,' observed a visitor in 1751,[8] and it would be natural to assume that it was demolished. But there is an intriguing alternative. On Lord Cobham's death Stowe entered the possession of his widowed sister, Hester Grenville of Wotton Underwood. At Wotton, an estate twenty miles to the south where Lancelot Brown had been briefly employed before moving to Stowe, several garden pavilions appeared in the middle of the century, one of which was a Chinese House. According to tradition it was erected at Wotton in about 1750. But it is surely equally likely that Hester Grenville and her eldest son Richard (who took the title of Earl Temple on his mother's death in 1752) were reluctant to destroy the little hut at Stowe whose paintwork had been so carefully protected through a dozen winters; and that they simply transferred the Chinese House from Stowe to Wotton. It so happens that this hypothesis can be put to the test, for Wotton's Chinese House still exists – although in 1957 it was moved to Harristown in County Kildare, Eire. If the little building at Harristown is compared with Benton Seeley's engraving of the Stowe Chinese House, it is plain that the two coincide. The stilts have been removed, of course, but the general proportions of walls and gambrel roof, the diagonally latticed windows, the projecting eaves and even the cross motif above the front roof accord closely with the engraving. And the Wotton pavilion's distinctive exterior panels, painted with landscapes and bouquets, correspond well with the reports of Francisco Sleter's chinoiserie at Stowe. There can be little doubt that the bright little building now in Ireland is Stowe's Chinese House, twice transplanted, and thus the earliest recorded oriental structure in Britain.

18

17

46

18 The Chinese House at Harristown, Co. Kildare, Eire

Lord Cobham's estate at Stowe was fertile ground for architectural innovation. But we may still ask what inspired its Chinese House, and why no Chinese pavilions were built in England until the late 1730s, while chinoiserie in general had been fashionable since the turn of the century. Well before 1700 it was possible to see representations of oriental buildings on many kinds of surface – painted, printed, woven, lacquered or glazed. In 1664 John Evelyn examined 'such a Collection of rarities, sent from the *Jesuites* of *Japan* and *China* . . . as in my life I had not seene', including scenes painted on calico and 'Prints of Landskips'.[9] But depictions of Chinese life were soon to become more familiar to Evelyn, who in the course of his diary refers on half a dozen occasions to collections of screens, hangings and cabinets from the Far East. Evelyn particularly admired the 'Jopan Skreenes . . . representing the manner of living, and Country of the Chinezes' which he saw at the house of his

neighbour, Christopher Boone of the East India Company.[10] In the year 1700, when Evelyn visited Samuel Pepys at Clapham, he observed 'all the Indys and Chineze Curiosities' with appreciation, but by now he could add that these were 'almost anywhere to be mett with'.[11] We can be certain that several of the characteristic features of Chinese buildings, their curving tiled roofs, multiple storeys and open arcades supported by slender wooden columns, must have been familiar to many Europeans at the turn of the century.

Besides the variety of goods imported into Europe from the East, imitations of oriental art were now being produced in several European countries. Cabinets *à la Chinoise* are recorded in the second decade of the seventeenth century; blue-and-white pottery with chinoiserie patterning was in production at Nevers in France in the 1650s, and at Delft in the 1670s. (German and British factories followed in the eighteenth

19 Design for japanned work, pl. 21 of J. Stalker & G. Parker, *A Treatise on Japanning and Varnishing*, 1688

is in the Victoria and Albert Museum.) But as the fashion for japanning gathered momentum, so did the sophistication of designers increase; and today there are hundreds of japanned snuff-boxes, chests and clock-cases which can testify that, by the opening years of the eighteenth century, there were many English craftsmen who could represent the essentials of oriental land-scapes and architecture with a very fair degree of competence.

Nevertheless it was clearly a different matter to construct on English soil a building with oriental characteristics. Some further prompting must have been necessary, and one possibility is that such a stimulus was provided in the theatre. In 1692, for example, an operatic adaptation of Shakespeare's *A Midsummer Night's Dream*, en-titled *The Fairy Queen*, was performed at The Queen's Theatre to the music of Henry Purcell. Towards the close of the final act came the following remarkable episode:

While the Scene is darkened a single Entry is danced. Then a Symphony is play'd; after that the Scene is suddainly illuminated, and discovers a transparent Prospect of a Chinese Garden, the Architecture, the Trees . . . quite different from what we have in this part of the World. It is terminated by an Arch, through which is seen other Arches with close Arbors, and a row of Trees to the end of the View. Over it is a hanging Garden, which rises by several ascents to the top of the House . . .[13]

This spectacular-sounding set was probably no more recognizably Chinese than are Stalker and Parker's engravings. But it is tempting to suppose that this sort of stage scenery, which occupies an intermediate position between the second and third dimensions, might have served as a link between paintings of Chinese scenes and build-ings in a Chinese style. We may imagine that some architect-designer such as William Kent, having tried his hand at an oriental stage set, was inspired (or commissioned by a theatre-going patron) to try out something more substantial in the same vein. This is little more than conjec-ture;[14] but there is at least one report of such a transition in the later eighteenth century, at the court of Catherine the Great of Russia. Augustus Bozzi Granville, a nineteenth-century English traveller in Eastern Europe, visited the environs of Tsarskoe Selo, the imperial park which Catherine had filled with exotic monuments of every kind. One of these, which still stands, was the Great Caprice, a monumental arch sur-

century.) Oriental lacquer work was widely imitated, and Mr Boone's 'Jopan Skreenes' could have been made in England. English 'japanned' work of this period could be crude in design: the buildings depicted in Stalker and Parker's *Treatise on Japanning and Varnishing* (1688), purportedly representing the 'bright and radiant' temples of Japan,[12] are concocted from a wild assortment of bell, cone, pyramid and crescent shapes, and the concave roofs and many-storeyed towers which appear in the exotic panels painted by Robert Robinson are no less fantastic, yielding an effect which – despite the accompanying coconut palms and American Indians – is unmistakably European and bar-oque. (The most flamboyant set of Robinson's panels, signed and dated 1696, can be seen in Sir John Cass's Schools, Aldgate, London; a more subdued series, attributed to Robinson on the grounds of similarities of style to the 1696 panels, mounted by a Chinese Kiosk. Granville passed on the story of its creation:

The Empress Catherine, happening to be at the theatre one night, was struck with a painted scene, representing the perspective view of a small town, at which she expressed her great pleasure to Orloff, who was with her. The next time she visited Tzarsco-çelo, she was agreeably surprized with the sight of her favourite scene, which she found there delineated in reality . . . viewed from the gate of the Caprice, this little town presents itself precisely like a perspective town projected upon an even surface.[15]

A second possibility is that the Chinese House at Stowe was inspired by the publication of a compendium of Chinese lore, edited by Jean-Baptiste Du Halde from the writings of twenty-nine missionaries, 'printed or in manuscript'. Père Du Halde's *Description géographique, historique . . . de l'empire de la Chine* was published in Paris in 1735, and at once gained attention on the other side of the Channel. Edward Cave, the proprietor of *The Gentleman's Magazine*, arranged for a translation to be made, which appeared in weekly numbers from February 1737; a rival version translated by Richard Brookes had already been published in four octavo volumes in 1736, but *The Gentleman's Magazine* was quick to point out its shortcomings. In the midst of the interest aroused, Samuel Johnson wrote an essay in the issue of July 1738 eulogizing the ways of the Chinese.

Du Halde's volumes did not contain much information that was entirely new to Europe; on the 'Porcelain Pagoda' of Nanking, for instance, Père Le Comte's remarks were reprinted, and although Du Halde and his contributors passed a few scattered observations on Chinese arches, bridges, temples and pagodas, sometimes with guarded praise, they added little that was not known in the seventeenth century. Du Halde did, however, organize his material usefully into sections, on geography, institutions, customs, maxims of morality, herbal remedies (tea, ginseng, elephant's gall), and travellers' reports. Of these last the most substantial was written by Père Gerbillon, who travelled extensively in the emperor's entourage between 1688 and 1691 – visiting, incidentally, the ruins of Shang-tu, where the Emperor shot a large boar. Gerbillon was interested to see an ancient octagonal pagoda of eight storeys, 'each of eleven Foot at least, besides the first, which exceeds fifteen without the ceiling, so that the whole Height is over 100 Foot . . . Its Architecture is quite different from ours, and tho' a little rude, has its Beauty, and pleases the Eye'.[16] The emperor's halls of state did not greatly impress Gerbillon, but in the spring of 1690 he and his fellow Jesuits were privileged to attend the emperor in one of his pleasure-houses, where they instructed him in geometry and logarithms. This small building and its surroundings were much more to Gerbillon's taste, and his admiring words must have enhanced the reputation in Europe of Chinese gardening:

The Beauty of their Houses and Gardens consists in a great Propriety, and Imitation of Nature, as Grotto's, Shell-work, and craggy Fragments of Rocks, such as are seen in the wildest Desarts. But above all they are fond of little Arbors and Parterres, inclosed with green Hedges which form little Walks. This is the Genius of the Nation. The Rich lay out a great deal of Money in these sorts of Whims . . .[17]

20 'A Chinese Wedding Procession' (detail), engraving from J.-B. Du Halde, *A Description of the Empire . . . of China*, 1741

21 The Chinese temple (upper left) and Skell valley at Studley Royal, Yorkshire, painting attributed to Balthazar Nebot, *c.*1750

Both French and English versions of Du Halde's book contained a number of engravings, but when Stowe's tourist of 1738 wrote that Chinese buildings were 'well known from prints',[18] I doubt whether he or she was referring to Du Halde's. Prints of China circulated in England from the 1660s onwards: on 10 January 1668 Samuel Pepys came across 'an excellent book . . . on China' at a bookshop, and four days later he acquired it, 'a most excellent book with rare Cutts';[19] Pepys's editors suggest this book was Kircher's *China . . . Illustrata*, published in Amsterdam in 1667, but it could equally well have been the Dutch or the French edition of Nieuhof's *Embassy* (1665 and 1667).[20] At any rate, the many engravings in each of these two great works gave rise to a multitude of reproductions which must have been familiar to many people by the 1730s. Du Halde's engravings are of poor quality and small architectural interest. A view of a wedding procession shows the bridegroom's house in the foreground, and some small houses in the background, which may have been responsible for the belief held by designers

of English pattern-books that Chinese architecture was punctured by a succession of cusps and rococo swirls. Otherwise Du Halde's influence was probably not specific; but the composite picture he conveyed of a people 'mild, tractable and humane', with manners strange but unobjectionable, might easily have captured the imagination of Lord Cobham as he considered what curious new artefact he should add to his famous pleasure-ground.

The vogue for Chinese architecture had little or no impact in Scotland, Ireland, Wales or the more remote parts of England. It principally affected landowners who were wealthy, fashion-conscious and in close touch with the latest developments in the capital and its outskirts. (A pattern-book of Chinese designs set out to rescue that style from 'the many bad Consequences usually attending such light structures, when unskilfully erected: Which must unavoidably happen at a Distance from this Metropolis . . .')[21] But one interesting and early specimen was built well beyond the normal orbit of the architect earls and the leading arbiters of taste, at

20

Studley Royal in Yorkshire. In September 1744 this great park, laid out by John Aislabie, was visited by Philip Yorke, later the 2nd Earl of Hardwicke, who admired the varied beauties of the land and the way in which they were exploited:

Mr. [William] Aislabie designs to erect a Chinese house of a pyramidal form, with a gallery encircling every story, upon the point of a ridge which encloses on each hand a valley finely wooded and washed by a rivulet. One side is formed into a number of small terraces interspersed with rocks, which makes a Chinese landscape.[22]

Two months later a stonemason began work on 'Ye Chenieys building', as the estate records show, and in 1746 the plasterwork was executed by Cortese of York.[23] But when the same visitor returned in 1755 he was disappointed. 'The Chinese seat lately erected commands a delightful valley, but it is in very bad taste and not at all like their architecture.'[24] In 1751 a Frenchman noted its lead roof, red upswept eaves, blue-and-gilt decoration and fine plaster ceiling, but he most admired its prospect – 'une vallée enchantée'.[25]

Fortunately there is a painting (attributed to Balthazar Nebot) in Fountains Hall of the pavilion overlooking the Skell valley, which makes it possible for us to understand the attitude of these tourists. From this picture it appears that the pavilion was circular and of one storey only, with a conical roof and eaves which curled upwards like ear-flaps on a Mongolian warrior's helmet. But it stood on the brink of a precipitous gorge, with a narrow river running at its foot. If any pavilion in England was inspired by Ripa's views of Jehol, it was surely this one; especially since Lord Burlington, the possessor of a set of Ripa's engravings, was a close friend of the Aislabies.

The Chinese House survived for a century and a half, without great renown, perhaps because tourists seem to have been discouraged from entering this part of the grounds.[26] The circular stepped base of stone is still in place.

One of the few Chinese pavilions in England with a claim to authenticity is the Chinese House which stands at Shugborough Park, near Stafford. As Thomas Pennant travelled south in 1780, he was much impressed by the architecture at Shugborough, which included 'the chaste buildings of Athens, exemplified by Mr. Stuart' and 'the genuine architecture of China, in all its extravagance'. He added that the Chinese House

was 'a true pattern of the architecture of that nation, taken in the country by the skilful pencil of Sir Percy Brett; not a mongrel invention of British carpenters'.[27]

The park at Shugborough is the result of the complementary resources of two brothers, Thomas and George Anson. As a founder-member of the Society of Dilettanti, Thomas Anson was one of the first to make use of the architectural designs drawn in Athens by Stuart and Revett in 1748–55. Shortly before, George Anson had returned from his triumphant naval expedition around the world, having captured the Spanish treasure-galleon which sailed each year from Acapulco to Manila; his share of the booty, which was paraded through the City of London on 32 wagons, contributed to the architectural projects on his elder brother's estate at Shugborough. Moreover, George Anson had spent many frustrating months at Canton, where Lieutenant Peircy Brett would have been able to make sketches of Chinese architecture. A drawing which may well be Brett's original design for the Chinese House has recently come to light in a private collection.

The Chinese House may have been the earliest of the Ansons' garden buildings; certainly it was complete by August 1748, when it was mentioned in the journal of Philip Yorke.[28] Originally it stood on an island in the river Sow, but the course of the Sow has been altered and the pavilion is now approached from the hall by land. The external walls, now white, were formerly pink, and painted in a fret pattern. By Chinese standards it is solid-looking, relieved only by trellised windows positioned at one end of the room, but in the eighteenth century it had at least one other entrance at the side, with a tent-like canopy over it. The broad eaves of the saddle roof curve upwards attractively, and a two-tier finial sits in the centre of the ridge-pole. The interior furnishings were arranged by the admiral's wife; today there is still a small three-bay alcove in red lacquer, with gilt singerie painted above. The Imari vases, elaborately framed Chinese mirror-pictures and rococo plasterwork ceiling were removed from the Chinese House in 1885 and are preserved in Shugborough Hall.

The park is well documented in two series of paintings carried out respectively by Moses Griffith and the Danish-born Nicholas Dall. It is these oils and watercolours that record the early appearance of the Chinese House, and show in

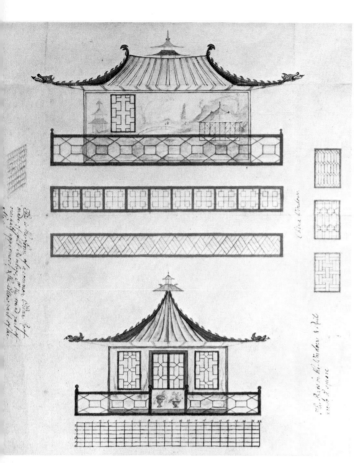

22 Design for the Chinese House at Shugborough, Staffordshire

addition a pair of Chinese-trellised bridges connecting the island to the mainland. (The present cast-iron bridge, built in 1813, is called 'Chinese' sometimes but for no good reason.) On one of Griffith's paintings one can see beside the Chinese House a boat-house which also possessed a Chinese roof and topknot.

On the other side of the hall from this outcrop of chinoiserie was one further, dramatic reference to Admiral Anson's voyage to the East: a wooden hexagonal pagoda of six diminishing storeys, each bearing a balcony with red corner-posts, which was said to have been based on a Chinese original. This too appears on several of

III the views of the park, perched improbably on a very small island in the Sherbrook. In November 1752 the admiral learnt from his wife that the pagoda was under construction and 'promising greatly'.[29] Its architect is not recorded, but it has been suggested[30] that the astronomer Thomas Wright was responsible. Wright is known to have

put forward oriental designs for the estate of Badminton House – a 'Chinese temple coigned with umbrellos', and 'a Chinese garb' for Swangrove, a pavilion on the edge of Badminton park. But by the turn of the century the pagoda and the cascade beside it had disappeared, swept away perhaps by the great floods of 1795.[31]

Twenty miles from Stowe, at Lord North's estate at Wroxton Park in Oxfordshire, a more ambitious programme of Chinese building was undertaken in the late 1740s and 1750s, supervised probably by Sanderson Miller. 'There are several paltry Chinese buildings and bridges, which have the merit or demerit of being the progenitors of a very numerous race all over the kingdom: at least they were of the very first,' wrote Horace Walpole in 1753,[32] but his remark reflects his own disillusionment with chinoiserie rather than any particular shortcomings in the buildings, which are best illustrated in the margins of Francis Booth's plan of Wroxton.

This splendid plan, undated but of about 23 1770, indicates that Chinese structures actually formed a majority at Wroxton Park. The arrangement of garden buildings is also revealing. In the immediate environs of the house appear the most familiar and domestic features of the estate – the village, a Gothick dovehouse, the parish church across the bowling green. In the middle distance two exemplars of Mediterranean cultures would have been visible, a Roman obelisk and (on an eminence across the Great Pond) an octagonal Moorish temple, domed, with scalloped arches over clustered columns. Then at the farthest extremities of Lord North's empire, spread along the river out of sight of the house, stood the representatives of the Far East, three Chinese houses and two Chinese bridges. The south-western building served as the gamekeeper's lodge; due south of the hall was the Chinese House proper, similar to Shugborough's in its upturned eaves, but with long vertical windows in the painted exterior walls; and at the south-eastern corner of the gardens was a Chinese seat beneath a tented roof hung with bells. Because the pleasure-grounds extended southwards from the house, almost any walk to the end of the gardens would culminate in a Chinese building. For the visitor who managed to row to the Chinese House (which was surrounded on three sides by a bend in the river) or found his way there through the woods to the north, there was the additional reward of cold meat and ice-cream.[33]

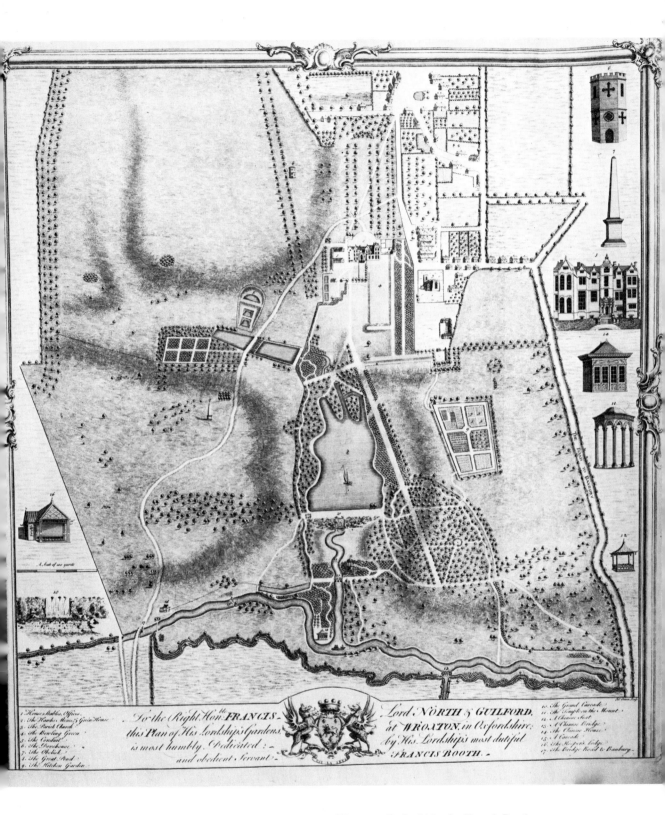

To the Right Hon.ble FRANCIS Lord NORTH & GUILFORD, at WROXTON, in Oxfordshire; this Plan of His Lordship's Gardens, is most humbly Dedicated; by His Lordship's most dutiful and obedient Servant FRANCIS BOOTH.

23   Plan of the gardens at Wroxton, Oxfordshire, by Francis Booth, *c.* 1770

If the stage was a possible source of architectural chinoiserie, then we should also consider the entertainments of the pleasure-garden, a likely location for a flimsy, mock-oriental structure which might catch the eye of a visiting gentleman seeking to furnish his own park with small decorative buildings. In the 1960s the influence of Battersea Fun Fair in London was felt in the stately estates of Britain; for less commercial reasons the pleasure-grounds of Vauxhall and Ranelagh may have affected the taste of landowners two centuries before, when the great gardens of London were patronized by all levels of society. Gray, Goldsmith, Reynolds and Johnson were to be seen at Ranelagh, and in 1744 Horace Walpole went there every night, complaining that he could not set down his foot without treading on a Prince of Wales or a Duke of Cumberland. The four principal London pleasure-gardens, Vauxhall, Ranelagh, Cuper's and Marylebone, all emerged as fully equipped centres of entertainment between 1732 and 1742, just as (or very shortly before) landscaped parks came to be regarded not merely as agreeable retreats, but as forms of cultural entertainment, in which visitors should be constantly surprised and stimulated by the variety of buildings and views displayed.

Vauxhall and Ranelagh, above all, offered a rich assortment of architectural curiosities. The young Lydia Melford in Smollett's *Humphry Clinker*, visiting London for the first time, was dazzled at Vauxhall by the 'wonderful assemblage of the most picturesque and striking objects, pavilions, lodges, groves, grottoes, lawns, temples and cascades, porticoes, colonades, and rotundos'; and Ranelagh seemed to her 'like the inchanted palace of a genie, adorned with the most exquisite performances of painting, carving and gilding, enlightened with a thousand golden lamps . . .'[34]

Both resorts had indeed been supplied with deliberately outlandish buildings. Vauxhall was no longer the pleasant floral garden where, observed by Samuel Pepys, 'the wenches gathered pinks'. It boasted a gothick bandstand, a rococo Prince's Pavilion and Tent, and a hybrid rotunda or music room 70 feet across, whose interior was again decorated in a thoroughly rococo style, extraordinary by British standards in the mid-1740s. Equally extravagant were the so-called Chinese pavilions, which were added in 1751 or shortly before. Samuel Wale's engraved views of these reveal nothing recognizably Chinese, but rather the squirming rococo-gothic that went under that name in several of the pattern-books of the 1750s. Domed kiosks were linked by a semicircular arcade with bulging, heavily cusped arches and a ray pattern in the spandrels. Some of the guide-books simply

24

24 The Chinese-Gothic arcade at Vauxhall, engraving after S. Wale

25 The Chinese pavilion at Ranelagh, engraving by C. Grignion

described this range as Gothic, albeit 'a peculiar, and very elegant Style of Gothic'.[35] All agreed that the ceiling of the middle temple was painted in the Chinese manner, despite the fact that it portrayed an episode of classical mythology, Vulcan catching Mars with Venus in his net.

By 1762 Vauxhall had also a Turkish Tent, situated behind the orchestra in the centre of the gardens. 'Turkish' in this context did not necessarily imply any affinity with the architecture of Turkey, nor even with the Islamic world, but merely a tented or domed structure not otherwise identifiable. At Vauxhall the dome of the Turkish Tent was supported by Ionic and Doric columns, with festoons hanging in between, and a plume of feathers above in place of the more usual crescent moon. Robert Morris satirized this capricious labelling of buildings by publishing (in his *Architectural Remembrancer*,

1750) a design for an octagonal domed construction with a pedimented block facing outwards from each side. Morris wrote that he had consulted several different people in order to determine the name and function of this building. A rabbi had told him that it was practically a synagogue; a 'Dervise' had seen it as a mosque; another man considered it to be a puritan chapel, and another thought it an admirable surgeon's dissecting-room. Morris then neatly deflated his imaginary advisers: 'I can only say my first Intentions were to make it for a cold Bath.'[36]

Ranelagh too had a rotunda, which preceded Vauxhall's and was no less remarkable. A visitor in 1742 wrote of this 'vast Amphitheatre, for structure *Roman*; for Decorations of Paint and Gildings, gay as the *Asiatic*'.[37] Ranelagh's Chinese pavilion was quite clearly oriental in intention, even though it bore the alternative title of

25

55

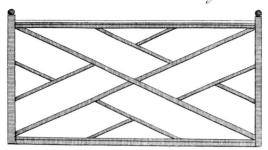

A Chinese Double brac'd Paling

26 'A Chinese Double brac'd Paling', pl. 2 of William Halfpenny, *Rural Architecture in the Chinese Taste*, 1750–52

Venetian Temple: it was a polygonal building, set in the middle of a canal, whose four conical roofs curved steeply upwards like tents. The roofing was supported by tapering columns with capitals in the form of oriental heads facing outwards; between the columns the pavilion was open to the elements (and the onlookers), except for a waist-high wall of intersecting diagonals which corresponds to the 'Chinese Double brac'd Paling' illustrated in William Halfpenny's pattern-book issued in December 1750.[38] The pavilion was in fact built earlier that year, and opened formally at the Jubilee Ball. It remained a centre of festivities, to judge by Grignion's engraving of 1759, which shows the Chinese pavilion thronged with figures dressed for a masquerade, while in a passing pleasure-boat a Chinese parasol is held aloft.

Such a building, in such a setting, would be capable of influencing the 'Chinese taste' in either of two opposite directions. It might inspire other essays in the same style – as perhaps occurred at Claydon House, Buckinghamshire, where the second Earl Verney, a prominent shareholder at Ranelagh, commissioned the most elaborate rococo-Chinese interior in Britain; or it might deter others from employing a style with the raffish associations of a London pleasure-garden. Lydia Melford's guardian uncle, Matthew Bramble, was less susceptible to the glitter of Vauxhall, which he described as 'a composition of baubles, overcharged with paltry ornaments, ill conceived, and poorly executed; without any unity of design, or propriety of disposition. It is an unnatural assembly of objects, fantastically illuminated in broken masses; seemingly contrived to dazzle the eyes and divert the imagination of the vulgar.' In the eyes of Matthew Bramble (and a good many others) the 'Chinese pavilions' appeared as 'a range of things like coffeehouse boxes, covered a-top'.[39] Something of the same contempt is implied in the words of Humphry Repton, when in 1806 he advised his readers to adapt their gardens to the character of the countryside. Wild scenery near a suburban villa was to Repton as incongruous 'as a Chinese temple from Vauxhall transplanted into the vale of Downton'.[40] Similarly Repton's contemporary William Marshall poured scorn on the cascades in the poet Shenstone's park at The Leasowes, likening them to 'the cascade of tin and horsebeans at Vauxhall'. This raised the question which Marshall might as pertinently have asked of Chinese pavilions – '*Quaere*, Did Vauxhall copy after the Leasowes, or the Leasowes after Vauxhall?'[41]

Chapter Five

Pavilions and Pattern-books, 1750–70

Scarcely, it would seem, is the Garden-house inferior
in respectability to the noble mansion itself.

Carlyle, *Sartor Resartus*

BY 1750 the fashion for Chinese garden architecture was spreading rapidly, and excited even Horace Walpole, who was later to regard the style with disdain. 'I wish you could see the villas and seats here!' he wrote. 'The country wears a new face! Everybody is improving their places ... the dispersed buildings, I mean, temples bridges etc. are generally Gothic or Chinese and give a whimsical air of novelty that is very pleasing. You would like a drawing-room in the latter style that I fancied and have been executing at Mr. Rigby's in Essex [at Mistley]; it has large and very fine Indian landscapes, with a black fret round them ...'[1]

Walpole had already made known his intention to build himself a Gothic house at Strawberry Hill. If he had set his mind on an oriental dwelling-place instead, this would have been no more and no less controversial, for while both Gothic and Chinese were winning acceptance in the garden, neither had yet been recognized as suitable for a gentleman's own house. When Sir Horace Mann queried his friend's choice of the Gothic style, Walpole defended it by reference to the Chinese:

I am almost as fond of the *Sharawaggi*, or Chinese want of symmetry, in buildings, as in grounds or gardens. I am sure, whenever you come to England, you will be pleased with the liberty of taste into which we are struck, and of which you can have no idea. Adieu![2]

Walpole rejoiced in this new-found 'liberty of taste', and was quick to see that the calculated irregularity which had changed the face of English gardens could be applied to architecture; and in the long term, the quest for asymmetry did promote the Gothic style at the expense of its rivals. But in the 1750s Gothic structures were seldom any less regular in plan than Chinese. Despite Walpole's definition of Sharawadgi as 'want of symmetry', the essential aspect of what he and many of his contemporaries admired at this time was not asymmetry of outline or plan but playfulness of line and intricacy of detail. Twists and curls, cusps, ogees and quatrefoils were at the heart of the early stages of the reaction against Italy and classicism. A Chinese summer-house was proposed for Walpole's new estate at Strawberry Hill, which, had it been built, would have served as an excellent demonstration against the solid little classical temples which had dominated English parks in the preceding decades. The summer-house was designed by Walpole's fellow-triumvir in the self-appointed Committee on Taste, Richard Bentley, 'for the corner of the wood at Strawberry-hill, where the chapel now stands';[3] the surviving drawing shows it to have been an exceptional design for a three-sided pavilion with large low-reaching window-openings, a double roof in the centre and sharp horn-like protuberances at the roof corners: an airy, spiky building with a small concession to Gothic in the form of a row of quatrefoils above the doorway, but with no concessions at all to classicism.

27 Design by Richard Bentley for a Chinese summer-house at Strawberry Hill, Twickenham

28 'A View of Twickenham', showing Lord Radnor's tower, engraving, *c.* 1755

A design for a Chinese pavilion for Holland House (now also in the Lewis Walpole Library) is perhaps from the same source, being similar in proportions and triangular in plan, although this time a square projects from each of the three sides. Walpole considered other exotic projects for Strawberry Hill, including a 'Mosque Gothic' swimming pool, complete with eunuch and houris. But none of these materialized, and the only oriental elements finally incorporated into Strawberry Hill were a pair of weeping willows on each side of the chapel, and 'Po Yang' – the name of Walpole's goldfish pond.

Presently Walpole began to lose interest in Chinese architecture. One reason for this may have been the appearance of a Chinese tower uncomfortably close to his Gothic showpiece, on the land of his immediate neighbour John

Robartes, 4th Earl of Radnor. Lord Radnor had converted a small hut into a conspicuous polygonal brick building of two storeys, which could be called Chinese only by virtue of its small upswept roof and trellised balustrade. This tower appeared in a drawing made by Bentley of the newly built Strawberry Hill, a drawing which Walpole sent to Mann explaining that the 'Chinese summer-house' belonged not to him but to Lord Radnor. Walpole continued, 'We pique ourselves upon nothing but simplicity, and have no carvings, gildings, inlaying or tawdry businesses.'[4]

Already the glittering image of chinoiserie seems to have acquired a little tarnish in Walpole's mind. Three months earlier the periodical *The World* had ridiculed the latest garden layouts, in which 'the eye is saluted with a

28

yellow serpentine river, stagnating through a beautiful valley, which extends nearly twenty yards in length. Over the river is thrown a bridge, *partly in the Chinese manner . . .*'[5] At the end of the same year the text of Hogarth's *Analysis of Beauty* was published, including the scornful assertion that 'There is at present such a thirst after variety that even paltry imitations of Chinese buildings have a kind of vogue, chiefly on account of their novelty.'[6] In August, Walpole had used the same epithet, 'paltry', to describe the Chinese structures at Wroxton.[7]

As the fashion spread in the 1750s, other critical voices joined Walpole's. Chinoiserie of all kinds lent itself to satire, and Chinese architecture was most vulnerable of all, although at this stage the tone of the satirists was generally mild. 'The simple and sublime have lost all influence almost everywhere, all is Chinese or Gothic,' wrote John Shebbeare in 1756. 'Every chair in an apartment, the frames of glasses, and tables, must be Chinese; the walls covered with Chinese paper filled with figures which resemble nothing of God's creation, and which a prudent nation would prohibit for the sake of pregnant women . . . Nay, so excessive is the love of Chinese architecture become, that at present foxhunters would be sorry to break a leg in pursuing their sport in leaping any gate that was not made in the eastern taste of little bits of wood standing in all directions.'[8] In the previous year *The Connoisseur*, a weekly composed by 'Mr Town, Critic and Censor-General', suggested that the Chinese taste, already introduced into gardens, buildings and furniture, would soon find its way into churches. 'And how elegant must such a monument appear, which is erected in the *Chinese* Taste, and embellished with dragons, bells, Pagodas, and Mandarins!'[9] (At a time when the first new Gothic churches had only just been completed, this was not such a far-fetched prediction, but it was not fulfilled.) An alternative line of attack can be observed in the same periodicals' depiction of a chinoiserie interior, which (it implies) revealed a suspect choice of decoration in a gentleman's room; at least, it was fit for men of 'delicate make and silky constitution'.[10]

If we distrust the satirists, we have only to read Dr Pococke's journals in order to gauge the extent of the Chinese invasion. Within a single week in April 1757, Pococke seemed to see China wherever he cast his eyes. At Valentine's, near Ilford, which was occupied in the 1750s by a Captain Raymond of the East India Company, Pococke saw in the canal a Chinese duck with wings upraised, reminding him of the ducks represented in Chinese pictures. Shortly afterwards he observed on the Duke of Portland's estate at Bulstrode 'Chinese pheasants of both kinds' in the menagerie, and beside it an open 'dairy' with a Chinese façade, surrounded by pools for the benefit of the waterfowl. And when Pococke called at Oatlands, near Weybridge, he found 'a basin for Chinese fish'.[11] The fashion for chinoiserie had surely reached its peak.

While Walpole was acquiring a taste for chinoiserie and losing it again, the style became established in the pattern-books – those portable collections of designs for furniture and architecture which had for several decades been gaining in popularity. The authors of mid-century pattern-books might be specialists in one art or the other, but in many cases they could move with facility from stools and fire-tongs to pavilions and elaborate bridges. Often it is hard to decide where furniture ends and architecture begins, as the reader is offered a range of equipment in consistent style, from seat to bed to alcove to garden temple, or from chair-back to railing.

The first to devote a pattern-book entirely to chinoiserie was William Halfpenny, who had been producing small volumes of architectural designs since 1722. His *Rural Architecture in the Chinese Taste* appeared in four parts from December 1750, the first part being entitled 'New Designs for Chinese Temples' and the others illustrating 'Chinese Bridges', 'Chinese Doors' and 'Chinese Gates'. The so-called Chinese temples shown are frivolous and crude, barely more oriental than the buildings illustrated by Stalker and Parker. They do not seem to have been derived from scenes on lacquered cabinets, nor even from home-produced chinoiserie, but we need not infer that their sole source was William Halfpenny's imagination. The crucial design is plate 13, 'A Banqueting House in the Chinese Taste', which bears a striking resemblance to a small building portrayed in the lower right-hand corner of one of the illustrations to Du Halde's *History of China*. In Du Halde's engraving this pavilion marks the conclusion of a wedding procession, and only the doorway and part of the roof can be seen, but it is nevertheless the most detailed rendering of any building which can be found in Du Halde's already Europeanized plates. The companion

29

20

29 'A Banqueting House in the Chinese Taste', pl. 13 of William Halfpenny, *Rural Architecture in the Chinese Taste*, 1750–52

30 'The Elevation of a Temple partly in the Chinese Taste', pl. 54 of William Halfpenny, *Rural Architecture* . . ., 1750–52

engraving depicts a funeral procession, and the medley of oddly shaped tombs in the background (again the work of a European draughtsman) may have suggested certain other details to Halfpenny. On this basis Halfpenny improvised, adding such well-known motifs as dragons, bells and multiple roofs, and balancing some of his structures on rocks. But for the most part his designs depended on simple trellis-patterns and endlessly repeated cusps. Halfpenny's formulas were applicable to any garden ornament, whether a 'gazebo', a 'termany seat', or a bridge with a pavilion placed on it 'for the Conveniency of Angling, Musick, &c.'[12] His work presented an easy target for satirists:

> The traveller with amazement sees
> A temple Gothic or Chinese,
> With many a bell and tawdry rag on
> And crested with a sprawling dragon;
> A wooden arch is bent astride
> A ditch of water four feet wide;
> With angles, curves, and zigzag lines,
> From Halfpenny's exact designs.[13]

Robert Morris, the author of *Rural Architecture* (1750), was sternly opposed to the Gothic style and was particularly scornful of the Chinese. He believed that all architecture should be pure, simple and regular, and therefore classical. Gothic was 'rude', Chinese was 'unmeaning', and both were meretricious. 'If you will be lavish in Ornament, your *Structure* will look rather like a *Fop*, with a Superfluity of *gaudy Tinsel*, than a *real decoration*.'[14] But in *The Architectural Remembrancer*, published in the following year, Morris relented to the extent of including an engraving of 'a chimerical seat, for a Garden', a half-hearted design for a circular building on a classical base, with bells and a turned-up octagonal tent roof. 'I have placed it here to keep in Countenance all true Lovers of the *Oriental Taste*, and to shew how Trifles may be esteemed, when it is the Fashion to be ridiculous.' Perhaps deliberately, Morris drew exactly the same roof elsewhere in the book, for a building whose style he described as 'partly *Persian*, and partly *Gothic*'.[15]

At about the same time Matthew Darly published *A New Book of Chinese, Gothic and Modern Chairs*, which in clumsiness and indistinctness of style is a counterpart to Halfpenny's *Rural Architecture*. In both architecture and furniture, Gothic and Chinese were closely related at this period, as equal representatives of the rococo counter-culture, the fanciful alternative to

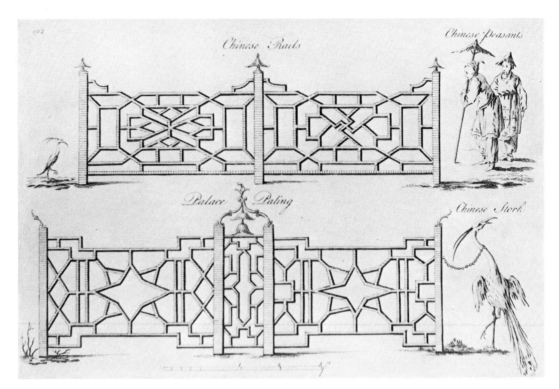

31 'Chinese Rails', design by Paul Decker after Edwards and Darly, 1759

classical tradition. Designers would turn from one to the other without any fundamental change of approach: a dragon or two added, a row of quatrefoils subtracted, and a Gothic pavilion could be announced as Chinese. Cusps and ogival curves were treated as the common property of both styles. One of Halfpenny's elevation is said to show 'a Temple partly in the Chinese taste', a description which could have been applied to many more. In this example the three-storey tower is undoubtedly Chinese, and the pointed gabled roof on which the tower sits is undoubtedly Gothic, but the outer windows, lower finials and star-shaped openings occupy a position which is just halfway between the two. Another book by William and John Halfpenny, *Chinese and Gothic Architecture Properly Ornamented* (1752), did not even attempt to distinguish between the styles promised in the title. At this time both Gothic and Chinese styles symbolized exoticism and deliberate disorder. Writing of the roofs of Chinese triumphal arches, Du Halde declared that 'even our Gothick architecture has not any things so odd',[16] while Hogarth seems to have regarded Chinese art as 'gothic' by definition; at least, he numbered China among the 'barbaric and gothic nations'.[17] Only in the course of the 1750s did the very different potentialities of Gothic and Chinese idioms become clear.

In 1754 an ambitious series of Chinese architectural and ornamental designs appeared, *A New Book of Chinese Designs calculated to improve the present taste . . . By Messrs. Edwards, and Darly*. It is unfortunate that practically nothing is known of Edwards, for this collaborative project is clearly superior to Darly's chair designs. (Darly also engraved many of the furniture designs in Chippendale's *Director* and in Ince and Mayhew's *Universal System*, and was in addition a caricaturist – a self-portrait of Darly on a donkey is inscribed 'The Political Designer of Pots, Pans and Pipkins'.) The 120 plates of Edwards and Darly enter more thoroughly into the world of chinoiserie. Their buildings are animated by figures, foliage and sometimes landscapes, while little vignettes of Chinese life, in the insubstantial manner perfected by Jean-Baptiste Pillement, appear in the corners of several plates. The architectural designs are largely conceived in two dimensions, to terminate views, and could as well be stage-sets. Some of the roofs are draped in a

32 'Temple Fronting a Cascade', design by Paul Decker after Edwards and Darly, 1759

stylized thatch, but in general these temples, bridges, ceremonial barges and trellis-patterns are more impressive and more fantastic than Halfpenny's. A group of landscapes, complete with hollowed-out rocks and small pavilions on stilts or islands, are as authentically oriental as any English landscape gardener could require.

Edwards and Darly's plates were plagiarized in *Chinese Architecture Civil and Ornamental* (1759) by Paul Decker, who added more grandiose titles to the buildings he reproduced. His book was in turn plagiarized in *The Ladies Amusement; or, whole Art of Japanning made easy* (undated), which included chinoiserie designs after Pillement. This volume explained that,

With Indian and Chinese subjects great Liberties may be taken, because Luxuriance of Fancy recommends their Productions more than Propriety, for in them is often seen a Butterfly supporting an Elephant, or Things equally absurd; yet from their gay Colouring and airy Disposition seldom fail to please.[18]

The question of which Chinese designs might be appropriate to the various uses proposed was scarcely considered, as may be observed in a design by Timothy Lightoler published in 1762. Lightoler, who was advertised as a 'carver' but worked also as an architect in the 1760s, had contributed several schemes for rococo-chinoiserie interiors to *The Modern Builder's Assistant* (by William Halfpenny and others), showing figures with Chinese hats and parasols linked in patterns with birds and foliage. A chimneypiece designed by Lightoler displayed a Chinese face hung between swags, and uprights in the form of palm-trees – a motif regarded as suitable for Chinese, Turkish and (later) Indian decoration alike. In 1762 his *Gentleman and Farmer's Architect* appeared, 'containing a great variety of useful and genteel designs'. One of the most genteel was surely a plan and elevation of a 'Lodge and Farm in the Chinese Taste', but we may safely assume that this design was never executed. At the corners of the crinkled eaves (representing the deeply-curved tiles tradi-tionally used in China), bells were suspended from the mouths of projecting dragons: a pleasant enough device on a pagoda at the bottom of the garden, but less satisfactory on a farm. At the ends of the pimpled wall which enclosed the farmyard were Chinese alcove seats, of standard design but not calculated to tempt the visitor to linger, since they backed on to the 'Hogg-sty' and 'Bog-house' respectively.

In William Wrighte's pattern-book of 1767, *Grotesque Architecture or Rural Amusement*, Chinese architectural design can be seen at its most absurd. Pride of place must go to his Oriental Hermitage, whose roof is 'covered with Thatch in the Chinese Taste' and supported by un-treated tree-trunks, while another tree seems to be growing from (or through) the rooftop. The ensemble would be hardly distinguishable from the 'Hermit's Cell' shown on the previous plate, but for the mock-Chinese inscription above the doorway and faintly oriental pattern formed by the roof-work of the accompanying Rustic Seats, which were to be composed of large rough stones and pollard roots cemented together. Wrighte's designs do not look practicable, but nor have

33 Chinoiserie design from *The Ladies Amusement*, after J. Pillement, *c.* 1765

they the flimsy fantasy which makes Pillement's rustic chinoiserie so acceptable; they are an uneasy compromise.

Wrighte's offerings also include three varieties of mosque (all variants on Chambers's mosque at Kew), two moresque buildings and five grottoes, one of which is 'an open Chinese Grottoe, to be placed at the Head of a Grand Canal'. Within this structure a bath and a Chinese temple, both ornamented with a mosaic of shells, were to be linked with arcades made of ice – 'or frosted Work', Wrighte added, for the benefit of those who required a less ephemeral building.

Of all the authors of pattern-books during these years, only a handful of the leading practitioners could expect that their designs would be at all widely adopted by craftsmen or builders. Just as cabinet-makers designed a great deal of their own furniture, and looked to the pattern-books for general trends rather than for immediate inspiration, so were architects apparently reluctant to borrow directly from the printed models – with the exception of those portrayed in Sir William Chambers's *Designs of Chinese Buildings*. It was perhaps felt more important to follow 'the true taste of the Chinese' in a pavilion than in a chair, moreover, and several of the pattern-designers, confident that their architectural designs would never be adopted, would have felt entitled to treat these purely as advertisements of their ingenuity and mastery of the style. In this spirit they produced a quantity of projects which were delightfully exorbitant but largely impracticable.

Even in the case of those Chinese structures which are known from paintings or engravings to have been built, we must bear in mind the possibility that the artist has made them appear more fanciful than they really were. We are especially liable to be deceived by the chinoiserie that appears in the paintings of Thomas Robins the elder, much of which has no literary documentation, and whose sinuous patterns wonderfully evoke the spirit of the English rococo garden. In contrast with the Brown-inspired expanses of later decades, the gardens drawn by Robins were full of objects, natural and artificial, often enclosed within a swirling border of plant-stems or trellage decorated with flowers, shells or butterflies, as if to echo the elegant profusion of the gardens themselves. Geometric and informal layouts are juxtaposed, and in the garden buildings Chinese and Gothic achieve scarcely less prominence than classical.

34 Portrait of Richard Bateman by Tournières le Vrac, 1741

35 Richard Bateman's estate at Old Windsor, detail from a watercolour by Thomas Robins, c. 1750

Among Robins's subjects was Woodside in Berkshire, where Hugh and Ann Hamersley began to reorganize the gardens soon after their marriage in 1752. The house itself received a Gothic front, chinoiserie papers were hung in the old greenhouse, and a Chinese kiosk and screen were set up in the grounds. Robins's view of the kiosk flanked by feathery saplings shows it to have been one of the most attractive of its kind, painted in red and white and partly enclosed by a decorative little palisade.

Another client of Robins was Richard Bateman, who lived at Old Windsor not far from Woodside. Bateman was an early and dedicated follower of the Chinese cult. A clear indication of his taste is a portrait (now in Birmingham City Art Gallery), painted in 1741 by Tournières le Vrac, in which Bateman appears beneath a Chinese porch decorated with openwork patterns in red, yellow and green, and adorned with sinuous creatures. This porch can just be discerned in one of a pair of undated paintings by Robins of Bateman's estate. A close scrutiny also reveals several other Chinese features – a polygonal kiosk, a bridge with a light trellis arch above the centre, a bizarre farmhouse with a Chinese finial, and an arched gateway in the Halfpenny manner.[19] In the 1750s these were apparently remodelled in a Gothic idiom, with the aid of drawings by Richard Bentley and Johann Müntz, two artists associated with Horace Walpole. 'I converted it from Chinese to Gothic,'[20] wrote Walpole triumphantly in the following year, and twenty years later he again recalled the episode with satisfaction:

I am as proud of such a disciple [Mr Storer] as of having converted Dicky Bateman from a Chinese to a Goth. Though he was the founder of the Sharawadgi taste in England, I preached so effectually that his every pagoda took the veil.[21]

In 1748 Robins painted Marybone Park, Benjamin Hyett's estate at Gloucester, where the most striking feature (to judge by Robins's picture) was a four-storey pagoda, thin-stemmed and heavy-based but unmistakably Chinese. It stood on a mound covered with serpentine paths, but again the main approach to the pagoda was a broad straight avenue, running parallel with the inner garden walls. In this 'transitional' garden there could be no subtly contrived or unexpected prospect of the pagoda. It would have been impossible to miss it unless one crouched behind the wall.

34

35

36 The park at Davenport, Shropshire, watercolour by Thomas Robins, 1753

37 The park at Honington Hall, Warwickshire, watercolour by Thomas Robins, 1759 (overleaf)

On the estate of Davenport House in Shropshire, where Robins was at work in 1753, placid, open scenery merged with torrents and craggy hills. Robins's depiction of the wilder elements at Davenport has a thoroughly Chinese feel; a suggestion of towering but delicate cliffs disappearing into the mist, and a trellis bridge on tall stilts spanning the rapids. A version of the Bristol High Cross in the centre of the picture tends to dispel the oriental atmosphere, but at the left the Gothic arbour is fenced off by 'Chinese rails'.

Robins spent much of 1759 in the Midlands.

His commissions included the park of Joseph Townshend at Honington Hall in Warwickshire, an estate laid out shortly before by Sanderson Miller. Townshend's Chinese House overlooked the river Stour and several structures on the farther bank (including the favoured 'double-braced' Chinese paling). It appears to have been the least substantial of pavilions, consisting of a small tent roof on an open cube, with swastika-patterned railings extending halfway round. Its four slim columns seem to mingle with the straight tree-trunks along the ridge.

Anyone who investigates the garden architecture of the mid-eighteenth century must be impressed by the web of family connections and personal friendships which determined its development. Having sprinkled his landscape with casinos and belvederes, the landowner did not expect to be left to contemplate them in private. Touring ladies and gentlemen would arrive in considerable numbers, often unannounced. If the owner was not in residence it did not greatly matter, since they would still be allowed to visit the grounds and probably the house also. If he was at home, on the other hand, he might well serve breakfast to any visitors with whom he was acquainted. They would learn of any new projects he had in mind, and gather ideas for improving their own gardens. The fashion for Chinese pavilions, relatively esoteric in their appeal, seems to have been transmitted largely in this way.

One of the most avid tourists was Jemima Grey, only child of the eldest daughter of the 1st Duke of Kent. The duke was an enthusiastic gardener who transformed Wrest Park; his straight canal, terminated by Thomas Archer's

38 The Chinese pavilion at Wrest Park, Bedfordshire, from the sketchbook of the 1st Earl de Grey

baroque pavilion, is still the pride of Wrest. In 1740 the duke saw his grand-daughter Jemima married to Philip Yorke, son of the 1st Earl of Hardwicke, then Lord Chancellor; a fortnight later he died, leaving Wrest and the marquisate to Jemima. She was then seventeen and her husband was twenty. Not surprisingly, they did not at once begin to alter the already celebrated gardens, but both spent a good deal of time travelling in England, noting their observations in journals and letters. By 1758, when with Lancelot Brown's help they finally set about the gardens at Wrest, they had seen and commented on the Chinese pavilions at Studley Royal (in 1744 and 1755), at Stowe (in 1748), at Wroxton (in 1748), at Richard Bateman's house (before 1756) and at Shugborough (on several occasions).

In the course of their travels they had become connoisseurs of garden architecture of all kinds, and the marchioness in particular developed firm opinions on style and arrangement. Her letter to Lady Gregory after a visit to Stowe in 1748 illustrates the aesthetic appeal that a Chinese pavilion offered at this time. Stowe had thirty-three garden buildings, predominantly classical, but the total effect left her dissatisfied, for although the park was vast and magnificent (she wrote) it lacked 'Variety and Surprise', and above all the buildings were too 'heavy'. Jemima was clearly tired of classical temples, and appreciated any departure from that norm. She admired the Elysian Fields and the shell-work of the grotto, and she found Gibbs's Gothic building 'the most uncommon & best in its way', but of all the structures on view she was most interested in what she described as the Chinese Room, 'the prettiest I have seen, & the Only One like the Drawings & Prints of their Houses'. The location of the Chinese House was not ideal – 'it stands in a little dirty Piece of Water' – but otherwise it fulfilled her criteria of lightness, attractive detail, authenticity and novelty.[22]

Jemima Grey was in the vanguard of taste, and her ideals prevailed in many landscape gardens of the 1750s and 1760s. By 1756 the avant-garde marchioness was 'almost tired of the Chinese' and preferred the Gothic of 'Mr Horry Walpole' at Strawberry Hill. In 1760 she revisited Bateman's Park at Old Windsor, which she had evidently known in its Chinese incarnation, and was now well aware that despite the Halfpennys and their ilk, Gothic and Chinese were not simply equivalent. The scale of

39 The Quarters at Alresford Hall, Essex

Bateman's Gothic was too small – 'One could suppose Oneself before in a Chinese Baby-House, but can never be reconciled to a Gothic One.' Gothic should be 'more Great & Solid & Awfull & Magnificent'.[23]

Two visits by Philip and Jemima to Studley Royal are recorded, although they probably paid more, for their second daughter subsequently married the 2nd Baron Grantham, inheritor of the Studley estate. But they were most familiar with the Chinese House at Shugborough, since Philip's sister Elizabeth had married Admiral Anson shortly after its construction. The chinoiserie at Shugborough figures often in Jemima's correspondence, and from her we learn that by September 1748 there was 'a Chinese Boat extremely pretty' in the canal by the Chinese House.[24] Among a group of drawings related to Wrest Park is a design for a Chinese vessel,[25] which must surely be connected with the boat at Shugborough. Peircy Brett was probably the designer of the latter.[26]

At last the alterations began at Wrest Park. The best of the formal gardens was allowed to remain, but around the Great Canal and Archer's pavilion encircling canals were linked and 'serpentized', and incidental buildings were added, including a Chinese House. In September 1761, when the external paintwork was completed, Jemima sent instructions for the painter to begin work on the interior. 'And he may begin first with the yellow paper . . . which he knows should not be made deeper than a straw colour . . .'[27] A delightful wash-drawing by her great-nephew the 1st Earl de Grey shows that this structure was the epitome of mid-eighteenth-century Chinese pavilions, light and airy, with scrolls and bells at the eight corners of its double roof, and a dragon placed proudly at the summit.

The pavilion survived (although as a ruin in its last years) until the 1950s. Fortunately the Department of the Environment are replacing it at the time of writing with an identical pavilion, albeit with fibreglass roofs; it stands on the original stone base. As a design which encapsulates much of the brief tradition of Chinese pavilions in England it is an excellent candidate for rehabilitation.

38

40 The pavilion on the Chinese Island in Virginia Water, drawing by W. A. Delamotte, *c. 1830*

In one respect the Wrest pavilion was untypical, for most Chinese pavilions built in England in the eighteenth century were placed beside – or over – water, and were often used for fishing or boating. A good example is the Chinese House in the gardens of Alresford Hall, Essex, where the vertical posts of the front portico were continued downwards into the shallow water to provide a fishing platform, although now the dry land extends for a few yards in front of the house. It is a happily designed building in other respects too, with fanciful but un-oriental windows and a steep verandah whose curve is echoed by the double curves of the pointed roof, which sits like a coolie's hat on the central octagon of the small 'banqueting-room' behind. An estimate exists 'for Building the Chinese Temple for Colonel Rebow', partly with the aid of materials taken from a cottage which previously stood on the site. The estimate, which totals £343 13s 6d, is apparently in the handwriting of a Richard Woods, who was employed by Colonel Rebow at Wivenhoe Park near by in 1765 and 1776–81.[28]

Chinese pavilions were *démodé* by 1776, so that unless Colonel Rebow's tastes were unusually independent, 1765 seems the more likely date.

In 1816 Colonel Rebow's son-in-law, General Isaac Rebow, asked John Constable to paint 'two small landscapes' on his estate, of which one was a 'scene in a wood with a beautiful little fishing house, where the young Lady (who is the heroine of all these scenes) goes occasionally to angle',[29] as Constable wrote to his fiancée Maria Bicknell. This commission was particularly satisfying for Constable, in that General Rebow was a generous friend who was aware – as Constable put it to Maria – 'that *we* may soon want a little ready money'. They were in fact married six weeks later. Both the painting and the fishing house survive, the latter (now known as The Quarters) being perhaps the only eighteenth-century Chinese pavilion that is fully in use today. In the 1950s it was extended and converted into living accommodation, without sacrificing the southern aspect of its triple-decked roofs or their reflection in the waters of the lake.

39

41 'The Mandarin', the Duke of Cumberland's yacht, detail from an engraving by T. Sandby, 1754

Islands were strongly favoured as sites for Chinese pavilions, and a large island temple was observed in the summer of 1768 in the middle of a ten-acre lake at Woburn, 'a very elegant and light *Chinese* temple, large enough for 30 people to dine in'.[30] In a wood on the shore was a kitchen, from which dinner could be ferried out to the 4th Duke of Bedford and his guests. Another sizable Chinese pavilion was built in 1759 for the Duke of Cumberland, second son of George II. His veteran troops were employed in excavating the large artificial lake of Virginia Water in Windsor Park, leaving an island near the bank. Seven years later it was described by Mrs Lybbe Powys:

From hence we went to the Chinese Island, on which is a small house quite in the taste of that nation, the outside of which is white tiles set in red lead, decorated with bells and Chinese ornaments. You approach the building by a Chinese bridge, and in a very hot day, as that was, the whole look'd cool and pleasing. The inside consists of two state rooms, a drawing-room and bed chamber, in miniature each but corresponds with the outside appearance . . . in short, the whole little spot is well worth seeing.[31]

A view of the pavilion on the Chinese Island survives, drawn in the 1830s by W. A. Delamotte. It shows an unusual construction of three adjoining octagons with umbrella-like finials above the pointed roofs. This was not, however, the duke's first Chinese pavilion, for in 1753 another had been built for him on the deck of a converted hulk. The Chinese yacht or junk, as it then became, was forty feet long, and the pavilion formed a 'grand room' twenty feet by fourteen. The ship was fitted with Chinese lanterns, rails and insignia, its hull was decorated with a snaking dragon, and it was christened *The Mandarin*. In the course of their many drawings of Windsor, Paul and Thomas Sandby recorded both the hulk, as it was dragged by oxen from the Thames, and the finished product on Virginia Water, with a huge standard flying at its stern, awaiting inspection by George III and Queen Charlotte.[32]

42 The park at Shaw Hall, Lancashire, watercolour
by Anthony Devis, 1767

If there was no lake available, it was possible
to place a Chinese pavilion in the curve of a river
and then form an island by cutting a canal, as
was done at Shugborough. Alternatively the
pavilion might form its own island, standing on
posts sunk into the river. The Chinese House at
Stowe was of this type, and another example was
erected by Sir William Farington at Shaw Hall
(subsequently called Worden Hall) in Lancashire. Sir William was something of a connoisseur, who is said to have brought back with
him from Italy frescoes from the ruins of
Herculaneum; in 1742 he inherited the estate,
and soon afterwards made considerable alterations to the house. The park in Sir William's
time exhibited the variety of styles typical of mid-
century gardening taste. A painting by Anthony
42 Devis, dated 1767, shows the 'Temple of Retirement', the Chinese House and the 'Gothick
Room' on successive bends of the meandering

72

river. In this case an island was evidently available (and occupied, in Devis's view, by a nude female figure skulking among its trees), but the Chinese pavilion was placed instead in midstream, in a broad curve of the river. It was a square open pavilion, hung with bells at the corners of upper and lower roofs, with shallowly curving bridges continuing the pattern of its trelliswork.

In no English landscape garden is water exploited to greater effect than at Stourhead in Wiltshire, where temples, cottages and a grotto are arranged around a triangular lake in such a way as to allow a series of sudden cross-views as well as a succession of surprises along the circuit. At Stourhead the classical allusions are so strong that it is difficult to imagine that a Chinese pavilion once overlooked the lake; and despite the fact that, rather unusually, it was not placed by the water's edge, it seems during its brief existence to have played a significant role in the drama which unfolded before the visitor's eyes. From the first, the gardens at Stourhead were conceived in a classical image: under the direction of Henry Hoare the Younger, the Temple of Ceres (now the Temple of Flora), the Grotto with its inscriptions from the *Aeneid*, and the Temple of Hercules (now the Pantheon)

were erected in the decade 1745–55, and part of the route around the lake may well have been intended to represent the travels of Aeneas. But by the mid-1750s Hoare was prepared to introduce a more cosmopolitan atmosphere into his gardens, partly by means of English Gothic – both medieval and revived – and partly through oriental features. Richard Pococke visited Stourhead in the summer of 1754, while the new developments were at an early stage. At that time there were two lakes 'which are to be made into one and much enlarged, for which a head is making at great expence,' Pococke wrote. 'There are to be three islands on it. with different kinds of buildings in them, one of which is to be a Mosque with a Minaret.'[33]

This would probably have been the first mosque seen in Britain, but it did not materialize. A little later, however, a Turkish Tent was built on the eastern bank of the lake, painted inside with a mosaic pattern of blue and white and hung with painted canvas.[34] Near by was a Chinese Parasol or Umbrella,[35] a mushroom-like construction which would also have been hung with protective fabric. In addition there was a Chinese pavilion or alcove, north of the Temple of Flora, and a timber bridge which was described as Chinese. In the summer of 1766 the

43 Bridge over the Thames at Hampton Court, wash-drawing by Canaletto, 1754

73

antiquary James Essex noted how the new oriental features took their place along the prescribed route which led anti-clockwise around the lake:

You first go down a Bowling-Green to a cast of the Belvidere Apollo, which leads you to the right into a shady walk[;] the first object that strikes you is a Chinese Pavilion, from thence you suddenly have a

fine view of the Lake and the Temple . . . you then descend and pass over a large Chinese Bridge of one Arch, and enter a grove; you walk some time in a beautiful gloomy path by the side of the Lake and are struck with the appearance of a rude arch of rock work. This is the entrance into one of the most beautiful Grottoes that can be imagined . . .[36]

'Chinese bridges' and 'Turkish tents' deserve a little explanation. Through the writings of Odoric, Pinto and Nieuhof, the bridges of China acquired a reputation for their quality and craftsmanship. Athanasius Kircher illustrated a great single-arched bridge of stone, 'the Flying Bridge' over the Yellow River, and he described another bridge suspended from iron chains, 'possessing the Passengers with giddiness and fear of the ruine and the fall of the Bridge'.[37] Fischer von Erlach reaffirmed the prowess of Chinese bridgebuilders, and Du Halde, who reported both stone and wooden bridges in China, wrote that even the former had 'Banisters each side handsomely carved'.[38] Wooden 'banisters' were adopted in Britain as the defining feature of Chinese bridges; so that in the second half of the eighteenth century almost any footbridge with a decorative wooden railing, however simple, was apt to be dubbed 'Chinese'. The 'Chinese' bridge at Stourhead, which was drawn by the Swedish architect Frederik Piper when he visited the park in 1779, was in reality derived from the sixth timber bridge illustrated in Leoni's edition of Palladio. A short-lived bridge over the Thames at Hampton Court, which was the subject of a wash-drawing made by Canaletto in 1754, appears to have consisted of seven arches on Palladio's model, with concave-roofed kiosks at the points of junction to lend an unmistakably Chinese flavour.

The Turkish Tent at Stourhead was removed (together with the Chinese pavilion and the Gothic greenhouse) in the 1790s by Sir Richard Colt Hoare, who was anxious to banish the unclassical frivolities of his predecessor. But it was only one of several semi-permanent exotic tents recorded at this period, which evolved no doubt from the notion that a small open pavilion might require a canopy in summer, to give protection against the sun or sudden showers. (A Chinese example was built on an artificial hill at Scraptoft Hall, Leicestershire, by a Mr Wigley.)[39] According to Mrs Powys, the Turkish Tent at Stourhead stayed up all the year round, but the fabric of most tents of this kind – others are recorded at Painshill, at Vauxhall and at

44 The polygonal tent at Boughton House, Northamptonshire, c. 1910

43

45 *Corps de garde*, Drottningholm Park, Sweden

Bellevue, Republic of Ireland[40] – was surely intended to spend each winter folded up indoors. An interesting specimen has survived at Boughton House, Northamptonshire, whose walls consist of latticework panels: in warm weather their upper halves swing upwards, to provide ventilation and shade. The roofing material is oilcloth, stamped 'Smith Baber London', painted on the inside with red dragons on a yellow ground. The polygonal tent is said originally to have stood in the gardens at Montagu House, Whitehall, and to have been moved from there to the Montagu estate at Boughton.

The Turkish Tent at Painshill may have been the prototype of several more ambitious structures in Sweden. Having sketched the Painshill tent during his visit to England, Frederik Piper returned to Sweden in 1780 to supervise the landscaping of Drottningholm Park, which was now the property of King Gustaf III, and here a large metal *corps de garde* was built in the shape of a tent. Piper also designed a Turkish Tent in the landscape garden at Godegård in Östergötland, together with a Chinese pavilion and a 'Cham-

pignon or Parasol' no doubt similar to the umbrella seat at Stourhead. At the royal estate of Haga near Stockholm, three large copper tents were built to designs by Piper's successor, Jean Louis Desprez, and one of these, deceptively painted with gatherings and tassels, now forms the entrance to what has become Haga Public Park.[41]

A slightly later variation is the 'Venetian Tent' illustrated in J. B. Papworth's *Hints on Oriental Gardening* (1823), iron-framed and covered in red-and-white striped canvas. Papworth claimed that this tent could be dismantled and re-erected in half an hour, if the sockets were set in place with care. And at the end of that decade a small encampment of tents was pitched opposite the royal Fishing Temple on the shore of Virginia Water: on every tent-pole was the inverted crescent which, since the publication of Fischer von Erlach's engravings of Constantinople a century before, denoted 'Turkish' architecture to the English. Exotically housed to the last, King George IV used to dine in these tents in the final summer of his life.[42]

Chapter Six

Sir William Chambers

THE INDIVIDUAL who did most to promote Chinese architecture in England, and subsequently in Europe, was Sir William Chambers. Chambers was a man of wit and enterprise, qualities that were never quite smothered by the series of royal commissions and public offices which he gathered in the course of his successful career. At the age of sixteen he had joined the Swedish East India Company, and within the next ten years made three voyages to the East, visiting Canton at least twice, but not, of course, the Chinese hinterland, from which European merchants were rigorously excluded. He had already displayed an interest in architecture, and made drawings in the course of his travels: his plan of the temple of Chidambarum, Madras, is preserved in the Royal Institute of British Architects. In the summer of 1749 he returned to England for a brief period, during which he may have met Frederick, Prince of Wales, before leaving to study architecture in Paris and then in Rome. By 1755, when he returned once more to London, he had gained some useful friends and a considerable reputation.

Prince Frederick had died during Chambers's absence, but Chambers now established a firm connection with the royal family, preparing his *Designs of Chinese Buildings* with the encouragement of the new Prince of Wales. In May 1757 the book was published; that summer he was appointed architectural tutor to the young prince (who was shortly to become George III) and architect to his mother, the Dowager Princess Augusta.

Although *Designs of Chinese Buildings, Furniture, Dresses, Machines, and Utensils* was much the most ambitious work of its kind, it was published at a time when Chinese architecture was regarded as unworthy of a serious architect. In September 1756 John Adam mentioned Chambers's project in a letter to his mother, observing that 'a book of Chinese affairs he is publishing cannot raise his reputation high among the truly learned in architecture'.[1] Chambers was aware of the danger, however, and in the month before the *Designs* appeared he publicly announced his intention to bring out a book of classical patterns, in order to establish his credentials as an orthodox architect. In the event, the *Designs* was a success: a handsome folio with an impressive list of subscribers, and (according to Boswell)[2] introductory remarks supplied by Dr Johnson. And far from damaging the reputation of Chambers, it managed to confer a degree of respectability on Chinese architecture in England.

In his preface Chambers trod warily, not only criticizing 'the extravagancies that daily appear under the name of Chinese' but conceding that Chinese architecture as a whole was far inferior to classical, and seldom appropriate in Europe. It might be employed in the less important features of parks and gardens, Chambers wrote, for it had at least the merit of originality, and it had much in common with the architecture of the Greeks – a cunning argument, supported by the classical proportions of the designs which followed.

It is possible that Chambers deliberately incorporated European elements into his designs, in order to make them more acceptable to his readers. But there are several statements in his text that should make us suspicious – such as his declaration that he had omitted most of the examples he had seen in Canton, and that he intended 'only to give an idea of Chinese architecture', for 'exact measurements of Chinese structures are of small consequence to European Artists'. He offered no elevation of Canton's principal pagoda, on the grounds that 'to be of a proper size it would occupy at least three Plates'. And a year before the book was published, Chambers had written to his brother in Gothenburg requesting drawings for Chinese buildings;[3] all of which indicates that Chambers was exaggerating in his claim that all the engravings in the *Designs of Chinese Buildings* were

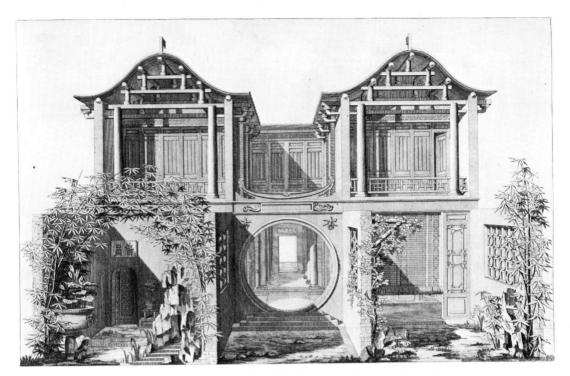

46 Section of a Chinese merchant's house, pl. IX of W. Chambers, *Designs of Chinese Buildings . . .*, 1757

based on sketches and measurements he had taken at Canton.

The plates themselves provide the strongest evidence. They form a mixed group, ranging from a magnificent section of a merchant's house to some unconvincing pots and cups. Seven pavilions or small temples are included, together with a triumphal arch, a bridge, a small pagoda (with plan) and the merchant's house, plans of another large house and the Ho-Nang pagoda, and a detailed presentation of columns and roof-beams. Even if these were based on drawings obtained or drawn by Chambers in Canton, the proportion of authentic Chinese design which they exhibit is certainly smaller than Chambers would have had his readers believe. Most of the plates appear to be the work of a draughtsman playing with oriental detail but imbued with classical principles. All the buildings drawn have a weighty look, even the open pavilions impressively described as 'tings', and for all their distinctive bases and brackets the columns are firmly Roman in proportions. Much of the background information is borrowed from Du Halde; on the other hand there are finials, curlicues, and trellis and fret patterns which could easily have been inspired by the English pattern-books of the early 1750s. To these Chambers no doubt added a few mannerisms of his own, such as the sudden sharp upward twist given to the corners of many of the roofs, a feature which is neither Chinese nor in the tradition of chinoiserie. The final impression is of an uncomfortable compromise between faithful Chinese design and the zestful, unpretentious exaggerations of the Halfpennys, Wrighte and Lightoler.

The designs were taken seriously, nevertheless, and became the prime source of architectural chinoiserie in Europe. French designers drew freely on Chambers's publications, and for Frederick II's new palace of Sans Souci at Potsdam Chambers adapted his own bridge design in preparing a Chinese Bridge in 1763.[4] In the following year the architect received an inquiry as to the number of bricks required to build a replica of the Turkish mosque;[5] and one of his 'Cantonese' open temples, containing a tripod bearing an urn 'in which the Chinese sacrifice gilt paper to their idols on their festivals', reappeared in 1767 on an island in the grounds of Ansley Hall, Warwickshire.[6]

On plate XII Chambers compared six different kinds of 'Chinese' column, which he distinguished almost entirely by their bases. Batty Langley's attempt to organize Gothic columns into the classical scheme of five orders, which had been published twice in the preceding decade, had not yet become notorious, and Chambers's plate was clearly prompted by the same urge to sort his subject into neat categories. Although Chambers did not try to give capitals and entablatures to all his columns, as Langley had done, he could not resist likening the bases of his columns to Grecian models – one to Attic, another to Tuscan – and he varied their roof-brackets as if they were the Chinese equivalents of Greek and Roman capitals. As Langley had tried to codify Gothic along classical lines, so Chambers aspired to be the Vitruvius of Chinese architecture.

Soon after the publication of the *Designs*, Chambers had an opportunity to confirm his reputation in this sphere. The Dowager Princess Augusta asked him to undertake a radical remodelling of the royal gardens at Kew, a commission which offered valuable prestige and great scope for his inventive talents. Chambers did not waste his chance. It was his achievements at Kew that firmly established him as the pre-eminent authority on oriental building in England and on the Continent. When in the later decades of the eighteenth century European garden designers wrote admiringly of English parks, Kew was their favourite example, and to the French in particular the pagoda at Kew (which was based on the best of the *Designs*) was a conspicuous symbol of new and exciting developments in garden architecture.

The adjacent grounds of Kew and Richmond Gardens, which together comprise the present Kew Gardens, had undergone considerable alterations in the early 1730s, largely at the hands of William Kent, who at the same time built the White House (Kew Palace) for Frederick, Prince of Wales. By 1749 the prince had set further operations in motion, and this may have been the occasion of Chambers's first involvement at Kew – Kent having died the year before. Chambers returned from his final voyage in the summer of 1749; the Prince's accounts refer to an 'India House' built at Kew in that year;[7] and in October 1750 Vertue observed a 'new Chinese Summer hous painted in their Stile & ornaments the story of Confucius & his doctrines'.[8] (As at Stowe and elsewhere, 'India House' and 'Chin-

ese House' were synonomous.) This may possibly have been the first Chinese building designed by Chambers.

But there is still a certain mystery attached to the House of Confucius, as it came to be known. In 1763 Chambers wrote of it as 'built a good many years ago, I believe from the designs of Mr. Goupy . . . its walls and ceiling are painted with grotesque ornaments, and little historical subjects relating to Confucius . . . the soffa and chairs were, I believe, designed by Mr. Kent, and their seats and backs are covered with tapestry of the Gobelins.'[9] As John Harris has argued,[10] this is not altogether convincing. If Chambers had been genuinely in doubt as to the architect, he could easily have discovered his identity – from the Dowager Princess Augusta, for example, or from the workmen concerned, or even from Joseph Goupy. Chambers's ascription of the pavilion to Goupy, who is not known as an architect, is also a little surprising, as is his suggestion that the furniture was designed by the deceased Kent. And, more compellingly, the engraving of the House of Confucius carried the inscription 'W Chambers Architectus'. So it may be that the forty-year-old Chambers, author of the carefully considered *Designs of Chinese Buildings*, had no desire to be known as the architect of a playful pavilion which he himself had designed in his twenties, and therefore covered his tracks effectively enough to deceive posterity for two hundred years, forgetting only to remove his name from the engraving.

But the case for Chambers's authorship is far from conclusive. Although not an architect, Goupy had turned his hand to many kinds of design; he painted snuff-boxes for George I, interiors for Prince Frederick and stage scenery for the King's Theatre, and he was renowned for his skilful copying, in gouache, of the drawings of eminent masters: 'he knows how to accommodate his pencil to their different manners of designing and painting.'[11] So versatile an artist as Goupy could have been thought better qualified to design an exotic pavilion than a practising architect trained in the orthodoxies of his profession. (Only a small minority of the oriental pavilions built in English parks are attributable to established architects.) Then there is the question of the furniture. Even if this was not based on an existing design of Kent's, or made in Kent's lifetime and moved from another location, Chambers had no reason to be deceitful: since the 'soffa and chairs' were not illustrated in

47 Sacrificial temple, pl. IV of W. Chambers, *Designs of Chinese Buildings . . .*, 1757

48 'Chinese columns', pl. XII of W. Chambers, *Designs . . .*, 1757

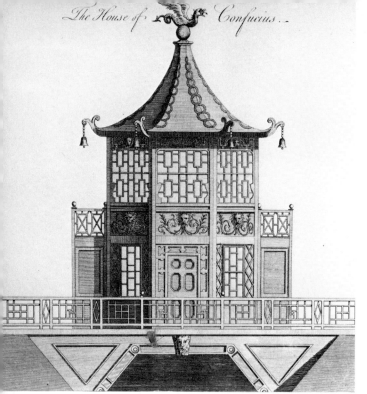

The House of Confucius

49 'The House of Confucius', pl. 15 of W. Chambers, *Plans . . . of Kew*, 1763

from the mongrel designs of the pattern-books, than the House of Confucius; if anything, its roof ornament (which is partly based on the bridge pavilion in *Designs of Chinese Buildings*) curls with a more impish twist. What reason, then, had Chambers to be ashamed of the earlier building? When he reorganized the Kew estate in 1757 – 63, he did not pull down or alter the House of Confucius, but relocated it at the head of the lake.[12] So, far from despising it for its frivolity, Chambers may indeed have been influenced by the decorative little kiosk of 1749 in preparing his own plans for the menagerie pavilion, which – on this line of reasoning – was the first of his Chinese designs to be put into execution.

The light, open character of Chinese architecture was well suited to 'menageries' (which in the eighteenth century housed birds as much as animals), since a barrier of Chinese trelliswork allowed the spectator to view the inmates as they moved from one part to another. As Arthur Young toured the north of England he admired the menagerie at Wentworth Woodhouse, which consisted of 'a little light *Chinese* building of a very pleasing design; it is stocked with Canary and other foreign birds, which are kept alive in winter by means of hot walls at the back of the building; the front is open network in compartments'.[13] At Kew the menagerie contained exotic birds, including 'great numbers of Chinese and Tartarian pheasants',[14] but the Chinese pavilion in the pool afforded little protection to the delicate birds which were supposed to live there, acting simply as a perching-place linked by a straight bridge to the shore.

Kew epitomizes the mid-century vogue for variety in garden architecture. Its five-arched 'Alambra' of 1758 followed the Moorish style, although much less faithfully than did the original drawing by J. H. Müntz on which Chambers's executed design was based.[15] Chambers evidently could not resist adding classical bases to the columns and Gothic finials to the balcony. The Gothic Cathedral was also the work of Müntz; a cattle bridge took the form of a Ruined Arch, through which one of the nine classical temples could be seen; and the Turkish Mosque, triple-domed and flanked by minarets, was derived from Fischer von Erlach's engravings published in England thirty years before. Above the Gothick ogee arches of the mosque doorways were inscriptions from the Koran picked out in golden characters, and the interior was decorated with stuccoed palm trees, their

his Kew volume, he need not have mentioned them at all. Finally the inscription on the engraving could be an engraver's error, understandable in the context of Chambers's other designs.

There is one further factor which, in my mind, tips the balance in favour of Chambers's innocence – the evidence of the second Chinese pavilion engraved in the *Plans . . . of Kew* (1763). It was an open octagon, built in 1760, which stood on a small island in the middle of a circular pond which was itself the centrepiece of the 'menagerie' or pheasant ground. Chambers wrote that he had designed it in imitation of a Chinese open 'Ting'. But the engravings clearly indicate that the pavilion in the menagerie was more similar in design to the House of Confucius than to any of the 'Tings' shown in Chambers's *Designs of Chinese Buildings* of 1757. The later pavilion had an additional roof, and open arches in place of the continuous trelliswork of the House of Confucius, but in general proportions, in curvature of roof, in balustrades and painted swags, the two structures resemble each other quite closely. The overall effect of the menagerie pavilion is no less rococo, no further removed

51

50

50

50 'A View of the Wilderness with the Alhambra, the Pagoda and the Mosque at Kew', pl. 43 of W. Chambers, *Plans . . . of Kew*, 1763

51 'A View of the Menagerie and its Pavilion at Kew', pl. 40 of W. Chambers, *Plans . . . of Kew*, 1763

branches spreading outwards towards a sunny sky painted by Richard Wilson.

The most celebrated oriental structure in Kew Gardens (and perhaps in Europe) was the Great Pagoda, which still stands, some 160 feet high and seemingly even taller, since its ten storeys successively diminish in both height and diameter. After a slight revision of the original plan the pagoda was built in the winter of 1761–62, of grey brick, with balconies at each level and a wooden spiral staircase inside. At the points of each roof crouched winged dragons, 'covered with a kind of thin glass of various colours, which produces a most dazling reflection'.[16] It is unfortunate that these dragons have not survived, for the prospect of eighty dragons apparently poised to swoop down must have been impressive.

There can be little doubt that the Great Pagoda was inspired first and foremost by the so-called Porcelain Tower of Nanking, 'the highest and finest in China',[17] as engraved in Nieuhof's *Embassy* and subsequently in many travel books. It is true that Chambers would have seen several other pagodas in his travels, but the Kew pagoda bears a closer resemblance to the Porcelain Tower than to the pagoda near Canton which he reproduced in *Designs of Chinese Buildings,* or to any of the other pagodas illustrated in the English literature of China. Like the Porcelain Tower, the pagoda of Kew was given a broad basic storey with nine stages above, tapering slightly (although in Nieuhof's well known engraving the tapering effect can be attributed to perspective), a round-arched opening in each of its facets, and a series of rings suspended around its crowning pole. The roofs of Chambers's tower do not sweep upwards with as much verve as those depicted at Nanking, but in each case the upper and lower slopes of the roof-projections are approximately equal, and terminate in dragons. Even the glittering surfaces of the Kew pagoda, the roof tiles 'of varnished iron of different colours' and the 'dazling reflection' from the dragons, were probably intended to emulate the Porcelain Tower, which, as Chambers well knew, had been 'all Glazed over and Painted with several Colours'.[18]

Chambers's last excursion in the Chinese style had little in common either with the *Designs of Chinese Buildings* or with his operations at Kew. In 1772 he completed the reconstruction of the Chinese Temple on the Duke of Queensberry's estate at Amesbury Hall, Wiltshire. 'Temple' is the appropriate description of this porticoed rectangular block, which is a rare combination of classical and oriental elements. There is a heavy entablature and a triangular projection which could be taken for a pediment, while circular windows, slender hexagonal columns and a fret pattern along the frieze provide the Chinese flavour. The building stands solidly on an arch, straddling the stream which runs beneath it, and in this sense it forms a bridge, although far removed in its weighty effect from the ethereal bridge-pavilions designed in the name of Chambers on the continent of Europe.

A Chinese pavilion built on a stone bridge had existed at Amesbury at a previous date, presumably on the same site, and as early as 1750 'a Chinese House and Bridge' were reported in the 3rd duke's garden.[19] Five years later, however, this 'humble imitation of a Chinese house' was said to be 'yet unfinished'.[20] Perhaps it remained humble and incomplete until Chambers was called in to erect something more imposing. The Duchess of Queensberry's letters to Chambers show her concern for the details of the temple's interior decoration. She preferred the motif of '*Oake* leaves and Acorns' to 'old Eggs and Anchors', and she 'would have nothing done in black and white, but glowing and soft, not excluding the requisite light and shade'.[21]

By this time the Chinese style was no longer fashionable among the leaders of British taste. Chambers was occupied with a number of more orthodox commissions, public and private, and one might have expected him to allow his enthusiasm for Chinese art and architecture gracefully to subside. Yet in May 1772 appeared his most controversial publication, the extraordinary *Dissertation on Oriental Gardening.* The *Dissertation* was not a wholly new work, since its core consisted of his short essay 'On the Art of Laying out Gardens among the Chinese', which had appeared fifteen years before as a part of *Designs of Chinese Buildings.* Chambers claimed there that his information was derived from the small gardens he had seen himself in China, and from conversations with a celebrated Chinese painter. But it would be more accurate to describe the essay, like the designs it accompanied, as a skilful blend of borrowings (in this case largely from Attiret), imaginative infilling, and – perhaps – Chambers's own experiences at Canton and its vicinity.

The essay divided garden scenery into three classes, the pleasing, the horrid and the enchanted (categories attributed by Chambers to

Chinese artists, although clearly British in origin). As explained by Chambers, however, the 'enchanting' was scarcely distinguishable from the 'horrid', involving as it did such 'artifices to excite surprize' as underground torrents mysteriously rumbling, complicated echoes and wind effects, and monstrous birds and animals. The 'scenes of horror' were said to include caverns and cataracts, blasted trees and ruined buildings. From these gloomy prospects the visitor would suddenly be transported into delightful scenes of colour and harmony. 'Artifice' was the keynote of the essay. Varieties of buildings and rocks, grottoes, boats, mills and other hydraulic machines were all put forward as characteristic of Chinese gardening. But it was a difficult art, Chambers pointed out (as Temple had done), 'not to be attained by persons of narrow intellects'.[22]

The suggestion that a mild *frisson* of apprehension could form one of the pleasures to be enjoyed by a connoisseur of scenery occurred in the same year in a more substantial publication, Edmund Burke's *Philosophical Enquiry into Our Ideas of the Sublime and Beautiful*. One of the components of the Sublime, Burke believed, was 'a sort of delightful horror, a sort of tranquillity tinged with terror'.[23] To lend weight to this controversial proposition Burke reprinted Chambers's essay in the *Annual Register*, edited by Burke, of 1758. Further support came in 1770 from the pen of Thomas Whately, whose *Observations on Modern Gardening* advised that similar scenes of terror could be effectively introduced in England, with the aid of alarmingly suspended rocks, mines or thundering machinery. Or 'A house placed at the edge of a precipice, or any building on the pinnacle of a crag, makes that situation seem formidable, which might otherwise have been unnoticed'.[24]

Chambers knew both Burke's *Enquiry* and Whately's *Observations* well, and he was now encouraged to expand his short essay of 1757 into an uncompromising attack on Lancelot 'Capability' Brown (to whom Chambers had recently lost a commission) and on the Kent–Brown tradition of landscape gardening. Chambers claimed that English parks imitated 'nature' too slavishly, and with insufficient art; they offered little to amuse, occupy or even shade the visitor. Instead Chambers set out again the pleasures of the Chinese manner of gardening, this time placing still greater emphasis on its artificial aspects. The 'enchanted' scenes were now peopled with 'beauteous Tartarean damsels, in loose transparent robes, that flutter in the air'; there were pavilions occupied by the 'fairest and most accomplished concubines', menageries, decorated dairies, and structures built for wrestling, boxing and quail-fighting. And whereas Whately had on occasion come close to burlesque, Chambers's scenes of terror were turned into comically terrifying pantomime:

Bats, owls, vultures, and every bird of prey flutter in the grove; wolves, tigers and jackalls howl in the forests; half-famished animals wander upon the plains; gibbets, crosses, wheels, and the whole apparatus of torture, are seen from the roads . . . they sometimes conceal in cavities, on the summits of the highest volcanoes, founderies, lime-kilns, and glassworks; which send forth large volumes of flame, and continued columns of thick smoke, that give to these mountains the appearance of volcanoes.[25]

Electric shocks, showers of artificial rain, explosions and hideous cries and creaks were additional surprises which Chambers's vivid imagination allocated to the gardens of China.

It is inconceivable that the *Dissertation* was intended wholly seriously, although Chambers's antipathy to Brown was genuine enough. But how were its readers to react to such a book, written as it was by the Comptroller General of His Majesty's Works, and dedicated to the King? One reviewer was not amused, and practically accused Chambers of behaving in an unpatriotic manner by exalting the clumsy, tasteless Chinese, who lagged behind England (he wrote) in all the arts with the possible exception of politics.[26] Another review came nearer the spirit of the *Dissertation*, declaring that its accounts 'seem to pass the bounds of possibility. But the descriptions are highly entertaining . . .'[27] Other readers made the mistake of criticizing the book as if it were a serious thesis. Horace Walpole declared that it was 'more extravagant than the worst Chinese paper, and . . . written in wild revenge against Brown; the only surprising consequence is, that it is laughed at . . .'[28] Even in the scholarly journals of the twentieth century, articles have been published defending the *Dissertation* as a worthy contribution to garden design, with apologies for Chambers's fanciful aberrations ('Here, perhaps, he misinterpreted what he was told').[29]

The affair is confused by the fact that William Mason, aided by Walpole, published a satire on the *Dissertation* soon after it appeared – 'An

Heroic Epistle to Sir William Chambers, Knight' – which rapidly ran through at least fourteen editions. Mason's motives were political rather than aesthetic, and his 'Heroic Epistle', with its many references to contemporary figures and events, was an effective attack on Tory extravagance. As a parody of the *Dissertation* it merits are less obvious:

Giants from Africa shall guard the glades,
Where hiss our snakes, where sport our Tartar maids
  . . .
Hounslow, whose heath sublimer terror fills,
Shall with her gibbets lend her powder mills.[30]

But the original work, already something of a self-parody, was hardly capable of further exaggeration. Chambers's work remains a good deal more fantastic, and amusing, than Mason's.

Chambers responded to his critics by publishing a second edition of the *Dissertation* in 1773, which was even more transparently unbelievable than the first. He added a bogus air of authority by scattering the text with Chinese names of trees (taken directly from Du Halde) and inserting a poem on the willow in English, French, and transliterated Chinese. The new edition was prefaced by 'An Explanatory Discourse by Tan Chet-qua' – the name of a genuine Chinese modeller of portrait busts who had recently visited England. Chambers introduced the supposed Chet-qua:

. . . he was bred a face-maker, and had three wives, two of whom he caressed very much; the third but seldom, for she was a virago, and had large feet . . . He likewise danced a fandango, after the newest taste of Macao, played divinely on the bag-pipes, and made excellent remarks.[31]

Needless to say, this purportedly Chinese account consists of nothing but Chambers's fantasies taken to still more absurd lengths. The gibbets previously mentioned as elements in the 'horrid scenes' of China were now proposed as a means of enlivening England's duller stretches of countryside, and they were to have 'wretches hanging *in terrorem* upon them'.[32]

Once regarded as the authority on genuine architecture, Chambers now found himself in danger of being cast as a promoter of amusement parks, of Vauxhall-chinoiserie. But as he replied to a correspondent who had objected to the wilder passages of the *Dissertation*, those episodes were 'chiefly contrived to amuse the curious, the vulgar, or the childish . . . Holy-day folks'. The letter in which this admission occurs is altogether disarming, conceding his excesses while reaffirming that 'Art, nay even Whim' could find a legitimate place in a landscape garden. The following extract gives an idea of the provocative spirit in which the much-misunderstood *Dissertation* was written:

We may be puzzled perhaps in England, to find Islands large enough for Ostriches and Forests capacious enough for Elephants. Yet some such spaces might perhaps offer themselves upon a nice enquiry. I am however sorry that they are not often to be met with, as I know I should delight very much to wander in scenes where the enormous Roc (Roc, a large East Indian Bird often mentioned in the Arabian nights entertainments) would figure no more than a common Tom Tit, jesting however apart, I thought it necessary to move in an exalted sphere. Our Gardeners, and I fear our Connoisseurs too, are such *tame* animals, that much sparring is necessary to keep them properly on their haunches. Do not imagine my dear Sir, that this reflection extends to you. You are pleased to allow me some taste, & I cannot refuse you a great deal.[33]

Chapter Seven
Le Jardin Anglo-Chinois

If the English invented the 'natural' landscape garden, then the French took the architecture of the landscape garden to its most theatrical extremes. Yet it was only in the last third of the eighteenth century that French gardens succumbed to *anglomanie*. Until then, grand formal arrangements reigned supreme, and French writers continued to declare, not without reason, that the finest gardens in Europe were French. They were not on the whole impressed by English parks; one authority complained of their lack of fountains, and remarked that English gardening had nothing to offer but lakes, avenues of trees and stretches of lawn called 'Boulen-greens'.[1]

By the early 1770s the first landscape gardens had begun to appear in France, at Ermenonville, at Le Raincy, at the Petit Trianon and at Monceau. Even at this early stage, however, it was 'the garden of incident' which appealed to most French garden designers, rather than Capability Brown's expansive lawns, or the wilder, more overgrown natural effects which were beginning to gain adherents in Britain. In fact the notion of a garden which displayed a variety of architectural styles was espoused by the French just as the English were turning away from it. Partly for this reason, several French designers in the new idiom were reluctant to declare that they drew inspiration wholly from English parks, and spoke instead of '*le jardin anglo-chinois*'. They were inclined to believe that China, and not England, was the home of the landscape garden. Perhaps they also felt that Frenchmen should be better informed about Chinese gardening, through their Jesuit missionaries to China, than were their English counterparts. As one of the greatest connoisseurs of gardens wrote in 1781, 'France is beginning to acquire a number of Chino-English gardens, or Anglo-Chinese, for there is no difference between the two. The French could have had these before the English: but their missionaries were too concerned with conscience and with commerce'.[2]

Chinese architecture had gained a measure of acceptance in France, in principle at least, well before the *jardin anglo-chinois* brought opportunities for its exploitation. In the second (1755) edition of his influential *Essai sur l'Architecture*, Marc-Antoine Laugier admitted that the architecture of China had its own particular merit, and that it received in Europe 'la justice qui est dûe'.[3] Laugier admired Attiret's account of Chinese gardening, and hoped for 'un ingenieux mélange des idées Chinoises avec les nôtres', although he does not seem to have envisaged a landscaped park in the contemporary English manner.[4] We have seen also that several so-called Chinese pavilions were built for the royalty of Europe during the first sixty years of the eighteenth century, including the outlandish summer-houses of Lunéville, which owed little to English fashions in gardening. But these early examples were dubbed 'Chinese' largely by virtue of their interior chinoiserie, and in some cases also because of their treatment of certain details of roof, cornice and column, which by convention came to be regarded as oriental. On the other hand, the flimsy pavilions which appeared in the landscape gardens of Europe captured far more of the spirit of their prototypes in China, both in the lightness of their construction and in their relationship to the surrounding scenery. Many of these garden kiosks were based on English models or English designs, but it was the French belief that the landscape garden was essentially Chinese that provided the impetus for a fresh tradition of oriental architecture in France.

In the autumn of 1775 Horace Walpole visited France, and was naturally interested in the 'English' gardens recently developed there. He went to see *Moulin Joli*, Watelet's island in the Seine, and was not impressed: it was 'joined to *terra firma* by two bridges, one of which he calls Dutch and the other Chinese, and which are as unlike either as two peas'.[5] To Walpole's mind such gardens were pale imitations of the English – 'Anglo-Franco gardens' – and he objected to the idea (for which he blamed Chambers) that English gardens had in turn been 'stolen' from the Chinese. 'I shall tell them another tale when I publish my last volume.'[6] And indeed, when the last volume of his *Anecdotes of Painting in England* was belatedly published in 1780, it made good his promise.

This volume contained Walpole's perceptive essay, 'The History of the Modern Taste in Gardening', which traced the idea of 'natural irregularity' through Pliny, Temple and Kent before discussing the vexed question of the Chinese. It was true that Chinese gardens were irregular, he wrote, but whereas English landscape gardens were irregular insofar as they followed the principles of nature, Chinese gardens were *whimsically* irregular; they were unnatural. Having read Attiret's account of Yuan-ming yuan, he declared (surely untruthfully) that he could find nothing, beyond a determined irregularity, to suggest attention to the ways of nature. The pierced rocks, the many palaces, the arched, twisting bridges and colonnades were too artificial for Walpole's taste. It was a 'fantastic Paradise' far removed from the delights of a truly rural life.[7]

In the second edition Walpole reinforced his argument with a long footnote, reasserting that the French formal garden and the Chinese 'fantastic Sharawadgis' stood at opposite extremes of artificiality, but going on to make some revealing remarks about current French attitudes to gardening. He observed that the French preferred to use their garden architecture rather than simply to pass it by or glimpse it from afar. A French visitor to Strawberry Hill had objected to the English fashion for imaginary temples and fictitious terminations of views; he wanted activity, and functional garden features such as a watering-place at which horses actually drank. One can imagine Walpole raising an amused eyebrow at so naïve a suggestion. 'Such Gallo-Chinois gardens . . . will rarely be executed,' he wrote.[8]

But Walpole underestimated the capacities of French gardeners. He also underestimated the influence of Chambers's *Dissertation on Oriental Gardening*. A timely French edition published in 1773 stimulated the imagination of Frenchmen who, with the enthusiasm of recent converts, hardly cared whether or not Chambers was accurately describing the gardens of China.

Scenes of terror, drama and contrast were rapidly adopted in French garden projects. Even Père Cibot, a Jesuit missionary in Peking and author of an 'Essai sur les jardins de plaisance des Chinois', wrote of Chambers as the creator of 'a happy mixture of Chinese ideas and European ideas'.[9] Elements of Chambers's *Designs of Chinese Buildings* were freely borrowed, although they may have been considered a little lacking in fantasy. Chambers had for many years maintained strong contacts with patrons and architects on the continent of Europe, and now these stood him in good stead.

In 1774 the persuasive prose of Watelet lent its support to the *jardin anglo-chinois*. Much of Watelet's *Essai sur les jardins* is a defence of 'Les Parcs Modernes' and an exposition of the various characters which could be represented therein – the Noble and the Rustic, the Serious and the Melancholy. Watelet believed that artifice was an essential element of the new genre. He pointed to the example of the Chinese, who exploited their temples, altars and triumphal arches in performing dances and mock ceremonies in appropriate costume – although he gave a warning, as Sir William Temple had done, that Europeans could not expect to achieve such perfection. A little later Watelet recommended 'des sites un peu sauvages et dénués d'ornement' as a useful contrast to the more elaborate scenes, a suggestion which indicates the influence of Chambers. Watelet left his readers in no doubt that a landscape garden should not afford merely rational pleasures; it should be a land of enchantment – 'c'est à Sybaris qu'il faut se transporter' – created by borrowing from every period and every culture. In conclusion he quoted at length from a lyrical Chinese portrayal (previously published in the Peking missionaries' *Mémoires*) of a Chinese garden, and added a similarly evocative description of a French garden as it might be. The combination of Watelet's elegant reasoning with Chambers's flights of fancy lent a distinctly oriental flavour to many of the French landscape gardens which followed their lead.

In England the landscape gardening movement had often resulted in the destruction of formal gardens laid out at an earlier date. Not without reason was 'Capability' Brown known to his opponents as 'the destroyer'. But on the Continent formal and informal systems coexisted more peaceably, with the result that when the *jardin anglo-chinois* waned in the nineteenth century, the geometrical layouts of previous centuries could still be maintained and appreciated. A case in point is the Château de Beloeil, situated near the French border in the Belgian province of Hainaut. The formal gardens which survive are largely the conception of the 6th Prince de Ligne, Claude Lamoral II, who described them as 'Les Jardins de l'Intelligence'. But his son Charles Joseph landscaped a portion of the estate, and created 'Les Jardins du Coeur'.

The brilliant and versatile 7th Prince de Ligne became the friend and adviser of several of Europe's leaders of fashion, including Catherine the Great and Marie Antoinette. His *Coup d'oeil sur Beloeil*, which was first printed on his private press in 1781, is considerably more than a catalogue of his own intentions and achievements, for the prince wrote with as much wit and enthusiasm about the other great gardens of Europe as about his own. He greatly admired English gardens, especially Kew and Wilton, although he had a few reservations – 'Stau' (Stowe) he thought had too many buildings ('Mylord Temple s'est trop laissé aller à son nom'), and he claimed that there was not enough water in English parks ('On y meurt de soif . . . En vain faites-vous vos ponts Chinois sur des creux, pour faire croire qu'il y a quelque chose là dessous').[10] The prince's tastes were catholic, and ranged from the architecture of 'Inigo de Jones' ('très noble et très simple') to the Chinese pavilions at Retz, Dornbach, Tsarskoe Selo and Sans Souci. But he warned against an overdose of chinoiserie:

Not too much Chinese, which is too tawdry and becoming too common. If you have a region of wilderness where you want to build some ethnic dwellings clothed in exotic garb, then the Chinese is sure to be most acceptable. Even the design of pleasure-grounds requires discretion, and a building in a foreign idiom is appropriate to a location of the same character.[11]

For himself the Prince de Ligne arranged a Tartar village, composed of thatched buildings in 'le style sauvage' and occupied by singing peasants and picturesque livestock. An existing ice-house or dairy was given the superstructure of a mosque, with two minarets which served as dovecotes. Originally the prince had intended his pigeons to inhabit a Chinese pagoda, and he had hoped also for 'un Temple Indien pour y manger de la crème', whose ground floor would be an open hall with some twenty small columns arranged in two rows; a smaller room would lie above, and there was to be a third stage, smaller still, which would be a false storey without access. This last project seems to have come to nothing, since the proposal was omitted from the 1795 edition of the prince's book, but in its place there was a Tartar cemetery with marble tombstones crowned with turban domes, and fountains in the *genre turc*, such as the prince had seen near Belgrade. He was clearly searching for exotic alternatives to the Chinese style, which by the last years of the eighteenth century seemed to him more appropriate to the boulevards and the fairground. Gothic buildings, he added, were also becoming too common, and (equally damning) 'c'est le fort des Anglois'.[12]

The most accessible landscape garden in France must be the Parc Monceau, once known as the Folie de Chartres, situated near the Arc de Triomphe in Paris. Today prams are wheeled gently past the few features which survive from the park's outlandish prime in the late eighteenth century: a tomb in the form of a pyramid, a cascade and the 'Naumachie', a placid lake flanked by columns which was once the scene of explosive battle-effects. The park was originally laid out in the mid-1770s by Louis Carrogis, better known as the author and artist Carmontelle, for the Duc de Chartres, later Duc d'Orléans. In 1779 Carmontelle published a set of engravings of his achievement, and we can see among its attractions a Dutch windmill, a Gothic ruin, a minaret, Turkish tents, a Chinese bridge, a Tartar tent (depicted by Carmontelle with a camel outside it), and a *jeu de bague* or roundabout beneath a parasol. The roundabout had four seats, two in the form of cushions held by Chinese figures and two in the form of dragons; as the visitors were whirled round, powered by three attendants in Chinese costume, they were supposed to propel some missile at rings which were placed at the edge of the apparatus. A two-seater model was designed for the Folie Saint-James, and another could be found at the Petit Trianon, where the men rode dragons and the women rode peacocks. We can well imagine that Marie-Antoinette spent a few pleasant hours in her abbreviated life travelling at high speed on the back of a wooden peacock.

In the text which accompanied the engravings Carmontelle set down his intentions with admirable clarity, and they may be taken to represent those of a dozen other garden designers who followed his example:

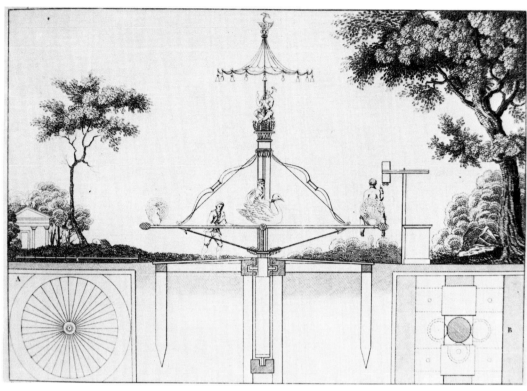

52 *Jeu de bague*, Montbéliard, engraving from J. C. Krafft, *Plans des Plus Beaux Jardins . . .*, 1809

At Monceau we have not tried to create an English garden; we have tried to do exactly what a critic has accused us of – to unite in a single garden every era and every place. It is a fantasy pure and simple, an attempt to form an extraordinary garden, for sheer enjoyment, and not an imitation of a nation which, in laying out natural gardens, runs a roller over every lawn and ruins nature by applying to it the art of a gardener bereft of imagination.[13]

By English standards Monceau (like many other French landscape gardens) was extremely crowded. Carmontelle's defence was that he had filled his forty-eight acres with a large number of features in order that a visitor might be able to tour the gardens on foot in a couple of hours. In addition to the delights of nature, Carmontelle argued, there should be games, concerts and lively amusements. Monceau was conceived as a place for light-heartedness, not for dreams or austere philosophy; and it took account of the requirements of ladies, he claimed, instead of leaving them to their own devices as Englishmen did. A garden must be continually stimulating: 'True art lies in the knowledge of how to retain the visitor's interest, by a variety of objects, without which he will turn to the open country in search of what is not to be found in that garden – the image of Liberty.' We can see again how easily 'liberty' may be invoked in support of almost any cause. The proprietor of the 'Folie de Chartres', however, was less fortunate in borrowing another current catchword: when the Revolution broke out, the Duc d'Orléans joined the Jacobins and styled himself Philippe Egalité, quickly earning the distrust of both sides. After his execution in 1793 the National Assembly claimed his gardens for the state, and for twenty years they were open to the public. Evidently the Revolution did not discredit the *jardin anglo-chinois* entirely. Napoleon himself seems to have appreciated the fashion, for he suggested in 1807 that the Parc Monceau should become 'un jardin véritablement beau *dans le genre chinois*', to complement the formal gardens of Luxembourg and the Tuileries.[14] What further chinoiserie the emperor could have had in mind is not clear.

Under Louis XVIII the Parc Monceau was returned to the heirs of the Duc d'Orléans, who lost it again to the state in 1852. Finally the City of Paris took over the whole district; the park was reorganized in 1861, since which time the remains of Carmontelle's elysium has provided a pleasant haven for strolling Parisians and overfed pigeons. Ironically, Victorian England reacted strongly to the *jardin extraordinaire*, and an English guide to the gardens of Paris illustrated three 'ugly and needless structures in the Parc Monceau', an obelisk, a solid bridge and an octagonal Chinese aviary. The author longed to see the end of 'these sham ruins, sham pools, sham pyramids, toy bridges',[15] for which England had been at least partly responsible.

There was no French equivalent to Chambers, no established architect of chinoiserie or supplier of designs in that genre. But if any individual was pre-eminent in the architectural aspects of landscape gardening, it was the versatile François-Joseph Belanger. In 1769 he was introduced by his mistress, Sophie Arnould of the Comédie-Française, to the Prince de Ligne, whom he subsequently assisted in the prince's operations at Beloeil and at Baudour (where two Chinese towers were built, and a 'château sauvage'). In the 1770s Belanger probably visited England twice, once early in the decade and once in 1777–78; his sketchbook contains numerous views of English parks drawn at both periods.[16] Subsequently he was in demand not only as a practitioner of neo-classical architecture but as a creator of intricate landscapes for very wealthy clients. Chinese designs by Belanger figure prominently in the bulky volumes of engravings compiled by Georges Le Rouge and by J. C. Krafft – a bridge and kiosk for a Parisian garden on the Rue des Victoires, a Chinese bath-house built at 'Madame Bellanger's Propriété Rurale'[17] at Sauteny, and a plethora of oriental buildings located in two of the most spectacular *jardins anglo-chinois* ever laid out, at Bagatelle and Saint-James in the Bois de Boulogne.

The circumstances of their creation were as reckless and excessive as the gardens themselves. Bagatelle was the result of a wager of 100,000 francs between Queen Marie Antoinette and Charles-Philippe, Comte d'Artois (brother of Louis XVI and later to be Charles X), who undertook that he would entertain her in a 'Palais de Fée', built within the three months of the court's sojourn at Fontainebleau. Belanger provided the design, a huge workforce was employed, and building materials were commandeered on the highways; by November 1777

53 The Great Chinese Tent, Bagatelle, engraving from J. C. Krafft, *Recueil d'Architecture Civile*, 1812

54 The Philosopher's Hut, Bagatelle, engraving from J. C. Krafft, *Recueil . . .*, 1812

the Comte d'Artois had won his bet. It was then necessary to transform the gardens of the new Bagatelle into a pleasure ground for the amusement of Marie-Antoinette. The Scottish gardener Thomas Blaikie proposed a landscape garden on English lines, which Belanger converted into *un jardin à la mode*, full of writhing paths and architectural incident.

In this garden the dominant architectural style was Chinese. Most remarkable was the Great Chinese Tent, a cube-shaped room with circular windows, held high off the ground by four draped columns, and apparently prevented by guy-ropes from taking off. Swans curved their necks over the corners of the roof. One of the Chinese bridges linked craggy cliffs at a considerable height, beside a thunderous cascade, while another supported a Chinese pavilion with an exaggeratedly tall ringed mast. A tent-roofed 'Philosopher's Hut', sometimes referred to as Gothic, was balanced on rocks hollowed-out in the Chinese manner, and had to be approached by a spiral staircase inadequately sheltered by a parasol.

In July 1789 the Comte d'Artois made his escape, and in 1793 the Convention decreed that the park should be dedicated to the public. It remained popular under the Directoire and the Empire; in 1809 Napoleon took over Bagatelle as a hunting-lodge, in 1830 the park passed to Louis-Philippe, and in 1835 it was bought at auction by Lord Richard Seymour Conway (later the Marquis of Hertford), who removed many of the surviving garden features but imported one of the pavilions from the Chinese Baths on the Boulevard des Italiens. Today the piled-up rocks can still be seen, but apart from the Bagatelle lodge itself, none of the architecture remains.

Close to Bagatelle in the Bois de Boulogne was an estate purchased in 1772 by Claude Baudard de Saint-James, 'Trésorier général de la Marine'. Anxious to outdo his neighbour, Saint-James engaged Belanger to create a similar but still more opulent landscape garden. The essential component of Belanger's plan was a steam-pump; he harnessed the water of the Seine near by and pumped it in a circuit around the gardens. A waterfall fed a lake, which narrowed into a river and divided to encircle the 'Île d'Amour' and the 'Île des Magnolias', before going underground and reappearing to cascade down the face of a rock. Lastly the system supplied the dwelling-house, and then returned to the Seine. Around this waterway Belanger organized his architectural effects.

Saint-James's pavilion was (and is) a relatively conventional rectangular building, comparable in scale to that of the Comte d'Artois, with a small portico on the garden front which early visitors described either as Chinese or as Moorish. The only other significant survivor is the Grand Rocher, an enormous rock grotto with a Doric colonnade set into a cave. The Turkish temple and bridges are gone, as are the Gothic monument, the swing and *jeu de bague*, and the many structures which housed plants and animals. One of the Chinese pavilions was built above a grotto, and another stood on stilts in the lake, on which visitors could cruise in a Chinese pleasure-boat of matching design.

Baudard de Saint-James enjoyed his private elysium for a few years, and probably succeeded in outdoing his rival in conspicuous consumption. In 1787, however, he was admitted to the Bastille, where he died a bankrupt.

The outstanding source of information about oriental buildings in pre-revolutionary France is a huge but unsystematic series of engravings organized by Georges Le Rouge, known as *Détails des nouveaux jardins à la mode*. The engravings were published in 21 *cahiers* (with slightly varying titles) between 1774 and 1789, displaying gardens and garden buildings from all over Europe. Most are justly described as 'Jardins Anglo-Chinois', for the Chinese contribution is strong, especially in the French contingent. Four *cahiers*, a total of 97 plates, are devoted to Chinese woodcuts which show the emperor of China's many pleasure-houses – some from the French royal collection, 'traced from the paintings executed on silk in Peking', and others copied from the woodcuts of Yuan-ming yuan which Ch'ien Lung had commissioned in 1744. When Le Rouge published these in 1786, the public at last had access to the visual counterpart of Attiret's literary evocation of that most famous of Chinese gardens.

It is unlikely, however, that these *cahiers* had much effect in altering the nature of *jardins anglo-chinois*, which had by now been fashionable for a decade and a half. A typical, though unexecuted, project was the '*jardin anglo-français chinois*' intended for the Venetian ambassador in Paris, the Cavaliere Delphino, which Le Rouge published in his first *cahier* in 1774. Every kind of scenery and artifice was to be incorporated, from a 'désert affreux' to a starlit Temple of the Moon.

55 The Chinese pavilion, St. James, engraving from J. C. Krafft, *Recueil . . .*, 1812

The park was to be divided into such sections as a 'French-Italian' formal garden, a Chinese district whose oriental structures included underwater rooms encrusted with shells and coral, a Dutch shrubbery and a smooth English lawn in the manner of Brown. But the chief novelty was the house itself, which presented four quite different façades. Seen from the grand avenue between the geometrical parterres it appeared as a French château in the grand style. Seen from the lawn its frontage was unmistakably English, with pedimented doorway and windows of mid-Georgian proportions. The visitor who approached the third side had to pass through a grotto which largely obscured a rustic, farm-like aspect of the house; while the fourth side, which gave on to the Chinese garden, was not only Chinese but deliberately irregular: the wings on each side of the central rotunda and the flanking towers outside them were drawn as unlike one another as the designer's imagination would allow.

Another early project published by Le Rouge, a *jardin à l'anglaise* 'designed by the Prince de Croy on his return from London', again indicates that garden chinoiserie was well established in France by the mid-1770s. The prince's palace was to be Italianate, but in the gardens the classical colonnade and antique column were balanced by a five-storey pagoda, a Chinese pavilion and a Chinese bridge leading to an island. A later plan for a 'superbe jardin anglais' to be executed for the Comte de Sévigné shows no fundamental change of emphasis. Again the scale is quite small, there are no broad expanses of grass, and both trees and architecture are assiduously varied. A river, issuing from a cascade, flows past an island which bears a Chinese kiosk approached by Chinese bridges. The kiosk has a moon doorway and is built upon rockwork. The classical temples are not the focal points of the garden, but serve as retreats surrounded on three sides by trees at the perimeter of the gardens.

At the Petit Trianon, however, we can observe a development away from such elaboration towards something simpler. Le Rouge reproduced two plans for Marie Antoinette's gardens on the fringe of the formal parterres of Versailles. The first, by Antoine Richard and dated 1774, exhibits a profusion of architectural features situated among ever-winding paths and rivulets. But in the second plan, dated 1783, the paths and streams serpentize less furiously, and

the exotic buildings have gone; only the two classical temples built by Richard Mique are shown. Even so, the arrangement was too crowded for English tastes. 'There is more of Sir William Chambers here than of Mr. Brown, more effort than nature – and more expence than taste', wrote Arthur Young of his visit to the Queen's gardens in 1787.[18]

In the first six *cahiers* Le Rouge displayed a large number of English garden buildings. Stowe and Kew were both well represented, and several timber bridges caught Le Rouge's eye. Since he relied largely on pirated English engravings, he must have had difficulty in exhibiting Chinese

56

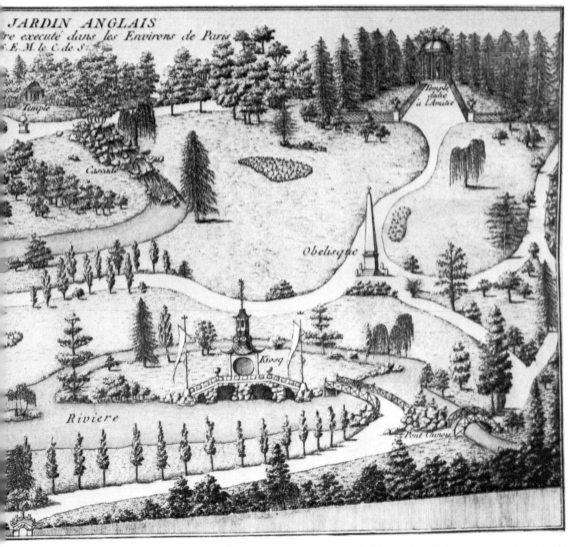

Within the image:
JARDIN ANGLAIS
re executé dans les Environs de Paris
E.M. le C. de S

Temple

Cascade

Obelisque

Kiosq

Riviere

Pont Chinois

56 Projected gardens for the Comte de Sévigné, engraving from G. Le Rouge, *Détails des nouveaux jardins à la mode*, 1774–89

pavilions from English parks (the Chinese House at Stowe had long been absent from the guide-books), and so introduced some inventions. To a plate which contained fairly accurate engravings of buildings at Kew and Stowe, Le Rouge added a Chinese temple adapted from one of Chambers's *Designs*, and a wholly imaginary pagoda. Under the heading of 'Ponts Chinois à Kew', moreover, appeared the wooden bridge at Kew which in fact followed a design by Palladio, and a bridge which, although more oriental in aspect, has never been seen at Kew. The group of oriental designs was reinforced by views of the supposedly Chinese semicircle at Vauxhall and

the polygonal Chinese pavilion at Ranelagh, and by some of the Halfpennys' designs.

Among the many French gardens portrayed by Le Rouge is the Désert de Monville or Désert de Retz, which occupies the thirteenth *cahier*. In September 1774 the cultivated and well connected Chevalier Racine de Monville bought a country estate at Retz, near Chambourcy, and in the next ten years created a magnificent *jardin anglo-chinois* with the aid of a little-known architect named Barbier.[19] A few of the buildings of the Désert de Retz can still be seen: the pyramidal icehouse, the remains of a medieval Gothic church, the Temple of Pan, and – most

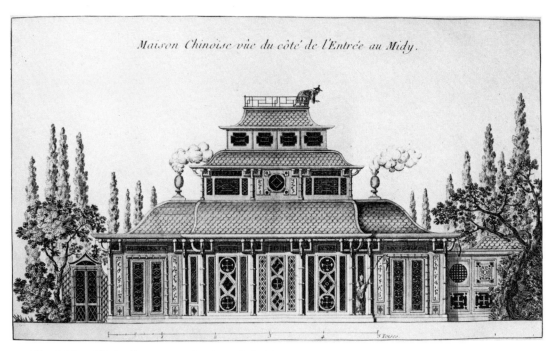

Maison Chinoise vûe du côté de l'Entrée au Midy.

57 The *Maison Chinoise*, Retz, engraving from G. Le Rouge, *Détails des nouveaux jardins à la mode*, 1774–89

spectacular of all – the gigantic stump of a fluted column worthy of Piranesi, built in 1780–81 as a habitable ruin some fifty feet in diameter, with a spiral staircase at its core.

57   For his own residence, however, Monville built a *Maison Chinoise*, one of the few oriental buildings in Europe to be used as a dwelling-house. The outer curves of its roofline are a little reminiscent of Louis XIV's Trianon de Porcelaine, but otherwise the *Maison Chinoise* at Retz is recognizably Chinese, with triple roofs of diminishing size, broad eaves, and intricate geometrical patterning on the exterior panels divided by mock-bamboo columns and brackets. It was built in teak on a stone base, with three ground-floor rooms, the central room containing a divan in an alcove upholstered in appropriately eastern style. A hidden staircase led up to the library, where the oriental motifs were continued, and what appeared from the outside to be a third storey was in reality a lantern lighting the library from above. Oriental vases hung from the eaves, and two others disguised the chimneys. Outside stood two Chinese figures, one holding a parasol and the other a lantern, while close to the ground a Chinese head spouted water which formed a stream and supplied several ornamental ponds. According to contemporary engrav-

ings, another Chinese figure leant negligently over the trellis balcony on the topmost roof. Le Rouge's plate shows a gateway to the *Maison Chinoise* inscribed in oriental characters, but if this was built it has now disappeared, as have the Turkish Tent and the Chinese Orangery.

The Revolution forced Monville to abandon his properties, and in 1792 the Désert de Retz was bought by an Englishman, Lewis Disney Ffytch (or, as a French document prefers, Efytche), but was requisitioned by the District. In the wake of the Revolution the *Maison Chinoise* must have appeared to typify the extravagant frivolity of the *ancien régime*. In 1808 Alexandre de Laborde wrote of it severely:

This structure is an example of the bad taste current at that period, and of the expense incurred in this detestable manner of ostentation. Chinese architecture gives an impression neither of elegance nor of strength. What little merit it possesses lies in a kind of lightness and gaudiness, particularly appropriate in a garden. It should then be skilfully constructed. This pavilion once enjoyed a considerable reputation.[20]

In 1816 Ffytch was able to buy back the Désert, and through several changes of hands the *Maison Chinoise* was adequately maintained during the nineteenth century. But in the twentieth century it was allowed to decay, despite its classification in 1941 as a historic monument. The French government was powerless to intervene until '*le loi Malraux*' came into force in 1971, in time to consolidate the truncated column but too late to prop up the *Maison Chinoise*, which had collapsed in the previous decade. However, its panels have been rescued from the undergrowth, and Monville's unique retreat may yet be resurrected.

In France as in England, it was a commonplace of garden theory that each architectural feature should be in some way appropriate to its location or should harmonize with the natural phenomena around it. Interesting combinations were made possible by a great extension in the range of trees and plants available in France, some imported from England and others from much farther afield. Cedars and willows, laburnums and rhododendrons played an important role in the new gardens. One of those whose estate was landscaped by Belanger was the navigator Bougainville, who tried to grow sugar-cane brought back from Tahiti. At the *Jardin des Plantes* in Paris, botanical and architectural experiments went hand in hand, and at the centre of the labyrinth the twelve strokes of midday were beaten out by a terrestrial globe on a Chinese gong, in a kiosk designed by Verniquet. The two hundred animals exhibited at the *Jardin des Plantes* had cages and enclosures supposedly appropriate to their natural habitat – a rational by-product of the landscape garden.

The influence of China was also evident in the contorted rock structures which were common in French landscape gardens. Caverns and grottoes had been exploited in European gardens for centuries, but in several of the gardens of the late eighteenth century, boulders were piled up into extravagant shapes in emulation of the 'artificial rocks' familiar from descriptions and engravings of China. Often a hollowed-out pile of rocks would serve as a basis on which a Chinese pavilion could be placed: good examples were to be seen at Chantilly, Chanteloup, Bonnelles, Neuilly (Saint-James) and the Hôtel Montmorency, while at the Jardin Ruggieri in Rue Saint-Lazare a kiosk raised in this way acted as a launching-point for the 'saut du Niagara', a precipitous chute which swept foolhardy volunteers downwards in little cars.[21] All these pavilions were slight, however; for structures of any size, the practical problems involved in setting them on their apparently precarious perch must have been considerable. For the Chinese pavilion of Cassan at l'Isle-Adam to the north of Paris, these difficulties were overcome by using a stylized equivalent to a heap of convoluted rocks, in the form of a hollowed-out but eminently solid base of rusticated stone. The success of this solution may be judged by the fact that the Cassan pavilion is the only eighteenth-century Chinese structure of any size still standing in France.

The park of Cassan was bought in 1778 by Pierre Jacques Bergeret de Grancourt, who inherited from his father wealth and a love of the arts. In 1773 he had accompanied his father and the artist Fragonard on a leisurely tour of Italy, where, according to Balzac, the younger Bergeret ('ce bourgeois Sardanapale') was so inspired by the Italian countryside that on his return he spent a huge fortune in recreating the landscapes which – thanks to Fragonard – he had in his portfolio.[22] A plan dated 1790[23] of the new landscape garden at Cassan shows a typical *jardin anglo-chinois*, with a meandering river enclosing a dozen islands, and temples scattered about the grounds. But most of these seem never to have been built, and today only the *Pavillon Chinois* survives. By 1970 it had become a ruin, but the intervention of the municipality of l'Isle-Adam and the architectural skills of M. Olivier Choppin de Janvry saved the pavilion from following its predecessors into oblivion. When the programme of restoration began in 1971, enough of the structure was still in place to permit a substantially accurate reproduction of the eighteenth-century building. It stands on a stone base punctuated by round arches, which encircle a pool of spring-water and an inner vault supported by eight Tuscan columns. This substructure was evidently envisaged from the outset, for it also appears (in abbreviated form) in two alternative designs submitted to Bergeret.[24] In each of these, and in the executed design, the pavilion itself is octagonal, with double roofing and the sharply upturned roof-ends typical of Sir William Chambers's designs, and indeed Chambers's 'Temple of the menagerie' at Kew appears to have been the designers' chief source. Inside, the twentieth-century restorers have appropriately followed the Chinese interiors engraved in Chambers's *Designs*, in painting the wall-panels between the French windows. The bands of triangular patterning on interior and exterior friezes are in keeping with the elegant geometry of the whole.

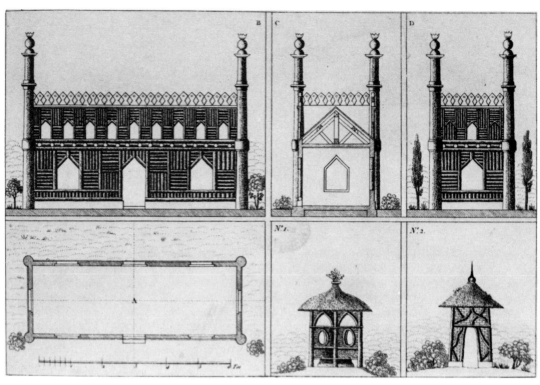

58, 59 'Structure in the Oriental Style', Montbéliard (above), 'Chinese Triumphal Bridge', Montbéliard (below). Engravings by J. C. Krafft, *Plans des Plus Beaux Jardins* . . ., 1809

It is clear that Chambers had more influence in France than in England, through his *Designs of Chinese Buildings* and his *Dissertation on Oriental Gardening*. As M. de Marigny considered how best to construct a Chinese belvedere on his estate at Rond-de-Cour, Menars, he regretted that he did not have Chambers's *Designs* at hand: 'Je suis fâché de n'avoir pas ici l'oeuvre de Chambers qui doit être bon à consulter sur pareille construction,' he wrote to Soufflot in 1771.[25] Adaptations of Chambers's engravings of pavilions and pagodas appear repeatedly in French designs for garden architecture in the last quarter of the century, two significant examples being a pavilion at Arminvilliers for the Duc de Penthièvre and the pagoda at Montbéliard. Moreover, the spirit of the *jardin anglo-chinois* was receptive to the *Dissertation*, especially in its macabre aspects. The park of Monceau had a Wood of Tombs, Bagatelle had an Island of Tombs, and the gardens at Betz, to the north-east of Paris (designed by the Duc d'Harcourt and Hubert Robert for the Princess of Monaco) had a Valley of Tombs whose tragic atmosphere was reinforced by cypresses. The 'fearful wilderness' projected for the gardens of the Cavaliere Delphino was to include blasted trees, ruined shells of buildings, blackened rocks split as if by lightning, an artificial volcano fired by anthracite, and grottoes inhabited by monsters.[26] Chambers could not have hoped for a more wholehearted response.

In France as in England, chinoiserie was favoured at public amusement parks, most notably at Michel Mellan's successful *Redoute Chinoise* which opened in 1781 on the fairground of Saint-Laurent. But the wealthy French landowner, unlike his English equivalent, was encouraged by current fashion to transform at least a portion of his own estate into a 'Vauxhall' of his own. The *jeu de bague* was a favourite plaything; another was the *jeu de quilles*, or ninepins; a third was the *escarpolette* or *balançoire*, a decorative swing. At the *Redoute Chinoise* the *balançoire* consisted of a shell-seat with a grinning Chinaman as its pommel, suspended between male and female Chinese figures. Perhaps the ultimate in exotic garden architecture is to be found in the designs for the Prince de Montbéliard's park in Alsace, reproduced in eight *cahiers* of J.-C. Krafft's trilingual *Plans des Plus Beaux Jardins Pittoresques* (1809). Here the *jeu de bague* is Chinese, the *balançoire* Egyptian and the *jeu de quilles* Persian. Every conceivable style is

60 The pagoda at Chanteloup, Loire Valley

represented, from the Tyrolean mill and Polish cottage to the Persian reading-room and the Moorish Tomb of Chivalry. The designs are often elegant, but sometimes over-ambitious: Krafft observed that the Doric balustrade of the ice-house and the Turkish parasol above it were 'not, perhaps, sufficiently in harmony'.[27] The Chinese buildings included an aviary, a swan-house evidently based on the Grand Pont de Bois at Bagatelle, an elaborate little temple, a triumphal bridge and a brick pagoda of six storeys. An imaginative curiosity is a Mughal temple recreated in logs of rough deal. 'Many of these buildings are to be met with in India; they are built of granite . . .' The surplus branches may have been used to build two tiny huts pictured on the same plate, intended for 'sheltering one's self from the rain'.[28]

After such a glut of exotica it is a relief to turn finally to the tall stone tower of Chanteloup, which stands aloof in a meadow – formerly a lake – near Amboise in the Loire Valley. Its architect was Louis-Denis Le Camus, who built the tower

59

58

60

Vue de la Place et du Sallon Chinois.

61 Sallon Chinois, Steinfort, near Münster, Westphalia, engraving by G. Le Rouge, *Détails des nouveaux jardins à la mode*, 1774–89

in 1775–78 for Etienne-François, Duc de Choiseul, formerly a powerful and liberal minister. Choiseul had then been exiled from the court of Louis XV, and the tower seems to have been dedicated to those friends who stood by him; he had their names inscribed on tablets inside.

The tower has often been described as a pagoda, but it scarcely deserves that title, since the roofs do not overhang the storeys below them and there is no subtly tapering outline. The building consists simply of seven storeys placed one upon the next in the best traditions of the wedding-cake. At the ground level is a peristyle of Doric columns, the second storey is encircled by pilasters, and the upper storeys are all octagonal, but differ in details of windows and balconies. The various patterns carved in the stonework are classical. Only the wrought-iron railings can be recognized as Chinese, although the plaques over the lower windows were once inscribed with Chinese characters.

The tower, 131 feet high, is indeed so little reminiscent of a pagoda that we cannot simply regard it as an amusingly inept folly. Its proportions are majestic, and its solid structure supports an inner stone staircase which twists gracefully upward at the perimeter, unlike the central spirals of Kew and Montbéliard. The ascending visitor could pause at each stage in a vaulted room or '*reposoir*', rewarded by increasingly splendid views over the forest of Amboise. Originally the rooms were furnished, and two tourists in 1800 could describe them as pretty;[29] today they are bleakly impressive. It is an accomplished and individual building, which owes little or nothing to Chambers, and whose peculiar dignity puts to shame many of the short-lived contrivances of the *jardin anglo-chinois*.

The fashion for landscape gardening spread rapidly throughout Europe in the last decades of the eighteenth century, and in many cases Chinese pavilions were built to adorn the newly created parks. A most elaborate 'Jardin Anglo-Franco-Chinois', as Le Rouge described it, was laid out at Steinfort, near Münster in Westphalia, between 1780 and 1787 for Count Ludwig of Bentheim and Steinfort. The garden structures included a triple-roofed Chinese palace similar to the pavilion at Retz, containing views of China taken from Nieuhof, and a 'Sallon Chinois en Treillage pour prendre le Frais'.[30] Patrons of this pavilion were supervised by Chinese deities who nodded their carefully balanced heads; similar figures can still be seen

61

in the corridor of the Royal Pavilion at Brighton. In Le Rouge's engraving Steinfort appears to have had a fairground atmosphere, with patently artificial rocks, hills and islands, and an open-sided ferry which might have been inspired by the Chinese kiosk in the canal at Ranelagh.

If Steinfort was dedicated to casual amusement, the Chinese village at Wilhelmshöhe near Cassel represented a more earnest attempt to combine novelty with function. The village (known as 'Moulang') was the conception of Friedrich II, Landgrave of Cassel: in the course of the 1780s and 1790s several cottages, a dairy, a barn, stables and cowsheds, together with a single-storeyed 'Pagoda', were built in a purportedly Chinese style consisting of bright colours and curved ornaments over the windows. Despite the assistance of Negro dairymaids (Chinese being unavailable), the dairying project was not a success, and the cottages were soon leased off.

In Hungary the Turkish occupation of the later seventeenth and eighteenth centuries had left its mark in the form of minarets and mosques; when landscape gardens subsequently became fashionable, the Moslem influence was revived, and domed kiosks and lodges took a prominent place among the customary variety of exotic garden buildings. The Esterhazy park at Csák-var, laid out in the last two decades of the eighteenth century, included a *Bâtiment Turc*, a *Temple d'Apollon* and a *Gloriette Chinoise*.[31] Similar developments were taking place elsewhere in Eastern Europe. In 1770 Frederick the Great was entertained by Count Albert von Hoditz at Rosswald (or Rudoltice) in Silesia, amid grottoes, pagodas and a fancy dairy. Chinese pavilions were among the apparatus at Cervený Dvůr (Rothenhof), near Krumlov, while at Vlašim, to the south-east of Prague, the park of the Auerspergs boasted a two-storey Chinese pavilion whose upper storey could only be reached by bridge from an adjoining tower. Near the Austrian border at Lednice (Eisgrub), a two-hundred-foot minaret was built in 1797 by Josef Hardtmuth for Alois Josef von Liechtenstein; it still stands.[32]

62 The gardens at Steinfort, engraving from G. Le Rouge, *Détails . . .*, 1774–89

Vue de la Grande Cascade Sauvage à Steinfort.

When Archdeacon William Coxe passed through Warsaw in 1778, he visited the grandest estates in the neighbourhood.[33] At Powazki he attended a *fête champêtre* and sat in a 'Turkish' tent; but at the island residence of Lazienki, Coxe was a few years too early to see the sets of interlocking Chinese canopies with which Johann Chrisostom Kamseter (better known as a neo-classical architect) created a pair of covered walkways from the shores of the lake to the central island. The surrounding Ujazdów Park contained a number of small structures built under the direction of the Italian Domenico Merlini, with the collaboration of Kamseter after 1780. Merlini was one of several Western Europeans employed on Polish parks at this time: he was probably the architect also of the hilltop Chinese temple in the nearby gardens of Jablonna.

As Archdeacon Coxe continued his travels eastward, he was gratified to find landscape gardens even in Russia. 'We could not avoid feeling extreme satisfaction that the English style of gardening had penetrated into these distant regions,' he wrote at the royal park of Miakulka.[34] The greatest devotee of this style was the empress herself, Catherine II, who in 1772 confessed that she was addicted to the *jardin à l'anglaise* – 'l'anglomanie domine dans mon plantomanie'.[35] She was already an admirer of chinoiserie, and in the early 1760s a 'Chinese Palace' (Chinese, that is, in its interior decoration) was built for her at Oranienbaum near St Petersburg. But when in the following decade she began to landscape her

63 The Chinese village at Tsarskoe Selo, near Leningrad

palace gardens at Tsarskoe Selo, with the aid of John Bush of Hackney, she decided to erect a complete Chinese Village in the grounds of Aleksandrovsky, one of the two palaces at Tsarskoe Selo. This project, which may have been stimulated by a Russian edition of Du Halde in 1774, seems to have preceded that at Wilhelmshöhe, although it took a number of years to realize: designs for it (perhaps by I.V. and V.I. Neelov) existed before the arrival of the Scottish architect Charles Cameron in 1778, but one of Cameron's first tasks was to design some additional Chinese pavilions and an eight-storeyed pagoda which was never built.[36]

At the time of writing the Chinese Village is being restored. Several of the houses have fresh supports for the upswept corners of their roofs and have regained their intricate wooden window-tracery. Vestiges of old paintwork can still be seen, in bands of blue and red.

Several other Chinese features may still be seen at Tsarskoe Selo. The Great Caprice is a rustic arch spanning the roadway, crowned by a small kiosk, which may have been inspired by a plate in Nieuhof's *Embassy*.[37] The Creaking Pavilion in the adjoining park of Yekaterininsky is a delightful composition, with some bizarrely shaped windows and doors; it was deliberately intended to creak, but whether the weather-vane or the floorboards were supposed to make the desired noise is uncertain. Near by is the cruciform bridge, on which an octagonal kiosk is approached by pairs of staircases on each side of the stream. All these structures were built in the later 1770s to the designs of Ilya Neelov, a young architect who had visited England. For the bridge Neelov made use of one of William Halfpenny's patterns; had Halfpenny been alive, he would have been pleased to learn that one of his designs, which were so seldom adopted in Britain, had met with the approval of the Empress of Russia.

One further outstanding example of oriental architecture in Europe may be mentioned here, although it has little connection with the *jardin anglo-chinois*. Indeed, the Chinese Palace of La Favorita at Palermo is entirely *sui generis*. Sicily may not seem an obvious site for a mock-Chinese palace, and it was not voluntarily chosen as such, for La Favorita owes its existence ultimately to the might of the French revolutionary army which caused King Ferdinando IV of Naples to transfer his court rapidly to Sicily in December 1798. In the following month he bought an estate just outside Palermo, where the architect Giuseppe Patricola erected for him a square four-storeyed palace. The Chinese elements are an octagonal tower with two bell-like cones above it, a polygonal upswept canopy above the giant columns of the semicircular portico, fret-patterned railings at the balconies, and mock-Chinese characters added in paint. To this blend of classical and Chinese, Patricola added Islamic features – a broad parapet halfway up the palace, and a pair of open-walled minarets exposing spiral staircases which lead up to the Turkish salon on the third floor. The exterior of La Favorita thus reflects the variety of its interior decorations, which include rooms in the Chinese, Turkish and classical styles.[38]

64 The Chinese palace of La Favorita, Palermo

Chapter Eight
Contact with China Renewed

'European artists are too cool and chaste,
For Mand'rin only is the man of taste.'

James Cawthorn, 'Of Taste'

JAMES CAWTHORN's satirical poem 'Of Taste' was published in 1756, but 'Mand'rin' was a remote figure indeed at that time. No Englishman had seen the Emperor of China, nor the Great Wall, nor the imperial palaces with their celebrated gardens.[1] Knowledge (and legend) of China had to be obtained from Jesuit missionaries and from the few embassies sent out by other European governments. There had been English trading links with China since the early seventeenth century, but all European traders were restricted to the outposts of Macao and Canton, where they were prevented from making direct contact with officials of the Chinese government. So any drawings made by English travellers, such as Brett and Chambers, could be based only on what they had seen in the provincial city of Canton, 1,500 miles from the Chinese capital.

The first British attempt to penetrate to the Imperial Court at Peking was made in 1787, under the command of Colonel Charles Cathcart. The embassy sailed in *The Vestal*, and included a capable topographical artist, Julius Caesar Ibbetson, who would no doubt have executed a useful series of drawings of China had he not been forced to turn back at the East Indies, where Cathcart died of tuberculosis.

A larger expedition was now prepared under the leadership of Lord Macartney, an experienced diplomat, in the hope of extending British trade with China and of establishing a permanent ambassador there. Julius Caesar Ibbetson was offered another chance to savour 'the Hookah and the Bamboo sofa' which he had enjoyed briefly on Cathcart's embassy, but he refused the post, and recommended instead William Alexander, one of his pupils; and Alexander was among the ninety-five men who set sail, in two ships, for China in 1792. Alexander was 'Draughtsman', and there was also a 'Painter', Thomas Hickey, an Irishman like Macartney whose portrait he had once painted: 'I believe he executed nothing whatever

while on the embassy,' wrote a fellow-traveller, 'but in conversation he was a shrewd, clever man.'[2]

The embassy sailed up the Chinese coast past Canton and reached Peking, before travelling north another hundred miles, beyond the Great Wall, to be received by the Emperor Ch'ien Lung at his summer residence of Jehol. The emperor was apparently well disposed towards the visiting party, but like his predecessors he saw little advantage in forming closer contacts with Europe. So Macartney had to return, his objectives unfulfilled, carrying an edict from Ch'ien Lung to George III which acknowledged the 'tribute' paid by the embassy and requested the King of England to swear perpetual obedience to the Celestial Empire. (Observers attributed the failure of the mission to Macartney's refusal to kotow to the emperor, but several other European delegations had carried out the three kneelings and the nine knockings of the head without any greater success.) In a month and a half, however, the visitors saw a good deal of the Chinese hinterland, which was duly recorded by Alexander and by Lieutenant Henry Parish, who commanded twenty artillerymen and drew some valuable sketches in addition.[3]

So spectacular an expedition brought a profitable opportunity for the returning travellers to publish their memoirs. Macartney's second-in-command, Sir George Staunton, brought out an 'Authentic Account' with engravings after Alexander in 1797; John Barrow, comptroller of the embassy, published four works related to the expedition, including about half of Macartney's own journal (which was published in full in 1962); and other accounts were provided by Staunton's son's tutor, by a private in the dragoons, and – the first to reach print, but thoroughly ghost-written – by Aeneas Anderson, Lord Macartney's valet. Three other members of the embassy left journals which have not been published.

The most perceptive of all these is Macartney's own record, which describes the daily progress of his mission and also includes detailed observations of many aspects of life in China. In the present context it is interesting to compare his descriptions of Chinese gardens with the *Dissertation* of Sir William Chambers, for Macartney and his entourage were probably the first Europeans other than missionaries to see the imperial gardens at Jehol, and they enjoyed the additional privilege of being conducted around the many features by Ho-shen, the emperor's chief minister. Macartney was evidently familiar with the literature of landscape gardening; Ho-shen was surprised to discover that his guest knew the gardens of Jehol were the creation of the Emperor K'ang Hsi.[4] And unlike many of his fellow countrymen, Macartney appears to have been more impressed by the characteristics shared by Chinese and English parks than by the differences between them. He found himself reminded, at various stages in his tour, of the gardens of Stowe, Woburn, and Painshill – all gardens noted for their architecture, appropriately enough, since Macartney was taken to forty or fifty palaces and pavilions in the course of his voyage around the garden's lakes. But he appreciated also the rural aspects of the scenery. 'Had China been accesible to Mr. Brown or to Mr. Hamilton I should have sworn they had drawn their happiest ideas from the rich sources which I have tasted this day.'[5] The contrasts of shape and vegetation, the succession of unexpected views, and the carefully sited ornamental buildings all appealed strongly to Macartney's English tastes.

Lancelot Brown had in fact been 'improving' the park at Luton Hoo for Lord Bute, Macartney's father-in-law, at the time when the *Dissertation* was published, and one might guess that Macartney did not admire Chambers's book. When the accompanying Chinese minister pointed out a private imperial enclosure in the distance, Macartney was careful to observe that

from everything I can learn, it falls very short of the fanciful descriptions which Father Attiret and Sir William Chambers have intruded upon us as realities. That within these private retreats entertainments of the most novel and expensive nature are prepared and exhibited by the eunuchs who are very numerous (perhaps some thousands) to amuse the Emperor and his ladies, I have no doubt; but that they are carried to all the lengths of extravagance and improbability

those gentlemen have mentioned I very much question . . .[6]

Nevertheless, when Macartney visited the western gardens at Jehol, which were wilder and more mountainous than the eastern gardens he had seen before, he described their raging cascades, gloomy pools and yawning chasms in language not far removed from Chambers in his more moderate vein, and his journals contain one outburst of purple prose which can stand beside anything in the *Dissertation*. A few days before reaching Canton on his return journey, Macartney had set off in a small shallop for the temple of Pusa. After a dramatic journey through frowning mountains, startling precipices and sullen floods, 'an ancient bald-headed bonze issued from his den, and offered himself as our conductor through this subterranean labyrinth'. Presently they confronted the god Pusa himself – 'a gigantic image with a Saracen face, grinning horribly from a double row of gilded fangs . . .' Opposite the god was a view to match: 'The convoluted rocks above shooting their tottering shadows into the distant light, the slumbering abyss below, the superstitious gloom brooding upon the whole, all conspired to strike the mind with accumulated horror and the most terrifying images'. To complete the Gothick picture Macartney reported a group of fanatical devotees of the cult existing in wretched condition, 'buried under a mountain and chained to a rock, to be incessantly gnawed by the vultures of superstition and fanaticism'.[7]

Summing up his observations of Chinese gardens, however, Macartney came down against the idea that horror played a significant part in them. He had seen no artificial ruins, caves or hermitages, he wrote, and 'cheerfulness' was the dominant impression he had received. Chinese garden architecture pleased him particularly:

All the buildings are perfect of their kind, either elegantly simple or highly decorated according to the effect that is intended to arise . . . The architecture of the Chinese is of a peculiar style, totally unlike any other, irreducible to our rules, but perfectly consistent with its own. It has certain principles from which it never deviates; and although, when examined according to ours, it sins against the ideas we have imbibed of distribution, composition and proportion, yet upon the whole it often produces a most pleasing effect; as we sometimes see a person without a single good feature in his face, have [*sic*] nevertheless a very agreeable countenance.[8]

Together with the seven literary accounts published in the years immediately following the embassy's return, a series of views of China was made available to the English public, which for the first time was able to see the celebrated scenery and architecture of the Chinese interior depicted in an idiom which it could understand and appreciate. Alexander's paintings of Chinese figures, ships and buildings, exhibited at the Royal Academy between 1795 and 1800, are in the finest tradition of English topographical watercolour, detailed and yet delicate. Sometimes he might exaggerate the curve of a roof, but in the main he resisted the temptation to romanticize his subjects, and we may concur in the judgment of the embassy's comptroller that 'Mr. Alexander drew beautifully and faithfully in water-colours, and omitted nothing that was Chinese'.[9]

Engravings based on Alexander's drawings reached a wider audience. Among the forty-eight plates in his *Costume of China* (1805) were admirably clear (if not especially glamorous) representations of Chinese brickwork and tiling, in 'A Pagoda near Soochow', 'The Habitation of a Mandarin', 'South Gate of Ting-hai, Tchusan'

65

65 'The Habitation of a Mandarin', aquatint from W. Alexander, *The Costume of China*, 1805

and 'A Pagoda near Tin-hai'. But it was the folio volume of engravings published with Staunton's *Authentic Account* in 1797 which did most to reveal the mysteries of Chinese architecture. The western gates of Peking, the gardens of the imperial palace crowned by its white marble dagoba, the Great Wall, the Lama temple known as the Potala near Jehol, and the hall of audience at Yuan-ming yuan, together with a sluice-gate, a waterwheel and a variety of pagodas, bridges, arches and domestic buildings, became familiar to English readers through the medium of line engraving. Alexander's views remained unrivalled until the era of photography; well into the nineteenth century they were used, often without acknowledgement, to illustrate books on China, such as *The Chinese* by John Francis Davis (published first in 1836 and many times subsequently). By 1843, when the four volumes of the Rev. G. N. Wright's *China, in a Series of Views* appeared, it was possible to utilize the drawings of Lieutenant Frederick White and Captain Stoddart, R. N., who had been involved in the first Opium War, but for many of the plates the publisher relied still on Alexander's works, redrawn by Thomas Allom for the steel-engraver.

Many of the significant monuments in the history of Anglo-oriental architecture have been inspired by drawings brought back by European travellers – Peircy Brett, William Chambers, William Hodges, Thomas and William Daniell, and perhaps Matteo Ripa. It would be surprising if William Alexander's accomplished drawings did not play a considerable role in the renewed interest in chinoiserie which affected England in the two decades following his return from China. Macartney's embassy had been an expensive failure and a blow to British pride; even before the expedition had left England, Gillray had skilfully depicted the humiliation which the enterprise was likely to incur. British merchants continued to be outmanoeuvred and frustrated by the Cantonese bureaucracy, and there was increasing evidence that the willow-pattern image of a gentle, carefree China dominated by benevolent rulers was an illusion. Yet the reports of Macartney and his colleagues were not unappreciative of Chinese culture; and however displeased the Prince of Wales may have been by Ch'ien Lung's uncompromising message, he was at any rate not deterred from adorning his Music Room at Brighton with scenes derived from Alexander's drawings.

Thus Macartney's embassy brought about a renewal of interest in China and its artefacts. But a revival of architectural chinoiserie depended on the additional influence of a skilled architect capable of breathing fresh life into the moribund forms of Anglo-Chinese design. In the years between the publication of Chambers's *Dissertation* and the French Revolution, oriental architecture was at its most fashionable on the Continent, but almost completely neglected in Britain. Only at the end of the 1780s, when events in France had stemmed the tide of the *jardin anglo-chinois*, was any oriental project of note begun in England, and it is no accident that the architect concerned, Henry Holland, had visited France shortly before. If Chambers had exported oriental architecture across the Channel, Holland re-imported it with an added element of sophistication.

Holland was on three occasions chosen to complete projects which Chambers had begun, although the latter was still professionally active, and on two of them – at Carlton House and at Woburn Abbey – the work involved oriental designs. There is a certain irony in the fact that Holland thus inherited the mantle of Chambers, for Holland was the son-in-law of Lancelot Brown, on whose ancestry and abilities Chambers had poured so much scorn. Chambers must have particularly regretted losing the Carlton House commission after his forty years of connection with the royal family; but the Prince of Wales, dissociating himself from his father's Tory associates, turned instead to Henry Holland, whose undertakings for Whig patrons included Brooks's Club in St James's Street. Prince George became a member of Brooks's when he reached his majority in 1783, and when in the same year he was voted a palace of his own, he decided that the remodelling of Carlton House should be placed in the hands of Holland. Chambers carried out some initial repairs in his capacity of Surveyor-General, but by 1784 Holland seems to have taken charge of the operations.

In the autumn of 1785 Henry Holland was in Paris. His work had already suggested affinities with French neo-classical design, and some of his subsequent achievements indicate that he took a close interest in the latest building projects in the French capital. The Hôtel de Salm, completed by Pierre Rousseau in the year of Holland's visit, boasted an Ionic screen comparable with the screen which Holland was soon to extend across the forecourt of Carlton House, and on the Hôtel's garden front a rotunda encircled by stone statues resembles the arrangement designed by Holland in 1787 for the Marine Pavilion at Brighton. The semi-peristyle of eight columns at Brighton bears an even greater resemblance to Ledoux's Hôtel Thélusson (1783). Bagatelle would also have attracted Holland, and there is further reason to suppose that he paid a visit to the Comte d'Artois's wager-winning pavilion. Two of those who helped to create Bagatelle, the decorator Alexandre Louis Delabrière and the furniture-dealer Dominique Daguerre, came to England subsequently to work for Holland. At Bagatelle Holland would of course have inspected the copious chinoiserie in the gardens and, emboldened by what he saw, would have returned to submit oriental designs to the Prince of Wales and the Duke of Bedford.

Under Holland's direction Carlton House received a solidly Palladian exterior, with a central Corinthian portico and rusticated façade. The interiors were largely in a delicate and restrained classical idiom, whose French inspiration did not escape notice. In 1790 the Chinese Drawing Room came into existence; fortunately it is documented by two engravings in Sheraton's *Cabinet Maker and Upholsterer's Drawing Book* (1793), and by an inventory of the room's contents. One engraving shows the south wall, with a pier table in the Chinese taste between the windows; the other shows the rest of the room, with another pier table on the left, a chimney-piece on the right (both of these have ormolu mounts of dragons, and Chinese terms), and along the north wall an ottoman capable of being warmed mechanically in winter. The pier tables and chimney-piece are now at Buckingham Palace.[10]

For the details of the Chinese Drawing Room, Holland certainly referred to Chambers's *Designs*, borrowing discreetly and selectively. The arrangement of Chinese wall-paintings within bamboo frames seems to derive from Chambers's engravings of interiors, but Holland added a series of thin columns around the room, with 'collars' (as he described them) similar to those illustrated in the first of Chambers's 'Different Kinds of Columns'. At the top of each column was a pair of lei-wen spirals hung with bells – an elegant adaptation from one of Chambers's 'Tings' (*Designs*, plate VIb), also the source of the trellis-patterned dado which ran around the lower part of the Drawing Room walls.[11]

66 The Chinese Drawing Room at Carlton House, looking north, engraving from Thomas Sheraton, *The Cabinet Maker and Upholsterer's Drawing Book and Repository*, 1793

Holland was at the same time working on a Chinese exterior, in the grounds of Woburn Abbey. Chambers had been employed there by the 4th Duke of Bedford, but the young 5th duke, also a member of Brooks's Club, engaged Holland to continue the alterations to the house and to add a number of outbuildings, including the Chinese Dairy which still remains. It is a most successful piece of lakeside architecture, but the oriental flavour is mild: the lines of the roof and even the octagonal lantern above are not particularly Chinese in effect. A colonnade follows the curve of the lake and continues slightly modified as the porch frontage of the dairy, whose trellised railings at the waterside are repeated above the arches, forming an open balcony at first-floor level. The regular and unambitious pattern of the trellis, which is maintained in the painted windows of the dairy, has no precedent in the *Designs*; nor has the geometrical pattern with which the interior walls and ceiling are painted, probably by John Crace, who also worked for Holland at Carlton House. But the decoration of the ledge which runs around the dairy is taken directly from the thirteenth plate of the *Designs*, and in the centre

of the room is a small octagonal table almost exactly like Chambers's prototype on the same plate, which stands directly under the octagonal lantern as if it had dropped from the cavity above. The glass windows of the dairy were painted by Theodore Perrache in 1789,[12] which we may assume was the date of the dairy's completion; since Holland's sketches for the Carlton House Drawing Room are dated January 1789, and since his bill for its furnishings is dated November 1789, the architect must have been at work on these two rather dissimilar Chinese enterprises simultaneously.

When Prince Pückler-Muskau visited Woburn in December 1826 he admired the Chinese garden, in which the dairy (then fully operational) was 'a prominent and beautiful object':

It is a sort of Chinese temple, decorated with a profusion of white marble and coloured glasses; in the centre is a fountain, and round the walls hundreds of large dishes and bowls of Chinese and Japan porcelain of every form and colour, filled with new milk and cream. The 'consoles' upon which these vessels stand are perfect models for Chinese furniture. The windows are of ground glass, with Chinese painting, which shows fantastically enough by the dim light.[13]

Something of the atmosphere of the dairy was communicated, in the form of little cupolas and semi-oriental trelliswork, to the Park Farm built on the Woburn estate in 1795–98 by Robert Salmon, who had worked under Holland at Woburn and at Carlton House. Even in the mid-twentieth century the tradition has been maintained, for the 'Flying Duchess Buffet', which stands between the dairy and the abbey, has trellised arches and a boldly sweeping roof which (as the guide-book explains) 'consists of two hyperbolic paraboloids'. Like the dairy, the buffet is oriental by allusion rather than by imitation.

While his palace in London was under construction, the Prince of Wales was forming an attachment to Brighton, where he first visited his uncle the Duke of Cumberland in the autumn of 1783. In the following year he fell in love with Mrs Fitzherbert, whom he married – secretly and without the consent of the king – in 1785, and

with whom he spent many pleasant weeks in Brighton. As well as the open company of Mrs Fitzherbert, Brighton could offer a congenial social atmosphere sufficiently removed from his disapproving father, and a salt-water cure for the prince's swollen glands. In October 1786 his steward, Louis Weltje, leased a timber-framed farmhouse close to the Duke of Cumberland's seaside retreat, with an option to purchase and rebuild; and in 1787 Henry Holland was asked to convert the farmhouse into a princely residence. The Marine Pavilion at Brighton was constructed almost as rapidly as Bagatelle in the Bois de Boulogne. Between April and July of 1787 Holland added a building similar to the existing farmhouse on its north side, creating two rooms out of each, and linked the two structures by a central circular saloon. Thus the five principal rooms formed a long, narrow suite, facing on their eastern side Brighton's broad thoroughfare, the Old Steine. To the west were servants' wings flanking a pedimented portico. The circular saloon projected into the gardens on the Steine side, its curve accentuated by an Ionic col-

67 The Chinese Dairy at Woburn, Bedfordshire

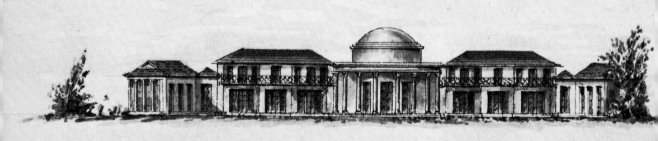

Elevation to the Steyne as executing.

68 Henry Holland's executed design for the Royal Pavilion at Brighton, 1801

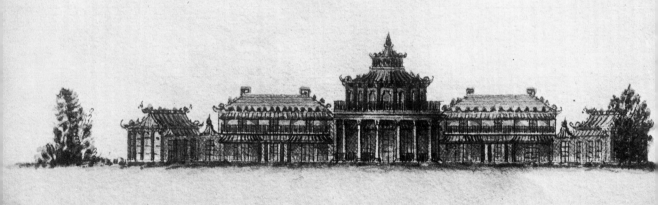

A Design for the Elevation to the Steyne.

69 Henry Holland's design for a Chinese façade at the Royal Pavilion, 1801

onnade, and above, a shallow cupola rested on a drum surrounded by classical statues in Coade stone. The interior of the saloon was decorated with painting by Biagio Rebecca. The accounts drawn up by the prince's steward show that 'John Crace, painter' was also employed,[14] and paid £141, but there is nothing to suggest that Crace was asked to carry out decorations in the Chinese style at this early stage.

Contemporary engravings show a pleasant, unpretentious building, its drum a little awkward but generally light and elegant; many of its early visitors commended its design. But even in its classical phase the Pavilion did not escape hostile criticism. A French visitor described it as a country parsonage,[15] and the *New Brighton Guide* of 1796, by 'Antony Pasquin', disliked its layout:

The Pavilion is built principally of wood; it is a nondescript monster in building, and appears like a mad house, or a house run mad, as it has neither beginning middle nor end . . .[16]

In the following year Staunton's account of Macartney's newly returned embassy to China was published, together with Alexander's views; and when, in July 1801, Holland submitted plans for enlarging the Marine Pavilion, these included a 'Design for the Elevation to the Steyne' which clothed the entire building in Chinese garb – upswept roofs, with dragons at their corners, chinoiserie finials and lei-wen spirals. The central dome would thus be converted into a two-storey pagoda, thereby ingeniously disguising the drum, which in any case had lost its classical statues. Another design in the same sketch-book, 'Elevation to the Steyne as Executing', shows the additions which were in fact carried out in 1801–02 (in Holland's absence, supervised by his nephew P. F. Robinson): an eating room and a conservatory, jutting out at 45 degrees north-east and south-east respectively from each end of the Pavilion. Since the Chinese design already included these extensions, it must have been put forward as a possible future adaptation. Only one element of that design appears to have been adopted: the green, outward-curving metal canopies (subsequently a fashionable feature of Regency architecture), which appear in the chinoiserie design but not in the 'Elevation to the Steyne as Executing'. They may be said to comprise the first oriental aspects of the exterior of the prince's Pavilion.

There is further evidence that the Chinese project was seriously entertained, in the form of

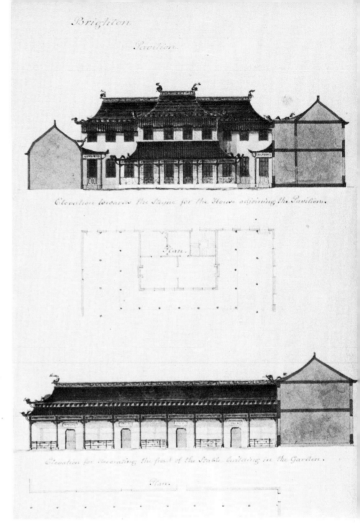

70 Designs by Henry Holland for buildings on the royal estate at Brighton, 1802

two coloured drawings made by Holland in November 1802. These designs, more clearly defined and confident than that of the previous year, proposed Chinese façades for the stable building and for the house occupied by Louis Weltje, which linked the stables to the end of the southern servants' wing of the Pavilion. At the same time the prince began to import through Crace and Sons large quantities of furniture, porcelain, figures and trinkets from China, envisaging, it seems, a complete Chinese empire in miniature at Brighton. According to Edward Brayley, chinoiserie was first introduced into the Pavilion as follows:

Whilst the improvements were going on in the year 1802, several pieces of very beautiful Chinese paper were presented to the Prince, who for a time was undecided in what way to make use of them. As the Eating room and the Library, which were between the Saloon and the new northern wing, were no longer required for their original purposes, Mr. Robinson, on being consulted, advised the Prince to have the partition removed, and the interior formed into a Chinese Gallery. This was immediately agreed to; the walls were hung with the paper described, and the other parts of the Gallery were painted and decorated in a corresponding style ... Such then were the circumstances under which the Eastern style of decoration was first adopted at the Pavilion.[17]

Brayley's story, written a generation after the events described, need not be accepted unquestioningly – Holland's design, and indeed the prince's interiors at Carlton House, suggest that the Chinese decorations at the Pavilion did not wholly depend on a gift of wallpaper – but Holland's accounts in the Royal Archives go some way towards confirming Brayley's date of 1802 as the turning-point in the Pavilion's interior design. Holland's bill for the years 1801–03 refers to 'making Designs for Chinese Decorations and directing the execution for Works and Furniture by Messrs. Saunders, Hale & Robson, Marsh & Tatham, Morell, Crace ...'[18] And in 1802 an account register was opened with the family firm of Crace, specialists in exotic design for five generations. Their greatest contribution, however, belongs to a subsequent phase in the development of the Royal Pavilion, in which Indian influences mingled with Chinese to produce the splendid fantasy that we may see today.

Although Henry Holland inaugurated a revival in certain circles, Chinese architecture was never again to become widely fashionable. By the last quarter of the century it was no longer considered necessary that a garden should display buildings from a variety of civilizations, and of such architecture as remained, sham ruins and crumbling masonry were gaining preference over the formality and symmetry of classical temples. In the 1790s the Picturesque came into its own, promoted by the writings and sketches of the Rev. William Gilpin and by the closely reasoned treatises of Uvedale Price and Richard Payne Knight. Neat Chinese pavilions were allowed no place among the irregular forms and shaggy silhouettes which Gilpin and his followers admired. It is true that the elegantly ramshackle hovels drawn by Pillement fulfilled many of the ideals of the Picturesque, but these were not enough to counteract the image of Chinese building as essentially artificial and precise. In *The Landscape, A Didactic Poem* Knight included two engravings, one of a river winding past smooth lawns and clumps of trees towards the symmetrical façade of a mansion, and the other a view from the same spot as Knight would have liked to see it – the mansion partly obscured by vegetation, the river banks overgrown and a fallen tree trailing in the water. The simple bridge visible in the first plate is replaced in the second by an even simpler one of rough wood framework. According to the text of the poem the first bridge is Chinese, and it seems to typify all that Knight most detested:

> But false refinement vainly strives to please,
> With the thin, fragile bridge of the Chinese;
> Light and fantastical, yet stiff and prim,
> The child of barren fancy turn'd to whim:
> Whim! whose extravagancies ever try
> The vacancies of fancy to supply ...

The Landscape thus not only attacks 'Capability' Brown ('whose innovating hand/First dealt thy curses o'er this fertile land') but associates his style with the 'whim' of Chambers, which

> With fairs and markets crowds a garden's glades,
> And turns the fishwomen to Tartar maids;
> Bids gibbets rise, and rotting felons swing,
> To deck the prospects of a pious king.[19]

If there was one Englishman of this time who might have been expected to create a thoroughly exotic garden, by virtue of his immense resources, his independence of fashionable opinion and his lifelong interest in the East, it was surely William Beckford. In his youth Beckford was taught the principles of architecture by Sir William Chambers, while Alexander Cozens instructed him in drawing and the nine-year-old Mozart taught him musical composition. Chambers may have communicated to Beckford some of his interest in China, and Alexander Cozens undoubtedly inflamed his pupil's imagination with eastern romance. (Unfortunately one of Beckford's less flamboyant tutors, the Rev. John Lettice, prevailed on Beckford to burn a 'splendid heap of oriental drawings and Arabian tales'.)[20] The young Beckford's fantasies must have been encouraged further by Fonthill Splendens, the house in which he was brought up. The original Elizabethan mansion, 'Fonthill Antiquus', was largely destroyed by fire in 1755, whereupon Alderman Beckford built himself a Palladian

71, 72 Alternative styles of gardening, engravings from *The Landscape, a Didactic Poem*, by Richard Payne Knight, 1794

mansion (completed in 1768 and demolished in 1808), which contained a Turkish Room and an arched Egyptian Hall eighty-five feet long, its ceiling designed by James Wyatt. The buildings in the park included a pagoda, constructed apparently before the fire.[21]

At an early age Beckford immersed himself in travel-books about China and Japan, and some of his reading-notes have survived: they include a reference to the illuminated tower of the Chinese Empress Tan-ki, perhaps a spiritual ancestor of the great tower Beckford was to build at Fonthill Abbey. In *L'Esplendente*, a novel which Beckford wrote before he was twenty, the boy-hero is shown some oriental manuscripts by an aged Jew (no doubt representing Alexander Cozens) and resolves to paint exotic scenes, including 'the antient King of China with his long nails, surveying his golden fantasies'. At a later stage architecture engaged this character's attention, 'and he built lofty towers in the morisco style'. In December 1782 Beckford himself was said by *The Rambler* to be preparing a lavish Eastern entertainment: 'a large temporary building' was to contain an artificial sun and a painted sky, and Indian music was to issue from its gallery.[22]

In 1787, after his wife's death and his own exile from polite society in England, Beckford left for the family estates in Jamaica. He was seasick, however, and got no further than Lisbon, which proved a happy chance both for himself and for readers of his diaries. Portugal had much to interest the orientalist, even after the earthquake which (in the same year, 1755, as the fire at Fonthill Antiquus) had devastated its capital city. 'From what I learn from every person, Lisbon abounded more than any city in Europe with precious Japan ware and Indian curiosities,' Beckford wrote soon after his arrival. A week later he was entertained in the Marquis de Marialva's 'gay pavilion designed by Pillement and elegantly decorated', with a sparkling chandelier hanging from a dragon's mouth.[23]

But Beckford's reactions to the great Manueline buildings of Portugal show that, for all his literary fantasies, he was at heart no admirer of oriental flamboyance in architecture. At Batalha he praised the proportions of the arches in the *Claustro Real*, and the elegance of their tracery, but the *Capelas Imperfeitas* were too much for him:

... the roofless, unfinished cluster of chapels, on which the most elaborately sculptured profusion of orna-ments had been lavished, as often happens in similar cases, to no very happy result. I cannot in conscience persuade myself to admire such deplorable waste of time and ingenuity – 'the quips, and cranks, and wanton wiles' of a corrupt, meretricious architecture ... Saxon crinklings and cranklings are bad enough; the preposterous long and lanky narrow-spoon-shaped arches of the early Norman, still worse; and the Moorish horse-shoe-like deviations from beautiful curves, little better.[24]

He professed himself glad that these chapels were never finished but decided that it would be indiscreet to criticize 'Don Emanuel's scollops and twistifications' in the presence of his hosts.

The *Recollections* quoted here were written by Beckford at the age of seventy-four, forty years after his visit to the Portuguese monasteries, but they do not misrepresent the tastes of his younger days. In September 1787 he had been un-impressed by the Manueline windows at Sintra Palace, 'which are all of an oriental fantastic shape'; and the eighteenth-century Palace of Mafra, huge but entirely free from any oriental influence, elicited a most conservative response from the English visitor:

On each side two towers, somewhat resembling those of St. Paul's in London, rise to the height of three hundred feet. They are light and clustered with pillars remarkably elegant, but their shape borders too much on a gothic or what is still worse, a pagoda-ish style, and wants solemnity.[25]

So it is not, after all, surprising that when Beckford came to reorganize the estates of Fonthill Abbey, he did not deck out the grounds with oriental oddments. He did enclose some 1,900 acres of landscaped gardens with a twelve-foot wall, possibly in emulation of the gardens of Yuan-ming yuan, whose great size and encircling walls were emphasized by several of the chroniclers of Macartney's expedition. The park at Fonthill also featured a good deal of rock-work, with grottoes and a hermitage; but none of the contemporary accounts or engravings yields any evidence of oriental buildings. Later, in his garden at 20 Lansdown Crescent in Bath, he had a little 'Moorish' summer-house built, with an onion dome, but he admitted that this style was not much to his taste. Beckford's love of the outlandishly oriental was manifested more fully in literature: *Vathek* (1786), with its callous caliph and countless concubines, is a worthy successor to the *Dissertation* of Chambers.

3

Chapter Nine
The Indian Revival

THE 'INDIAN REVIVAL' forms a short but fascinating episode in the history of taste. In several respects it was unlike its Chinese counterpart. Whereas chinoiserie entered Europe by degrees, adaptations of Indian art and architecture flourished rather suddenly in the last quarter of the eighteenth century. Moreover, the Indian Revival in English architecture had no parallel movement elsewhere in Europe, where commercial and cultural links with India were less strong; and since it was largely restricted to a small group of connoisseurs, the Indian fashion in architecture was characterized by a conscientious, often scholarly attitude unmatched by most patrons of chinoiserie. Yet the immediate sources of the movement are not intellectual but visual: they lie in the paintings and engravings of William Hodges and of Thomas and William Daniell.

These English travellers were by no means the first Europeans to record the architecture of India, for a line engraving of two Indian temples was made available in Europe as early as 1596, when Jan Huygen van Linschoten, a Dutchman who had lived in India for five years, published his *Itinerario*. Translations into English, German, Latin and French quickly followed. One of the most clearly delineated plates, engraved from the author's own drawing, shows at left a Hindu 'pagode' carved from the rock, while at right stands a 'mesquita' or mosque with three diminishing storeys and tiled roof. The columns

73 Indian architecture as portrayed in Jan Huygen van Linschoten, *Itinerario . . .*, 1596

and entablature of the 'mesquita' suggest the European eye of the artist. The Hindu 'pagode' was perhaps intended to represent the temple of Salsette, for the grandeur and intricate sculpture of the rock-temples at Salsette and Elephanta had been publicized through the Portuguese settlement of the west coast of India.

The first European to describe Elephanta thought that it might be Chinese in origin, 'seeing that it is so well worked'[1] – an interesting indication of the status of Chinese architecture in 1534. In 1590 Gasparo Balbi thought Elephanta must be an ancient Roman temple built by Alexander the Great. But by the seventeenth century Hindu architecture was generally respected in its own right. Other cave-temples were explored and praised, and in the north of India English visitors were appreciative of the monuments they saw. Sir Thomas Roe, English ambassador to Jahangir's court in 1615–19, lamented the ruin of the ancient stone-built city of Chitor, and admired its 'reverend and brave Reliques of Imagerie and carved workes, that few or hardly any where can be equalled'.[2] (Most Indian people, however, lived in houses 'of mudde, not so great as a Cottage on Hownslo-heath'.)[3] At the fortress of Mandu the imperial party was joined by the Reverend Edward Terry, who praised the house in which the emperor was staying: its 'many excellent Arches and Vaults speake for the exquisite skill of his subjects in Architecture'.[4]

By the second half of the seventeenth century the great Islamic monuments of Mughal India were beginning to rival the earlier Hindu and Jain temples in European eyes. François Bernier, one of a group of distinguished French travellers in the third quarter of the century, thought that Shah Jahan's Jami' Masjid at Delhi might be admired even if it were transported to Paris. He rated the Taj Mahal at Agra still more highly:

I believe it ought to be reckoned amongst the wonders of the world, rather than those unshapen masses of Aegyptian pyramids, which I was weary to see after I had seen them twice . . .[5]

In the eighteenth century this appreciative attitude was supplemented by studies in Indian religion and mythology, and in the iconography of Indian art. As British power in India grew rapidly in the second half of the century, so did British interest in Indian culture. In the 1780s the cave-temples near Bombay were accurately delineated. Sir William Jones founded the pioneering Asiatic Society in Bengal, and translations of the *Bhagavad-Gita* and *Sakuntala* were undertaken, the latter by Jones himself. The reputation of Chinese art, on the other hand, was at a low ebb, and Chinese architecture began to be compared unfavourably with Indian. The traveller Pierre Sonnerat was not an uncritical admirer of Indian temples, but he found in them 'something more noble and majestic than those of the Chinese, or even of any other people on the face of the earth'.[6] At this propitious moment William Hodges, a professional landscape artist who had accompanied Captain Cook on the *Resolution*, left England again to seek success in the infinitely promising yet unexploited terrain of India.

Hodges spent the years 1781, 1782 and 1783 touring northern India, recording its architecture and landscape under the patronage of Warren Hastings. The resulting sketches and oils were exhibited for several successive years at the Royal Academy, and forty-eight of the views were published between 1785 and 1788 as *Select Views in India*. Despite the impeachment of his patron, Hodges's work aroused a great deal of interest. Like his master Richard Wilson he was criticized for inattention to detail, but the sheer dramatic power of his prints presented Indian architecture to British eyes for the first time as something aesthetically admirable. Sir William Jones told his audience in Bengal that 'correct delineations' of Indian buildings would soon be published, and these might 'furnish our own architects with new ideas of beauty and sublimity'.[7] Sir Joshua Reynolds recommended Hodges's work with typically guarded praise: 'the Barbaric splendour of those Asiatick Buildings, which are now publishing by a member of this Academy, may possibly . . . furnish an Architect, not with Models to copy, but with hints of composition and general effect which would not otherwise have occurred.'[8] Hodges had just been elected an Associate of the Royal Academy, and in the following year he became a full member.

The text of *Select Views in India* reveals how deeply Hodges had been impressed by the architecture he had seen, both Moslem and Hindu. It was not merely a case of his capturing 'the most curious appearance of nature and art', as he had previously been commissioned to do on Cook's second voyage in the South Seas. In *Select Views* Hodges wrote as a proselyte eager to convert his readers. But he was careful not to overstate his case: the palace at Faizabad was 'in many parts very beautiful', while in a mosque elsewhere 'the swelling dome is certainly not a beauty'.

In 1787 he attempted a reasoned defence of Indian architecture in a *Dissertation on the Prototypes of Architecture, Hindoo, Moorish and Gothic*, which he probably intended to accompany a series of large stipple engravings, although the project seems to have been cut short.[9] Hodges had every respect for Greek architecture, he wrote, 'but must I admire it in an exclusive manner? or, blind to the majesty, boldness, and magnificence of the Egyptian, Hindoo, Moorish, and Gothic, as admirable wonders of architecture, find fault with them, and unmercifully blame and despise them, because they are more various in their forms, and not reducible to the rules of the Greek hut, prototype, and column?' There was no single standard of beauty, Hodges concluded; to the Chinese, even the Greek column must appear heavy.[10]

74 'View of the Musjid at Jionpoor', engraving from W. Hodges, *Select Views in India*, 1785–88

Hodges paraphrased these observations in *Travels in India* (1793), a book of small-scale engravings which did scant justice to the grandeur of their subject-matter. His earlier work however, had made a visible impression on English architecture. On 4 June 1788 George Dance, a fellow-Academician and neighbour to Hodges, submitted to the City Aldermen a design for a new south front of the Guildhall. It was accepted and executed, and most of Dance's façade is still visible. The original medieval porch was retained, but several of the details – the projecting turrets, the decoration above the central arch, and the scalloped arches of the windows – have an Indian flavour.

It is quite possible that the City Aldermen did not recognize the design as oriental, and that Dance, prudently, did not enlighten them. Hodges had pointed out that Indian and Gothic architecture had many motifs in common, including 'the lozenge square filled with roses'[11] of which a version can be seen in the Guildhall
75 façade, and (he might have added) the cusped arches, which in fact appeared in the earlier Gothic design by Dance for the same building; only in the context of the façade as a whole are they to be seen as Indian. And it is the façade as a whole which owes most to Hodges, in particular to his thirteenth 'Select View', entitled 'View of
74 the Musjid at Jionpoor' (Jaunpur). This plate shows the massive gateway of the Jami' Masjid

75 The Guildhall, London

punctuated with four storeys of dark-shadowed pointed arches above the entrance. Although the Guildhall frontage is divided by classical pilasters rather than the recessed arch depicted by Hodges, its resemblance to the 'View of the Musjid' is striking. And if the City Aldermen were unaware of the Indian origins of their Guildhall, others did recognize the 'Hindoo Gothic', not always with approval.[12]

Dance continued to draw on Indian design in his highly individual architecture. He developed a shallow dome and finial, ringed by curved anthemion-patterned 'battlements' similar to those which surrounded the Guildhall turrets. The first private house on which these turret-caps appeared was Cole Orton in Leicestershire. Dance rebuilt Cole Orton (partly in Gothic style) in 1804–06 for the collector and amateur artist Sir George Beaumont, who was no doubt more interested in the picturesque aspects of Dance's skyline than in any particular references to India, and indeed the oriental nature of Cole Orton's turrets is again ambiguous. But there is little doubt that Dance was influenced by the ideas of

Hodges. At dinner at the Beaumonts' London house in 1804, Joseph Farington observed that the architect 'derided the prejudice of limiting Designs in Architecture within certain rules which in fact, though held out as laws, had never been satisfactorily explained',[13] sentiments which echoed those of his friend Hodges who had died seven years before.

In 1806 William and Dorothy Wordsworth stayed in a farm near Cole Orton, and walked beside the Beaumonts' new mansion by moonlight: 'the turrets looked very beautiful tonight,' wrote Dorothy.[14] But Victorian additions muffled the originality of Dance's work, and today Virginia creeper curls around the famous turrets.

Dance's cap-domes reappeared at Stratton Park in Hampshire, the property of Sir Francis Baring. Since Sir Francis was a director of the East India Company, he may have felt that their Indian connotations were appropriate. The eastern gateway to Stratton Park was similar in proportions to a Mughal gateway, and the scroll moulding along the parapet can be seen as an

76 The eastern gateway, Stratton Park, Hampshire, executed design by George Dance

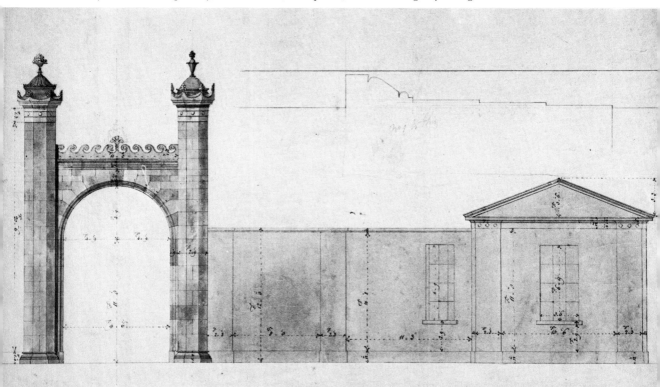

allusion to the crenellation of many Indian counterparts. A similar gateway served as *porte-cochère* in another of Dance's projects, at Ashburnham in Sussex (1807), where the house, the *porte-cochère* and a bridge in the gardens all displayed the characteristic turrets. They can be seen yet again in Dance's designs for Norman Court in Hampshire (1810).

One further, and earlier, country house bears the marks of Hodges's influence. In 1788 Warren Hastings bought the estate of Daylesford in Gloucestershire, which had been the property of his family earlier in the century, and commissioned Samuel Pepys Cockerell as his architect. Cockerell had strong connections with India, and was moreover a friend of Hodges, to the extent of serving as a guardian to Hodges's children after the artist's death. Hodges had remained equally loyal to Hastings, who when Daylesford House was built was not yet acquitted of the charges brought against him. At Daylesford Hastings hung Hodges's Indian oils, created an Eastern gaming-room in the basement, and installed two marble chimney-pieces with Indian figures carved by Thomas Banks. The exterior of the house was completed in 1793: it is a porticoed late-Georgian mansion, orthodox except in one prominent feature – a shallow, pleated dome, topped with a circular leaf ornament from which emerges a ball-and-needle finial. It is undoubtedly Indian, though subdued in shape, and several comparable domes can be found in the pages of its most likely source, Hodges's *Select Views*.

While Hodges was preparing his engravings in 1785, two other artists were sailing eastwards, Thomas Daniell and his nephew William. By August they had reached the Canton estuary, and they spent several months sketching the Chinese coastline. To judge by the Chinese views which they published in 1810, the Daniells were not particularly curious about Chinese methods of building, since of the twenty-four aquatints devoted to China and Macao only two or three are of much architectural interest, and one of these, depicting the Whampoa pagoda, allows this nine-storey structure to be upstaged by a passing boat. The Daniells admired Chinese gardening but described China as 'a country where good taste appears to be almost unknown'.[15]

Early in 1786 the Daniells arrived in Calcutta, where they published twelve engravings of the city. They then began a series of watercolour drawings which was to bear fruit in the 144 majestic aquatints known as *Oriental Scenery*. The Daniells travelled many thousands of miles in India, up the River Jumna and down the Ganges, and extensively in the south, sketching the landscape and above all the monuments of Islamic and Hindu architecture. In 1793 they returned to England. They expected to outdo Hodges in their engravings, and in the eyes of many Englishmen they succeeded; certainly their work was smoother and more detailed in its representation of architecture. Publication began in 1795, and the last instalment reached the public in 1808.

The first English building associated with *Oriental Scenery* was designed by Thomas Daniell himself, a small temple erected on behalf of a former soldier in India, Major Sir John Osborne of Melchet Park. Two engravings of the Melchet Park temple were published (both based on a drawing by William Daniell), a small line engraving reproduced in the *European Magazine* in December 1802, and a larger aquatint printed with an explanatory text. It seems that the building was erected in 1800, in artificial stone, under the supervision of John Rossi; it measured twenty-two feet by fifteen, and was a little under twenty feet high. Two Brahmin bulls sat above the porch, and the figure of Ganesa, god of wisdom and policy, was placed above the entrance to the temple proper. Thomas Daniell evidently based its design on a small temple near Rotas, in Bihar, which he had reproduced in the first series of *Oriental Scenery*.[16] It was a happy design for an English park, neat but distinctive in its features, and (as the text to William Daniell's aquatint observed) 'after the chastest models of Hindu architecture'.

The Melchet Park temple had an additional significance in that it was intended as a tribute to Warren Hastings, who was a friend of Major Osborne and a frequent visitor to Melchet. Anyone entering the temple doorway would have been confronted with a bust of Hastings 'rising out of the Sacred Flower of the Lotus'. This bust appears in another engraving by William Daniell, where its inscription can be read:

Sacred to the Genii of India, who, from time to time, assume material forms to protect its nations and its laws, particularly to the immortal Hastings, who, in these days, has appeared the saviour of those regions to the British Empire . . .

77 'The Temple at Melchet Park', aquatint drawn and engraved by W. Daniell, 1802

78 'An Ancient Hindoo Temple, in the Fort of Rotas, Bahar', aquatint from T. & W. Daniell, *Oriental Scenery*, 1795–1808, 1st series

So Warren Hastings was honoured as an incarnation of a Hindu deity – a point emphasized by the portrayal of the principal incarnations of Vishnu on the temple walls. It was hoped that such homage to Hastings would not be thought profane, but as the inscription observed, 'extraordinary characters can only be described in extraordinary language'.[17]

In about 1850 the temple was removed, because it was repeatedly plundered at midnight (or so the rector of the neighbouring parish recalled).[18] For a time, a few of the statuettes could be seen in the park, but these too were stolen, until by the end of the century all trace of temple and memorial had disappeared, except for a curious little poem written by Hastings and discovered among his papers a century after his death. Its title is 'On the Temple at Melchet':

> This monument which Osborne's ardent mind
> For real worth with erring aim design'd
> With blameless rapture I survey, though mine
> The bust, the tablet, and inscriptive line.
> With other eyes than his who bade it spread
> The beams of glory round my humble head,
> I view the splendid dome, its lustre thrown
> From mine reflected brighter on its own . . .[19]

In this modest vein the poem continues, concluding with a fulsome tribute to John Osborne. When Hastings was acquitted in 1795, Osborne had been one of the twenty-two guests at his celebration dinner,[20] and we may infer that Osborne had remained a staunch ally to Hastings during his impeachment. Though its stone was artificial, Osborne's temple stood as a gesture of genuine loyalty and affection which Hastings must have deeply appreciated.

The Melchet temple, however, was not the first of its kind to be built in England. In 1784 James Forbes (1749–1819), an assiduous student of Indian life, retired after twenty years in the East to Great Stanmore in Middlesex. By 1793 he had built an octagonal temple in his garden, to house a group of figures which were said to be the only specimens of Hindoo sculpture in England. They were presented to him 'by the Brahmins of Hindoostan as a grateful acknowledgement of benevolent attention to their happiness during a long residence among them'.[21] But before long the figures were removed, and the temple was dismantled early in the twentieth century.[22]

Possibly James Malton had this little building in mind when he complained in 1798 that 'the rude ornaments of Indostan supersede those of Greece; and the returned Nabob, heated in his pursuit of wealth, imagines he imports the *chaleur* of the East with its riches'.[23]

In the first decade of the nineteenth century Indian architecture became familiar to the gallery-going public of London, principally through the Daniells, who continued to exhibit finished oils and watercolours of Indian scenes at the Royal Academy and British Institution. *Oriental Scenery* gave rise to several rival sets of engraved views of India, less elaborate and less expensive (a full series of the first issue of *Oriental Scenery* cost £210), but the Daniells remained pre-eminent, and many of Thomas Pennant's *Views of Hindostan* (1798), of William Orme's *Twenty Four Views of Hindostan* (1808) and of the plates to Francis Blagdon's *Brief History of Ancient and Modern India* (1808) were engraved from originals by Thomas Daniell. When Thomas Hope bought his mansion in Duchess Street, and prepared to decorate it with a degree of eclecticism and originality which had seldom been witnessed in London, one of his first actions was to commission from Thomas Daniell an oil painting (executed in August 1799) of a 'Mosque in Hindostan', to serve as a pendant for a view of the Roman Forum by Giovanni Pannini. From this beginning, Hope's celebrated 'Indian Room' developed and came to serve as the principal drawing room of his house in Duchess Street, which was open to the public from 1804 onwards. Two further oils by Daniell were added in 1800, 'Temples on the Ganges at Benares', and 'Taj Mahal'. Although the Indian Room was 'principally fitted up for the reception of four large pictures, executed by Mr. Daniel', as Hope not quite accurately declared,[24] he was unable to match these displays of Indian architecture with appropriate examples of Indian interior design. The pattern of the ceiling was Turkish in inspiration, the carpet Persian, and much of the furniture Grecian. Similarly Hope's 'Closet or Boudoir fitted up for the reception of a few Egyptian, Hindoo, and Chinese idols, and curiosities' contained at one end 'a mantle-piece in the shape of an Egyptian portico', together with ceiling of bamboo laths hung with cotton drapery in the form of a tent, which no doubt alluded to China. The pillars at the side, not visible in Hope's engraving of this room, were very possibly 'Hindoo'.[25]

79 The Indian Room, engraving from Thomas Hope, *Household Furniture and Interior Design*, 1807

This mixture of cultural motifs within a single scheme of design, interior or exterior, is typical of several of the most ambitious exotic projects in the first twenty years of the century. But it is not true of Sezincote in Gloucestershire, the only Indian country house ever built in England or Europe. Colonel John Cockerell bought the Sezincote estate in 1795, and was soon succeeded by his brother Charles, a veteran of India who was created a baronet in 1809. His younger brother was an able architect, Samuel Pepys Cockerell, Surveyor to the East India House; and the Cockerells found a willing collaborator in Thomas Daniell, whom Charles had known in India. It is not clear which of these three took the initiative of proposing an Indian exterior at Sezincote, nor precisely when the building began. But some remarks by Humphry Repton indicate that by 1805 Charles Cockerell had the project in mind:

It happened that a little before my first visit to Brighton, I had been consulted by the proprietor of Sesincot, in Gloucestershire, where he wished to introduce the Gardening and Architecture which he had seen in India. I confess the subject was then entirely new to me; but from his long residence in the interior of that country, and from the good taste and accuracy with which he had observed and pointed out to me the various forms of ancient Hindû architecture, a new field opened itself; and as I became more acquainted with them, through the accurate Sketches and Drawings made on the spot by my ingenious friend Mr. T. DANIELL, I was pleased at having discovered new sources of beauty and variety . . .[26]

When was this 'first visit to Brighton'? The Windsor archives record that between 1797 and 1802 Repton was employed by the Prince of Wales at Brighton, and was paid £264 os 6d.[27] But Repton, as a rule not slow to disclose any connection with an illustrious client, makes no mention of this commission in his writings; presumably he was working on the gardens in some capacity which he thought inconsistent with his status as Britain's leading landscape gar-

V

dener. So Repton must in fact be referring to the subsequent occasion when he 'received the Prince's commands to visit Brighton, and there saw in some degree realized the new forms which I had admired in drawings'.[28] This would have been in 1805, when Porden's Stables were under construction; Repton's designs for a new pavilion were submitted to the prince in February 1806.[29]

Repton published his *Designs for the Pavillon at Brighton* in 1808, and in a footnote he made it clear that Sezincote House was now well under way:

Although I gave my opinion concerning the adoption of this new style, and even assisted in selecting some of the forms from Mr. T. Daniell's collection, yet the architectural department at Sesincot of course devolved to the Brother of the Proprietor, who had displayed as much correctness as could be expected in a first attempt of a new style, of which he could have no knowledge but from drawings, but who has sufficiently exemplified in various parts of his building, that the detail of Hindû Architecture, is as beautiful in reality as it appears in the drawings, and does not shrink from a comparison with the pure Gothic in richness of effect.[30]

It is not hard to detect in this footnote a trace of resentment over the fact that he had not been allowed a greater share in the planning of Sezincote. He must at least have hoped that the Cockerells would commission one of his celebrated 'Red Books', but none was required. Only a preliminary sketch in grey wash remains,[31] overlaid by a pair of Repton's characteristic fly-leaves showing the old farm buildings, pigs in the yard and washing on the line. Beneath the fly-leaves Repton has sketched the view southwards as he desired it, with the flower-garden leading up to the bank, and the new farm buildings (with a hint of crenellation) above. This is essentially the view which may be seen today; but how far that view was of Repton's own designing is still open to debate.

Sezincote House is beautifully situated on steeply rising ground, looking eastwards down a more gentle incline to the Stour Valley. Its plan is not unconventional, but in outward appearance it is unmistakably Indian. A single copper dome is raised clear of the roofline, with four well disguised chimneys at the corners of its base, and four chatris at the corners of the central block of the house itself. But the oriental effect does not depend on the dome, even at a distance: the broad, pointed entrance arch extending to the top of the upper storey, the generously projecting cornice or *chujjah* which extends around three sides of the building, and the hooded first-floor windows of the entrance front are all immediately striking and unparalleled in English architecture. And the colour of the masonry – a pale orange which has defied recent attempts to duplicate it – forms a pleasantly exotic contrast with the lush green surroundings.

At close quarters the architect's attention to detail becomes evident, and one can appreciate the precise carving of the window, spandrel and cornice ornament, and the delicate grille patterns of the cast-iron railings. The entrance front breaks forward slightly at the entrance, and again beyond the windows immediately beside it, providing an excuse for four entirely different window mouldings in the eight windows on each side of the archway. This arrangement might be thought over-elaborate, but there is ample precedent for such variety in Mughal façades, in particular in the gate of the Lahl Baug, the garden of Siraj-ud-Daulah's palace at Faizabad, where several British artists had worked for the Nawab and his family. The Daniells published an engraving of this gateway in October 1801. Although Sezincote is far from being an imitation of the Lahl Baug gate, it may be no accident that the two buildings have several other features in common – the small break in façade, the *chujjah* and parapet, and the four corner chatris.

80 Gate of the Lahl Baug, Faizabad, aquatint from T. & W. Daniell, *Oriental Scenery*, 1795–1808, 4th series

81 Sezincote, Gloucestershire, south front and garden, aquatint drawn and engraved by John Martin, 1817

The two principal elevations of Sezincote House, the entrance front to the east and the garden front to the south, follow Indian principles of symmetry rather than late-Georgian principles of the Picturesque, for in each case the dome is seen above the centre of a regular elevation. John Martin's views of Sezincote, drawn in 1817, show that the southern garden was from the start intended to be formal, and its principal axis is today neatly accentuated by a long rectangular canal flanked by cypresses. To the west of this garden, backing on to the hillside, an orangery sweeps round in an arc to terminate in a hexagonal aviary; a matching conservatory, now somewhat altered, originally curved away from the other side of the house, and the terminal hexagon was used as Sir Charles's bedroom.

The Indian theme is maintained in the gardens of Sezincote, where a narrow valley was planted with the most luxuriant vegetation available. Thomas Daniell seems to have been directly responsible for much of the garden architecture. At the head of the valley is the temple pool, where the Hindu goddess Souriya presides in a small shrine, its stepped roof echoing the flight of steps on which the shrine is raised. A stream flows down the valley, beneath a stone bridge solidly supported by rectangular Hindu columns. In the pool below the bridge a serpent coils around a tall tree-stump to emit a fountain of water. Daniell's drawings for Souriya's temple and for the bridge survive in the collection of the R.I.B.A., as does a group of letters from Daniell to Sir Charles Cockerell which give some indication of the artist's concern with the minutiae of design. On 12 December 1810 he recommended that Irish ivy be planted against the abutments of the bridge; on 30 December he thanked his patron for the turkey and hare which had arrived 'in good order' the previous night; and on 14–15 January 1811 he wrote in agitation about the positioning of Coade-stone Brahmin bulls (which he had used at Melchet Park) on the parapet of the bridge:

81

83

82

82, 83 Sezincote, the bridge (above) and the temple pool (below). Aquatints drawn and engraved by John Martin, 1817

84 Sezincote, farm buildings, aquatint drawn and engraved by John Martin, 1817

I am dreadfully alarmed about the Brahminy Bulls –
because I am certain they cannot be better placed –
could Viswakarma, the Artist of the Gods, of Hindoo's,
take a peep at Sezincot, he would say let the bulls
remain where they are . . .[32]

Unfortunately Daniell in his anxiety omitted
a few of the words which would enable us to make
complete sense of the rest of this letter, but it
seems that Daniell had originally proposed that a
bull should sit over each of the free-standing
columns of the bridge, forming a pair on each
side; instead, a single bull had been placed on the
middle of each parapet. Daniell's plea seems to
have been successful, for today two pairs of bulls
– replicas of the originals – welcome the visitor as
he approaches the house across Daniell's bridge.

The Indian style of the house and garden is
maintained in the farm buildings which stand on
higher ground a little to the south. The stables,
the dairy, the gardener's house and the surrounding wall all exhibit Indian motifs, and although
none of these outbuildings is as densely ornamented as the house itself, Cockerell has avoided the
effect of a group of English vernacular farm

buildings sprinkled incongruously with a selection of minarets and chatris. The farm com-
pound takes the form of an imposing square, and
the long buttressed walls are interspersed with
massive rectangular blocks, battlemented above,
giving an impression of a Mughal fort.

The furthest outpost of the Sezincote style is a 85
cottage in a village near by, Lower Swell; the
cottage was once the pump room of a spa that
failed. The 'eyebrow' hood above the door is
clearly derived from the upper windows of the
entrance front at Sezincote, but in the rest of the
cottage façade the anonymous architect has
allowed himself greater liberties – arched mouldings around the rectangular ground-floor windows on each side of the doorway, rectangular
mouldings surrounding scallop-arched windows
in the outer bays, a semi-classical frieze with
geometrical forms between the triglyphs, and a
pair of dormer windows whose concavely curving roofs hint at China rather than India. Fir
cones serve as finials to the dormers; a stone
pineapple appears in relief over the entrance.
The cottage is presumably contemporary with
Sezincote, and was therefore built at a time when

architects were exercising considerable imagination in designing both 'picturesque' and 'uniform' cottages of every variety. The cottage at Lower Swell bears no relation to any of the purportedly oriental cottage and villa designs set forward in the pattern-books of the time, but it is as happily designed as any of them, a cheerful, adventurous display amid the self-effacing cottages of the Cotswolds.

The Brighton and Sezincote estates are the two conspicuous survivors of Regency orientalism, but for sixty years these were rivalled by a third great structure, at Hope End in Herefordshire. Today Hope End is remembered as Elizabeth Barrett Browning's early home, built by her father Edward Barrett Moulton-Barrett. In 1809, when Elizabeth was three, he bought the site with a Queen Anne house; by the spring of 1810 he and his family had moved to Hope End, and he set about replacing the old house with an oriental stronghold. Hope End is less than forty miles from Sezincote, and like Sezincote occupies the side of a hill; its dates of construction (1810–15) overlap with those of the Gloucestershire house. But in other respects

the two houses are entirely dissimilar.

In the first place Hope End was conceived in a Middle Eastern idiom. Elizabeth later described it to Robert Browning as 'a Turkish house my father built himself, crowded with minarets & domes, & crowned with metal spires & crescents, to the provocation (as people used to observe) of every lightening of heaven',[33] and indeed the house flaunted stars and crescents not only on the skyline but on the façades above the windows. Second, its architect was not at all concerned with authenticity. Drawings and photographs of Hope End[34] show a nearly square block of three storeys, with windows in various forms – oval, rectangular or arched with depressed ogee curves – and a large Islamic dome at the centre. But the most distinctive and original feature of Hope End must have been the massive cylindrical concrete columns which clustered around the external walls. The corner columns were of uniform thickness and were punctuated by slit windows, while the intermediate columns were thicker at third-storey level than at the lower two storeys. All were capped by bulbous domelets and projected well above the roof, reducing the

85 Cottage at Lower Swell, Gloucestershire

86 Hope End, Hereford and Worcester, the stable block

prominence of the central dome. The architect's name is not recorded,[35] but Hope End was so unorthodox even in its parts, and so extraordinary in its stockade-like solidity, that Edward Moulton-Barrett may well have designed it himself. Like the Beckfords, the Moulton-Barretts had gained their wealth from the plantations of the West Indies, and Edward Moulton-Barrett shared some of William Beckford's characteristics. Brought up in Jamaica and unable to settle at Harrow and Cambridge, he was always regarded as strong-willed and isolated from public opinion. Hope End was his dramatic gesture of independence.

Some efforts were made to maintain an exotic atmosphere inside the house. The central dome was made of glass, and acted as a lantern to the main staircase; according to the sale catalogue of 1831, the vaulted billiard room had walls ornamented with Turkish views, and the doors of the principal bedroom were decorated in the Chinese style;[36] another bedroom was described by Elizabeth as 'the Turkish room',[37] and the hall reminded her mother of the Arabian Nights.[38] But otherwise the interior, like that of Sezincote, was English and unexceptional. Only at Brigh-

ton, where the royal proprietor could ignore the practical problems of family life, was it possible to achieve a thoroughly exotic interior.

For a brief period Hope End and its park were maintained in the grand manner, with deer and peacocks and landscaping by J. C. Loudon, successor to Repton as England's leading landscape gardener. In 1830 the Duchess of Kent and Prince Leopold paid a visit, and perhaps Princess Victoria also. But in the following year financial difficulties forced Edward Moulton-Barrett to leave the house, which the sale catalogue described as 'a chef d'oeuvre, unrivalled in this kingdom'.[39] Hope End was sold to the antiquary Thomas Heywood; in 1867 it was sold again and demolished by the new landlord, who replaced it with a Gothic mansion near by. A few clear traces of Hope End's oriental glory remain in the stables, which (like the stables at Brighton and Sezincote) were built in a style corresponding to the main residence. Seven thick 'minaret' columns, sixteen feet high and topped with flattened Islamic domes, still support the wall of the stable yard, and four more columns can be seen at the corners of the stables – which were evidently part of the earlier house which Barrett bought in

86

1809; they have been converted again, and serve their original function as living accommodation. The domed clocktower entrance to the stable yard has also been restored, although the four pinnacles which surrounded the cupola are no longer in place. Nor is the clock, whose installation the nine-year-old Elizabeth celebrated in verse: 'Hark! what deep tones proceed from yonder tower . . .'

The source of those deep tones has since been moved to the courthouse of Brown's Town, Jamaica, leaving the entrance tower with blank circles on three sides, and on the fourth side an empty cylinder where the pendulum once hung. Finally a Levantine minaret stands by the wall at the opposite corner, thirty-five feet to the iron crescent at the top. A watercolour by Arabella Barrett, Elizabeth's favourite sister, shows this IV   minaret with the house and stables, but in a later view all but the mansion is obscured by luxuriant foliage.

In its generalized exoticism Hope End is a true representative of its era, a phenomenon much more typical than Sezincote of Regency attitudes to design. Just as Thomas Hope mingled cultural themes in his 'Indian Room' and 'Boudoir', so were architects generally prepared (or compelled by a lack of detailed information) to blend different exotic styles within a single scheme. When Repton debated which style should harmonize with the Indian Stables, he assumed that not only Indian but Turkish, Chinese and Egyptian were candidates. Motifs derived from two or more of these might be combined even in the smallest projects. A drawing by George 87   Stanley Repton of a smaller circular conservatory,[40] based probably on a design by Nash, shows a hemispherical dome curving outwards at its base, and bells hanging from the upward-curling eaves in the Chinese manner; while between the windows beneath are columns formed by vertical trellis bars encircled by a spiral band of lead, whose capitals take the shape of a flattened globe, described by another writer as 'the globular-compressed cushion-form'.[41] Similar columns appeared in a conservatory designed by Nash at Sandridge Park in Devon, and in Humphry Repton's *Designs for the Pavillon*. No doubt their ultimate source is Elephanta or another of the many Indian temples displaying this form of capital, which is supposed to represent the seed-pod of the lotus flower – an appropriate choice for a conservatory.

The same tendency can be seen in the

87 Design for a conservatory by G. S. Repton

architectural fantasy paintings of Joseph Gandy and John Martin. Martin was commissioned to draw and engrave ten views of Sezincote at a time (late in 1817) when he was turning his attention to epic visions and immense architectural scenarios. But in attempting to recreate the palaces of Nineveh and Babylon in their prime, he was faced with an awkward problem. Practically no archaeological evidence was at hand, and the literary descriptions available, whether Biblical or classical, were incapable of furnishing the precise detail which Martin sought. The visual source which must have seemed closest to the spirit of his enterprise was of course the Daniells' *Oriental Scenery*, so that columns and vaults were carefully adapted from that work and made to play a prominent role in several of Martin's most spectacular Old Testament scenes. 'Belshazzar's Feast' (exhibited in 1821) 88 displays a mixture of Middle Eastern and Far Eastern motifs, but an Indian impression predominates, through the globular capitals in the massive colonnades and the stepped arches which link the columns at the far end of the palace. Martin justified his selection of styles by claiming, in the pamphlet printed to accompany the painting at its exhibition, that 'it was the

88 John Martin, 'Belshazzar's Feast', mezzotint after his painting of 1820

custom of Nebuchadnezzar, the conqueror of Egypt and India, to bring from these parts to Babylon all the architects, the men of science and handicrafts, by whom the Palace and the external parts of the temple of Bel etc. were built; therefore I suppose the united talents of the Indian, the Egyptian and Babylonian architects were employed to produce these buildings'.[42]

Joseph Gandy, Martin's rival in imaginative cityscapes, was also interested in exotic architecture, and put forward several implausible theories concerning the origins of Egyptian, Hindu, Persian and Chinese styles. 'A comprehensive mind will select from all sources',[43] he believed, and such paintings as 'The Tomb of Merlin' (in the R.I.B.A. library) bear out his doctrine. His designs for cottages, stark and streamlined, utilize Egyptian forms to great effect; but his oriental compositions, several of which were exhibited at the Royal Academy, are now known by their titles only.

The relationship between Indian architecture and more familiar styles remained a debatable issue during the first quarter of the nineteenth century. Whereas in the 1750s Chinese architecture had been closely associated with Gothic, Indian architecture now proved harder to categorize. In his designs, George Dance seemed to assimilate Indian to Gothic; on the other hand, it was suggested by several writers that ancient Indian architecture was the source of Greek architecture, and when Dance called on Thomas Daniell in September 1798 (shortly after Hodges's death), and saw a drawing of an Indian temple, he declared himself convinced 'that the Greeks borrowed from the East'.[44] But in truth, as Hodges had pointed out, the forms and proportions of Hindu and Islamic monuments 'will no more bear the comparison with Greek and Roman architecture than the Gothic' – although, like the Gothic in its majesty and grandeur, Indian architecture was liable to be rejected by that narrow-minded company which believed that all buildings should follow a Grecian prototype.[45]

The Indian style was occasionally represented in the pattern-books for villas and *cottages ornés*, without ever becoming a standard element in the Picturesque repertoire. Robert Lugar, an architect of ornamental cottages who later became County Surveyor of Essex, produced a series of drawings in which a Daniell-inspired Indian villa appeared in the category of 'fancy styles', together with crude but recognizable Turkish and Chinese summer-houses.[46] Only two designers wholeheartedly endorsed the Indian style, Humphry Repton and a young architect publishing his first book, Edmund Aikin.

Aikin dedicated his *Designs for Villas and other Rural Buildings* (1808) to Thomas Hope, and acknowledged his debt to Thomas Daniell; he distinguished carefully between Islamic architecture and 'the more antient Indian style', and listed the characteristics of the former: dome, minaret, projecting cornice, and surface panelling. He offered two sets of designs for Islamic-Indian buildings, 'a Villa of considerable magnitude' and (more elaborate) 'a large Villa or Mansion'. These elevations suggest that Aikin had seen designs for Sezincote, or perhaps the house in its early stages, for both include a prominent *chujjah*, a slight break in the entrance front, and projecting windows in the outer bays. The triple window over the entrance arch in Aikin's grander scheme is again reminiscent of the Lahl Baug gateway at Faizabad. But Aikin was anxious to demonstrate the flexibility of the newly discovered style. The principal elevation of his smaller villa presented an air of strength and seclusion, he explained, through its simple divisions and its low ratio of windows to wall (also advantageous if the villa was to stand near 'a large town or much-frequented road'). But the garden front was endowed with large and numerous windows, to demonstrate the cheerful character which he maintained the Indian style was equally capable of assuming.[47]

Humphry Repton's *Designs for the Pavillon at Brighton*, published in the same year as Aikin's *Designs*, proclaimed the merits of the Indian style even more forcibly, declaring that for a royal palace it was actually more suitable than Grecian or Gothic. Repton's designs will be discussed in the next chapter, but his arguments are worth outlining here. Repton could afford to champion the new style since he had no architectural practice to lose, and as a positive incentive he had an illustrious client who had already invested in the Indian fashion. Repton's polemical *tour de force* began by ruling out all the alternative styles:

89 Design for 'a large Villa or Mansion' in the Indian style, from Edmund Aikin, *Designs for Villas and other Rural Buildings*, 1808

129

The Turkish was objectionable, as being a corruption of the Grecian; the Moorish, as a bad model of the Gothic; the Egyptian was too cumbrous for the character of a villa; the Chinese too light and trifling for the outside, however it may be applied to the interior; and the specimens from Ava were still more trifling and extravagant.[48]

Neither Gothic nor Grecian would harmonize with the existing Stables, he continued, so that an Indian style remained as the only possibility. Repton now anticipated and countered several objections. The climate of India differed from that of England, but then so did the climates of Greece and Italy; relatively few models of Indian architecture were available to British architects, but the Daniells were about to publish more, and in any case a rigid set of proportions was unnecessary in Indian architecture; its ornaments might appear expensive, but in practice they could be turned on a lathe at less cost than the Grecian and Gothic equivalents. Later in the book Repton stressed again the variety of Indian architecture, illustrating nine examples of Indian columns beside the five classical orders, which appear uniform by comparison. Even cast iron, a material which Repton's generation was the first

to exploit in construction, was 'peculiarly adapted to some light parts of the Indian style'. The tendency of Repton's entire thesis was to present Grecian, Gothic and Indian as the three fundamental modes of building, each possessing its own principles of structure and decoration, which he encapsulated in neat little vignettes. Indian architecture should be considered not as a variant of either Gothic or Grecian, he insisted, but as an entirely distinct phenomenon. And English architects should select those Indian forms which bore the *least* resemblance to either of those.[49]

This last belief lies at the heart of Repton's attitude, and it may well have contributed to the failure of his project. At Sezincote, Repton had seen the successful results of this policy of architectural purism, and he had worked with Thomas Daniell, high priest of the faith in authenticity. When Repton wrote that a mixture of Indian with Grecian would be 'as disgusting to the classic observer, as the mixture in Queen Elisabeth's Gothic',[50] he perhaps had Daniell in mind. But the Prince of Wales was not 'the classic observer', and he was not averse to mixtures. The dashing eclecticism of John Nash, who eventually secured the commission to rebuild the Pavilion, was more congenial to the prince.

90 'Hindoo columns', aquatint from H. Repton, *Designs for the Pavillon at Brighton*, 1808

Chapter Ten

The Royal Pavilion at Brighton

Brighton appear'd in a fashionable, unhappy, Bustle, with such a harpy Set of
painted Harlots, as to appear to me as bad as Bond St in the Spring,
at 3 o clock, P.M.[1]

LIKE BRIGHTON itself, the Royal Pavilion has never been quite respectable. To many visitors the domes and minarets of Nash's seaside palace remain a 'set of painted Harlots' to this day, gaudy interlopers in the polite society of Brighton's tasteful squares and crescents. In contrast the great domed Stables near by, now constantly in use for concerts and conferences, has aroused much less controversy, although this building was perhaps the greater innovation: it was the first 'Indian' structure of any size to be built in Britain, and its style largely determined the Indian flavour of the Royal Pavilion.

Continental visitors often used to remark that the English lavish greater care and expense on their horses than on themselves, and this certainly seemed to be the case at Brighton, where the Prince of Wales remained modestly housed in his villa while a hundred yards away an enormous stable block rose high above him. Even the prince's thoroughbreds hardly deserved such spacious accommodation. Their stalls were arranged around a huge domed rotunda, sixty-five feet high and eighty feet in diameter – within twenty feet of the diameter of St Paul's, it was claimed. Today, as the Dome concert hall, it seats an audience of 2,500. To the west was a barrel-vaulted Riding House providing ten thousand square feet in which the prince and his horses might exercise; this later became the Corn Exchange, and is now an exhibition hall. The equivalent space to the east was to become an enclosed tennis court, but building on the site was postponed until 1832, when the new hall was used as Queen Adelaide's stables. It now houses Brighton's Art Gallery, Central Museum and Reference Library.

This colossal project was designed by William Porden, an architect less celebrated than Henry Holland, but what little is known of Porden suggests that he was well qualified for his task. He had worked for James Wyatt, architect of Fonthill Abbey, and for S.P. Cockerell, through

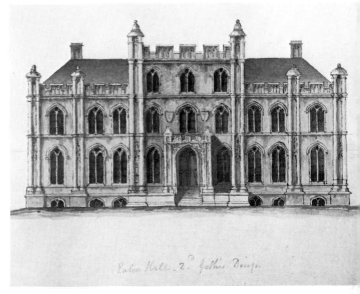

91 Unexecuted design by William Porden for Eaton Hall, 1804

whom he may have had some contact with the Daniells; in 1797 he exhibited at the Royal Academy a 'Design for a Place of Public Amusement, in the style of the Mahometan Architecture of Hindostan'.[2] The year 1803 saw his commencement not only of the Stables but of the remodelling of Eaton Hall, Cheshire, for the 2nd Earl Grosvenor. (It may be no coincidence that Eaton Hall was described in 1804 as 'Morisco Gothic'.[3] There was nothing Indian about the Gothic Eaton Hall as built, but an early design of Porden's for the house exhibits small domes capping the paired Gothic columns.)[4] 'Bold Porden', as Lord Grosvenor often described him, seems to have been a man of confident personality and grand visions, well suited to the temperament of the prince.

Two buildings inspired the design of the Stables. The plan and general form of Porden's rotunda were, on his own admission, modelled on

93

91

92 The Jami' Masjid at Delhi, aquatint from T. & W. Daniell, *Oriental Scenery*, 1795–1808, 1st series

the Halle au Blé in Paris, a cylindrical corn market which received a shallow wooden dome in 1782 and then lost it in a fire in 1803.[5] But the proportions and range of sizes of the scallop-arched windows in the Stables appear to follow the Jami' Masjid or Great Mosque at Delhi, of which a view was engraved by the Daniells and published in 1797. The main entrance to the Stables from the gardens is similar to the central wall-screen of the mosque entrance in its plain border within columns and crenellated lintel, and even in the series of receding arches within the gateway. The flattened shape of the dome above is the least oriental of the building's features. It is timber-framed, and divided into sixteen lotus-leaf panels of glass and eight narrower strips of stucco. It was widely believed that the dome would collapse, for on 29 November 1804 Porden wrote in triumph to his daughter, 'the cupola is now on, and the workmen are swarming about it like jackdaws. The whole proves fully equal to expectation. The dome now supports itself, without assistance from the scaffolding, and has *not yet* fallen.'[6] Another worry was that the lead-and-glass roof might make the Stables uncomfortably hot; but the lantern-cap and the arches of the stalls seem to have conducted sufficient draught to cool the amphitheatre.[7]

Although work on the Stables continued until 1808, the structure was substantially complete before building began at Sezincote in 1806. In

certain aspects of the latter one may detect the influence of Porden's design: the broad, ray-patterned windows of the orangery and aviary at Sezincote are similar to the north and south windows of his Riding House, and the conservatory wings of the Gloucestershire mansion closely resemble an unexecuted external corridor shown curving away from Porden's Stables in an engraving published by the *European Magazine* in 1806. Otherwise the Sezincote and Brighton estates seem to have developed without much reference to each other. It is true that Humphry Repton was involved in both, and that John Nash (and the Prince of Wales) must have been emboldened in remodelling the Pavilion by the knowledge that a Mughal mansion had already been successfully completed elsewhere in England. Nevertheless, Sezincote and the Royal Pavilion represent fundamentally different conceptions. The former was the product of a trio of enthusiasts, each devoted in his own way to Indian tradition and detail, who by careful planning unfolded a balanced and consistent composition in a style to which they were deeply attached. But at Brighton neither client nor architect had any personal commitment to India. Their resources were boldness and imagination, and a readiness to invent and combine forms without feeling themselves constrained by precedent. If Sezincote is an elegant tribute to Mughal India, the Royal Pavilion is an evocation of the wildest splendours of the East.

92

94

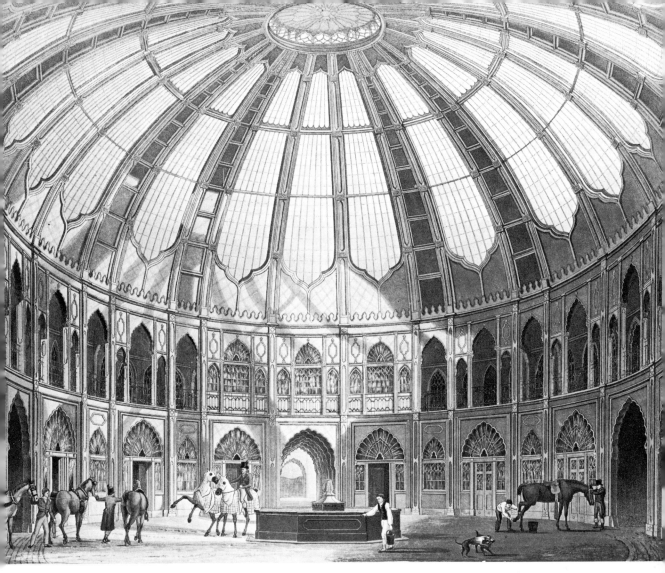

93 'Interior of the Stables at Brighton', engraving from John Nash, *Views of the Royal Pavilion*, 1826

94 'The Royal Stables at Brighton', engraving, 1806

133

95 Design by William Porden for a Royal Pavilion (east front) in the Chinese style, *c.* 1805

96 Design by William Porden for a Royal Pavilion (west front) in the Chinese style, *c.* 1805

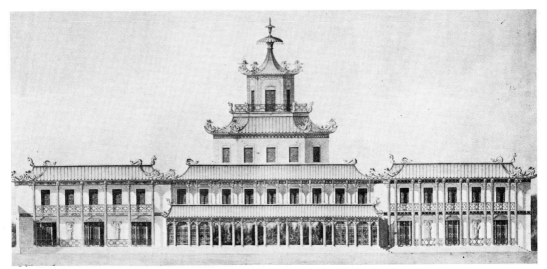

98 Design by William Porden for a Royal Pavilion in the Chinese style, c. 1805

As the Stables neared completion it became obvious that the prince would require radical alterations to his own residence. Contemporary engravings taken from the Old Steine show the huge, almost sinister mass of the Rotunda looming above the little cupola of the Marine Pavilion. It may seem natural that a predominantly Indian pavilion should have been built to match the character of the Stables. But in 1806, when exotic styles were more freely intermingled, there were alternatives to be considered. William Porden himself submitted designs for a 'Pavilion in the Chinese Style' at this time,[8] and three of his drawings, now in the Royal Pavilion collection, show that he was as adept a manipulator of Chinese detail as of Gothic or Mughal.

Two of the drawings form a pair, of east and west elevations. The eastern elevation retained Holland's pavilion, including the angled wings, but disguised it with blue-tiled roofs, golden dragons, scarlet columns and railings, and ornamental friezes. Each of the five bays of the existing building was to be shaded by a shallow roof supported by columns, and since the Saloon bay was already encircled by a peristyle, these columns would merely be painted red to match the others. Behind this reclothed structure Porden envisaged a new and taller range, again surmounted by five separate roofs, so that each dominated (and broadly corresponded with) one of the roofs of the eastern suite. The eastern front was thus extremely intricate in design. The western elevation was simpler and grander, a long double colonnade broken in the centre by four pairs of giant columns.

Porden attended to the decorative elements of his composition with great care, inscribing Chinese characters beneath the entrance canopies and placing life-size Chinese figures in niches at either side. Six different lattice patterns and twelve different friezes appear on the eastern elevation, and throughout Porden's Chinese designs there is a wealth of small-scale detail which contrasts with the boldly sweeping lines of the Stables. His sources were various: the topmost hexagon is firmly in the tradition of mid-eighteenth-century chinoiserie, but the shallow domes on each side of it seem to be entirely Porden's invention, while the general proportions of roofs and columns (slimmer than those illustrated in Chambers's *Designs of Chinese Buildings*) suggest that Porden had studied the architecture depicted by William Alexander. As a fellow-exhibitor Porden would have seen Alexander's views of China hanging at the Royal Academy each year from 1795 to 1800; also, he might have studied Alexander's illustrations to Staunton's official account of Lord Macartney's embassy. Plate 22, 'A Front View of the Hall of Audience in the Palace of Yuen-min-yuen', depicts a pavilion comparable to Porden's in conception and in several details. Moreover Yuan-ming yuan, the summer resort of the Emperor Ch'ien Lung, would be a suitable model for the Prince of Wales's retreat at

◄ 97 'A Front View of the Hall of Audience in the Palace of Yuen-min-yuen', engraving after W. Alexander, 1797

Brighton. Porden also follows Alexander's colour-scheme, from the roof tiles ('of a bluish, or slate colour')[9] to the red columns and yellow-gold embellishments.

98 Porden's third drawing is a little different, depicting three bays only and placing greater emphasis on the central block. Beneath the crowning hexagon is an additional storey, also hexagonal. No reference is made to Holland's building. In March 1805, when the prince was admiring the newly erected dome of the Stables, he observed that 'he should like to have a palace built on the same plan; the central area to be a vast hall of communication to the apartments ranged around, with four staircases'.[10] No such palace was built, but it is possible that the central octagon of Porden's design was prompted by the prince's words.

96 The western elevation was exhibited at the Royal Academy in 1806, after which no more was heard of Porden's Chinese designs. The prince may have set his heart on an Indian pavilion even before Porden drew up his proposals. For in February of the same year Humphry Repton delivered to the Prince of Wales his own designs for a new Pavilion, which were contained in a folio of twelve watercolours interspersed with text. Following his usual practice, Repton drew the scene as he found it on 'fliers' or flaps which could be folded back to reveal the altered prospect as he envisaged it. (The fact that the fliers never merged quite happily with the background made the 'View Before' less appealing still than the 'View After'.) Repton's designs for the Pavilion precinct included both a grand Mughal palace, drawn by his two architect sons, and his own speciality, a reshaped garden. In the latter he skilfully exploited the unpromising terrain. As he observed, the few acres owned by the prince lent themselves to a more formal and intimate arrangement than the existing landscape-in-miniature. Moreover, the Marine Pavilion as it stood was exposed to weather and public on each of the principal fronts; Repton suggested a screen of trees to the east, and a 'flower passage' or glazed corridors enclosing the garden to the west. The entrance to the new palace would be to the north, and on the south side the view across the lower Steine to the sea would be left open. Repton was well aware of Brighton's bleak winters, and the prince must have liked the idea of walking under cover from his new Pavilion to his Stables, by way of an orangery (convertible into an open 'chiosk' in summer); and thence to hothouses, a greenhouse and a pheasantry, and back past an orchestra and an aviary, protected all the while by glass and flanked by banks of flowers.

For the palace itself, Repton recommended that Holland's building be retained, but augmented by a much larger range to the west, which would be linked to Holland's rooms by a square central music room supporting the principal dome. Repton's master-stroke was a new set of private apartments projecting to the north-east and terminating in an octagon. This fulfilled several requirements at once: it provided a substantial northern façade suitable for an entrance front; it incorporated one of Holland's 45-degree extensions, which might otherwise have proved difficult to accommodate within the scheme; and it allowed the prince to remain in contact with the daily activity on the Steine. Repton perhaps knew that his client had previously set up a large mirror in his bedroom so that he could see the promenaders and the sea from the comfort of his bed. According to the new plan the prince would be able to use the roof of the octagon for the same purpose: in the Reptons' drawing a telescope was set up, pointed diplomatically seawards, although no doubt the prince would be able to train it on the human attractions immediately below him. 99

In detail the northern and western fronts were to be exclusively Mughal, from the single dominant dome to the subsidiary domes and minarets, the columns and the octagonal *chujjah*. The proportions of the two storeys and the scalloped arches corresponded to those of the Stables. Repton asserted that he had had access to Thomas Daniell's drawings,[11] but in practice the first published series of *Oriental Scenery* appears to have supplied most of Repton's needs. Large portions of his 'Pavillon' and garden buildings are drawn almost unaltered from the Daniells' engraved views. The octagon at the end of the private apartments is none other than the upper storey of the eastern bastions of Shahjahan-abad, near the gardens known as Qudsiya-Bagh, as depicted in the Daniells' 'View of the Cotsea Bhaug'. Repton's gateway to the town at the perimeter of the western gardens is taken from 'An Ancient Hindoo Temple, in the fort of Rotas, Bahar' – the building on which Thomas Daniell had based his temple in Melchet Park: Repton's design follows the engraving more faithfully than Daniell had done 100

78

99 Design for the west front of the Royal Pavilion, as seen from the Stables, from H. Repton, *Designs for the Pavillon at Brighton*, 1808

100 Design for the garden pool and gateway of the Royal Pavilion estate, aquatint from H. Repton, *Designs . . .*, 1808

102
101
104

103

himself. The upper part of Repton's Pheasantry is derived from the Daniells' 'View of the Palace in the Fort of Allahabad', while his Aviary design is a literal adaptation of the foremost of the 'Hindoo Temples at Bindrabund on the River Jumna'. (Thomas Daniell's oil painting of this subject was his diploma work at the Royal Academy in 1797.) Bindrabund (or Brindaban) is celebrated as the place where Krishna sported with milkmaids and stole their clothes while they were bathing; perhaps Repton thought this allusion appropriate to the prince's pleasure-ground.

The Reptons must have enjoyed toying with the Daniells' views, and the resulting project has undeniable panache. To utilize the outline of the ponderous, monolithic Bindrabund temple in designing an aviary, the least substantial of structures, is a neat specimen of architectural wit. In fact Repton's designs for lightweight buildings in an Indian idiom come close to contradicting his own characterization of Indian architecture as dignified and imposing. But there was a major flaw in his treatment of the east front. The existing suite of Chinese interiors, which constituted the glory of the Marine Pavilion, had to remain, and to judge by the drawings of Chinese exteriors put forward by Holland and Porden, the prince had envisaged a Chinese east front to match the interior decoration. Probably he had not yet abandoned this notion in 1805, for in proposing a screen of trees to the east Repton made this astonishing statement:

102 Design for a Pheasantry at the Royal Pavilion, aquatint from H. Repton, *Designs . . .*, 1808

101 'View of the Palace in the Fort of Allahabad', aquatint from T. & W. Daniell, *Oriental Scenery,* 1795–1808, 1st series

103 'Hindoo Temples at Bindrabund on the River Jumna', aquatint from T. & W. Daniell, *Oriental Scenery* (1795–1808), 1st series

104 Design for an Aviary at the Royal Pavilion, aquatint from H. Repton, *Designs for the Pavillon at Brighton,* 1808

105 'View from the Proposed Private Apartment', aquatint from H. Repton, *Designs . . .*, 1808

This Skreen will preclude the necessity of making much alteration in the east front, which may therefore retain the Chinese character EXTERNALLY, in conformity with the INTERNAL fitting-up of this suite of Royal Apartments.[12]

With these words Repton ended his book, leaving his readers to ask themselves how a Chinese east front could merge with the Mughal private apartments. Repton did not provide an elevation of the east front; if he had, it must have shown domes and minarets towering above small-scale Chinese detail. Only one small plate, 'View from the Proposed Private Apartment', allows a part of Holland's peristyle to appear at the right-hand edge of the picture, clothed in crudely 'Chinese' columns and upswept roof. Repton was never sympathetic to Chinese architecture, despite Peacock's caricature of him in *Headlong Hall* (1815), in which Marmaduke Milestone with Reptonian urbanity begs permission to wave his wand of enchantment over Squire Headlong's estate:

The rocks shall be blown up, the trees shall be cut down, the wilderness and all its goats shall vanish like mist. Pagodas and Chinese bridges, gravel walks and shrubberies, bowling-greens, canals, and clumps of larch, shall rise upon its ruins.[13]

Pagodas and Chinese bridges, however, were alien to Repton, who had written disparagingly of 'fantastic Chinese models' and of the 'puerile deceits' involved in Chambers's interpretation of Chinese gardening.[14] (The Chinese garden he proposed for Brighton's Pavilion consisted simply of small circular flower-beds scattered around the lawn.) Repton admitted that Chinese design could be suitable for interiors, but his only attempt at an interior design was, like his exteriors, inspired by India – a clumsy dining hall, whose Indo-Gothic fan-vaulting was supposed to allow the 'rarefied air and vapour' to escape between the pendants. Once again the Daniells' views were his inspiration, specifically the 'Interior View of the Palace, Madura'. The Daniells portrayed sacred cows in the end section, partly screened off; in Repton's version these were replaced by the prince and his companions at table. The simple circular columns of the seventeenth-century palace perhaps looked insufficiently exotic to Repton, who substituted a pair of Hindu columns adapted from another Daniell engraving.[15]

In 1808 Repton published the *Designs for the Pavillon at Brighton*, slightly amended,[16] as a folio of aquatints with printed commentary. The prince declared that he was delighted with Repton's plans, and settled his bill (£713 15s. 6d.) with unusual promptness. 'Mr. Repton, I consider the whole of this work as perfect, and will have every part of it carried into immediate execution; not a tittle shall be altered – even you yourself shall not attempt any improvement.'[17] But if this last quotation is accurate, then the Prince was deceiving Repton. There was no hope of 'immediate execution'; Repton's plan entailed the demolition of a number of buildings which the prince did not yet own, including Grove House (known also as Marlborough House), the largest private dwelling in Brighton. And the cost of the Stables was outrunning the prince's resources, to the great embarrassment of Porden and his subcontractors. As late as 1812, £11,000 was still outstanding, and the total expenditure was more than five times that amount. Repton's elaborate and expensive project had at least to be postponed. In fact, the prince seems to have abandoned it as rapidly as he had abandoned those of Holland and Porden, for in 1815, the year in which John Nash began to remodel the Pavilion, Repton found that his manuscript designs were still at the engravers, having remained there since the printed version was published in 1808. The prince had not asked for the designs in the seven intervening years. Repton returned the manuscript volume to his patron, enclosing a pathetic letter. 'I hardly know how to express my regret for the long delay and omission . . .'[18]

The fourth architect to fail in an attempt to build the prince a palace at Brighton was perhaps the greatest, James Wyatt. Unlike Holland and Porden, Wyatt could not point to any previous achievements in an oriental style, but he could nevertheless claim to be the most versatile architect of his generation. As author of the spectacularly domed Pantheon in Oxford Street, of the severely Grecian Dodington Hall, of the elegantly Gothick Lee Priory and of the legendary Fonthill Abbey, Wyatt might have been expected to design a Royal Pavilion worthy of its occupant. In 1812 he carried out extensive alterations at Brighton, largely it seems at Grove House (which the Prince had now bought and was soon to demolish); at the same time he was engaged on the fourth and final arm of Fonthill Abbey, 'killing himself with work', as his employer William Beckford wrote: 'every hour, every moment, he adds some new beauty'.[19] The qualities which endeared Wyatt to Beckford – his grand vision, his hedonism, his fitful energy – must also have appealed to the prince. Moreover, the prince had become regent in the previous year, and his financial circumstances were healthier. In 1813 Wyatt submitted to the prince

an estimate for unspecified 'improvements' at a cost of £200,000, a sum which must have included the building of a splendid new Pavilion. But on 4 September of that year Wyatt was killed in a carriage accident, after slipping away from Fonthill when Beckford needed him most. Even if Wyatt had lived on, it is doubtful whether this unpredictable prodigy would have been able to carry through his royal commission. 'Alas, my poor Bagasse had already sunk from the plane of genius to the mire,' Beckford lamented 'for some years now he has only dabbled about in the mud . . .'[20] The Prince Regent was scarcely less disappointed. According to Joseph Farington the news of Wyatt's death moved the prince to tears, and made him declare that 'he had just found a man to his mind, and was thus unhappily deprived of him.'[21]

Holland, Porden, Repton and Wyatt had now aspired and failed, but by 1815 the Prince Regent had at last secured all the prerequisites for a new Pavilion – finance, land and a congenial architect. John Nash had been of service to the prince for some years, both as an architect and through his wife, who was widely believed to be the prince's mistress. He had made his reputation as a designer of Gothick mansions and *cottages ornés*, including the Royal Lodge in Windsor Park. From 1812 he was engaged with the Prince Regent in the creation of Regent's Park and the great new Regent Street which was to link the park to Carlton House. Fanciful domes were a particular speciality of Nash's; throughout his life he delighted in small domes, caps, or 'pepper-pots' of every shape, some of them deliberately oriental. At the start of his career Nash worked at Hafod in Cardiganshire for the wildly idealistic Thomas Johnes, and may have been associated with Johnes's octagonal library, whose flattened dome was unmistakably Mughal. (Hafod 'is much esteemed, although it somewhat appertains to the *moresque*,' observed a contemporary architect.)[22] For Sandridge Park, near Dartmouth, Nash designed an oriental conservatory similar to the circular conservatory drawn in G. S. Repton's sketchbook. Aqualate Hall, Staffordshire, which Nash remodelled in 1808, was remarkable for its ogival domes, although these were Tudor rather than Islamic; he employed this device on several occasions, and a pleasant set of Nash ogees can still be seen near Regent's Park, emerging from the battlements of Park Village East. Even the tall hexagonal domes at Sussex Place near by, placed above a Corin-

106 The Pagoda in St James's Park, etching, published in 1814 by James Whittle and Richard Laurie

thian colonnade, were interpreted as oriental. The architect James Elmes described them (not at all accurately) as 'pagoda-like cupolas', and although he disliked the terrace as a whole, he confessed that these 'eastern-like cupolas', reflected in the lake, contributed to a picturesque silhouette.[23]

In 1814 Nash was involved in the Grand National Jubilee, celebrating the centenary of the Hanoverian dynasty. Firework displays were held in all the royal parks, but the chief attraction was St James's Park, where several thousand people paid half a guinea each to see the festivities. Over the canal Nash had erected a bridge with a pagoda in the middle of it, and a pair of concave-roofed kiosks at each end. *The Gentleman's Magazine* was uncertain 'whether such a character had or had not any thing to do with the matters of celebration', but the pagoda was functional as well as decorative: it was to display and to launch the fireworks. In the early part of the evening a hot-air balloon ascended, and the Chinese lanterns were lit, although inadequately. Then at ten o'clock Nash's edifice came into its own:

106

The Bridge, with its temples and pillars, and its towering superstructure, became an object of singular beauty and magnificence ... It appeared a blazing edifice of golden fire. Every part of it was covered with lamps, the glass reflectors, in proper places, relieving the dazzling splendour with their silver lustre; the canopies of the temple throwing up their bright wheels and stars, the pillars enriched with radiance, every rising tower of the Pagoda pouring forth its fiery showers, and rockets springing from its lofty top, in majestic flights, almost presuming to outrival the ancient inhabitants of the firmament.[24]

For two hours the gerbes and maroons, Catherine wheels, flower pots and girandoles whirled and exploded. But at midnight, as the fireworks were drawing to a close, the pagoda 'exhibited an appearance that excited much doubt'. It soon became clear that the upper storeys had caught fire. Before long the blazing fragments of the top five stages had fallen into the canal, killing two men and leaving the stump of the pagoda severely damaged. 'The fate of this erection was much regretted,' *The Gentleman's*

142

Magazine reported, 'as it was deservedly a favourite.'[25]

In January of the following year Nash went to Brighton and met the prince's equerry Sir Benjamin Bloomfield, presumably to discuss alterations to the Marine Pavilion. By this time the Prince Regent's mind was evidently made up. According to Nash, the determining factor was the size of the Stables. Even if the style of the Stables were altered, their enormous bulk would still dominate Holland's building. 'It was therefore determined by H.M. that the Pavillion should assume an Eastern character, and the Hindoo style of Architecture was adopted in the expectation that the turban domes and pinnacles might from their glittering and picturesque effect, attract and fix the attention of the Spectator, and the superior magnificence of the Dome of the Stables cease to be observed.'[26] In place of Holland's angled wings two large state rooms were to be built in line with the rest of the Pavilion. Nash set two alternative designs before the prince. In the less radical of these the Saloon 109 bay and the new state rooms were to be capped by three Mughal domes and surrounded by a fretwork colonnade, while the bays immediately flanking the Saloon were to be altered only in detail. The more radical design clothed the entire eastern front with oriental colonnades, placed pairs of smaller onion domes on each side of the central dome, and gave upswept tent-roofs to the new outer rooms. The first design offered a discreet sprinkling of minarets about its three domes; in the second, a forest of minarets and disguised chimneys at varying heights stood out against the skyline. Typically and rightly, the prince chose the second.

Rather than furnish an estimate for the entire project, Nash seems each year to have quoted the costs which he anticipated for the next twelve months. (Either the Prince Regent did not guess at the huge sum that would eventually be spent, or else he guessed, and preferred that it should not be committed to paper.) In March 1815 work began, at first on the corridor, staircases and entrance hall. The Chinese interior decoration 107 and the Mughal-inspired exterior developed together. The basic structure of the new state rooms was set in place in 1817, the Music Room to VI the north and the Banqueting Room to the south.

107 'The Corridor of the Royal Pavilion at Brighton', aquatint after A. C. Pugin, pl. 14 of John Nash, *Views of the Royal Pavilion*, 1826

A visitor to Brighton in 1818 would have had good reason to doubt whether Nash's project would fulfil its promise: he would have seen at the two extremities of Holland's pavilion a pair of large rectangular boxes, whose roofs, windows and crenellation matched neither one another nor the Marine Pavilion sandwiched in between. Everything depended on the final stage of 1818–22, during which the domes and minarets were added, and colonnades linked and unified the east front, screening it with pierced stone-work in patterns which swirl around the bud-shaped windows and cast a magnified pattern of light and shade on the wall behind. These screens are beautiful in themselves, with sinuous bands of star-shaped openings, but they are also essential to the psychology of the entire building. They serve as a veil to the body of the pavilion and prevent it from being apprehended immediately. Without them, the bold and symmetrical east front might appear blatant; as it is, the perforated tracery creates an atmosphere of elusiveness and mystery.

The effect of the west front is quite different, but scarcely less dramatic. The skyline bristles with domes and minarets in a manner that recalls the architecture of the sixteenth century – perhaps Richmond Palace was its Tudor counterpart. Its present asymmetry is not due to Nash, for the southern range which he planned has never been executed. But in other respects the composition is as Picturesque as anything in Nash's *oeuvre*. Rarely can such a variety of architectural forms have been combined in a single façade – domes, rectangles and cylinders cluster together above the octagonal entrance hall. (A hexagonal clock-tower built in 1816–17 was later dismantled.) The minarets, which are of three different sizes, offset the squat weight of the domes. The detailed work is uneven in quality, but the later is generally superior to the earlier, and it is difficult to believe that the elegant columns and windows of the King's Apartments, completed in 1821, are the work of the same architect who designed the graceless triangles above the entrance vestibule of 1815.

Today the west front is best seen in the winter, when the King's Apartments are not obscured by the leaves of three large elms, but the north front is delightful at any season. The last part of the Pavilion to be completed (in 1822), it is composed with an almost military neatness, an effect emphasized by the two ranks of chimney-pinnacles standing guard on the roof. Yet the north front has a certain delicacy, captured in A. C. Pugin's watercolour sketch, which the two main façades cannot rival.

In all three visible frontages (there have always been adjoining buildings to the south) the selection of motifs is astonishingly catholic, producing some unprecedented yet successful combinations. Mughal India is the dominant

108 Nash's Royal Pavilion under construction, from Wright's *Brighton Ambulator*, 1818

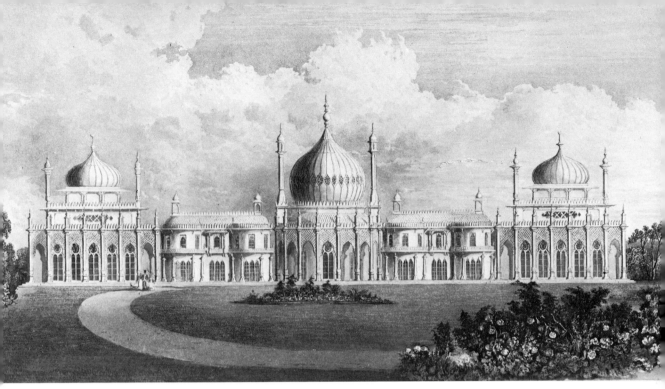

109 Rejected design for the Royal Pavilion, aquatint, pl. 11 of John Nash, *Views of the Royal Pavilion*, 1826

110 Richmond Palace, engraving of 1763 from an earlier drawing

inspiration, and some of the minarets, columns and windows are thoroughly Indian. Other windows are versions of eighteenth-century Gothick,[27] while others again are best described as *Style Métro* a century before its time. Two drum towers behind the main domes are unashamedly 'castellated Gothic', and the upswept roofs at each end, which contemporaries described as 'pagoda roofs',[28] are surely intended to be Chinese, overgrown nephews of the Chinese kiosks on Nash's bridge in St James's Park. Nash seems to have been determined to avoid expanses of unrelieved stucco. Even the domes are patterned into compartments and punctuated at the waist by a row of windows or (in the smaller domes) rosettes. The central dome appears to rest on four strips of decoration, the lowest of which bulges outward like cake-filling beneath the weight of the upper layers. Every parapet is occupied by balconies, battlements or miniature domes.

The new Pavilion was an easy target for the wit of tourists, especially those with literary aspirations. William Cobbett derided the building with references to squat decanters and Norfolk turnips; Hazlitt saw it as a collection of stone pumpkins and pepper-boxes, and Prince Pückler-Muskau likened it to a chessboard. William Wilberforce made the suggestion (also credited to Sydney Smith) that St Paul's Cathedral had come down to the sea and left behind a litter of cupolas. Several commentators, including Princess Lieven, wife of the Russian ambassador, likened the Pavilion to the Kremlin, which had recently been publicized in the plates of Ackermann's *Historical Sketches of Moscow* (1813). In 1820 the princess described the unfinished building as 'a mixture of Moorish, Tartar, Gothic and Chinese, and all in stone and iron. It is a whim which has already cost £700,000, and is still not fit to live in'.[29] Only a small minority of visitors recognized the true affiliations of Nash's structure. One of these was the artist and diarist Joseph Farington, who made his inspection in September 1818:

I walked to the front of the Regent's Palace & found the front nearly in scaffolding. The alterations carrying on were said to be in imitation of the *Kremlin at Moscow*. If so, the celebrated building must very much resemble some of the Palaces represented in Daniel's [sic] Oriental Scenery.[30]

Nash had undoubtedly looked at *Oriental Scenery*, for it is recorded that he borrowed from the royal library at Carlton House '4 volumes of Daniell's Views of India to make drawings for the Brighton Pavilion.'[31] He must also have consulted Repton's *Designs for the Pavillon*, which correspond with Nash's designs in several details, most obviously perhaps in the tall, scallop-headed windows which reach down to the floor of Repton's 'Dining Room' and which reappear as the principal windows of Nash's east front, the scallops now formed by the edge of the perforated screen. But Nash's art was not Repton's, and in any case Nash had nothing to gain from imitating an unacceptable set of designs. It is quite possible that he examined Repton's book not primarily for inspiration but from a wish to devise something entirely different.

Princess Lieven's figure of £700,000 was exaggerated – the total expenditure on the Royal Pavilion estate between 1804 and 1830 was about half a million pounds [32] – and her remark that it was 'all in stone and iron' overlooks the stuccoed brick which forms the core of the building. But Nash's pavilion was more solidly built than Holland's, both in external detail and in basic construction. Whereas Holland had placed statues of artificial stone around the drum of his building, Nash used Bath stone for his external colonnades. Cast iron, still something of a novelty as a structural material, was employed for the framework of Nash's great dome, for the central tubes of the disguised chimneys, and for the principal staircases, where the cast-iron balustrade was painted to simulate bamboo. The four columns in the Great Kitchen are also of cast iron, this time imitating the trunks of young palm trees which branch out into green copper palm leaves as they meet the ceiling. The domes and roofs were covered with an experimental stucco or 'mastic'. This last was a conspicuous failure. 'It has been represented to His Majesty that the Dihl Mastic employed on these Roofs has *completely failed*; that the covering of the magnificent Dining Room, the interior of which has cost so large a sum, is now in that state that to secure it from injury, pans are obliged to be placed over the surface, to guard the Interior from the Influence of the Rain . . .'[33] The mastic proved a constantly recurring problem, and in May 1827 a serious outbreak of dry rot was discovered.

By this time George IV had visited Brighton for the last time, and indeed since the completion of the Pavilion in 1822 he seems to have taken little interest in it, distracted perhaps by

111 The first South Gate to the Royal Pavilion, lithograph after Edward Fox, 1830

the rebuilding of Buckingham House and Windsor Castle. The Pavilion in its fullest glory was commemorated by the sumptuous volume usually known as 'Nash's Views of the Royal Pavilion' (dated 1826 but published in 1827). It would be fairer to describe the book as 'Pugin's Views', for most of the 31 plates were originally drawn by Augustus Charles Pugin. Twenty-eight of the plates are coloured aquatints, showing interiors, exteriors and a sectional view, and the remaining three are uncoloured outlines of decorative schemes which had been superseded. A number of Pugin's preparatory drawings also survive, some of them partly coloured to guide the engravers' colourists; it is clear that Pugin took great pains to ensure that the Pavilion and its contents were accurately reproduced. On the basis of his drawings and engravings, it has been possible to restore at least the ground floor of the Pavilion to the state which had finally satisfied George IV.

In 1830 William IV succeeded his brother. He liked Brighton, patronizing its Chain Pier and also its Pavilion, which he officially designated a royal palace. He and Queen Adelaide spent several winters there. Soon after his accession William was observed in the Pavilion grounds with John Nash, apparently planning alterations. But Nash did not return to the Pavilion, and the only additions made in William's reign were in the grounds. The unfinished eastern section of Porden's Stables, which had been intended for use as a tennis-court, was developed as further stabling ('Queen Adelaide's Stables') and kitchens; at the southern end of the estate a three-storeyed lodge gateway was built, with a 111 central scalloped arch between canopied sentry-boxes, and beside this South Lodge a range of white brick houses known as the Dormitories was erected for the use of the king's guests. Most of the work was carried out in 1831, under the direction of Nash's successor Joseph Good, Clerk of the

Works to the Board of Ordnance. But as an architect Good was no substitute for Nash, and after some public criticism of his work it was resolved that the Pavilion grounds should be enclosed by a North Lodge more impressive than the southern gateway. Again Good supervised the work, but this time the design was Nash's. The result was a grand and solid Mughal entrance, of Bath stone framing panels of lighter-coloured Portland stone. Completed in 1832, it still forms the main entrance to the Pavilion estate, and the military traditions of the guardsmen who once manned the gates are maintained by the car park superintendent.

Between the new North Gate and Queen Adelaide's Stables one house was still standing, the solitary survivor of an eighteenth-century terrace. In the 1820s it had been the residence of Lady Conyngham, George IV's favourite in his last years. This building (today known as Northgate House) was completely refaced, with corner turrets, Indian crenellation, and scalloped arches within panels around doors and windows. The oriental ensemble was now complete.

The Royal Pavilion and its outbuildings were scarcely influential outside Brighton, but within the town they produced a number of offspring. The first oriental project conceived after the Pavilion's completion was fortunately abortive. Henry Phillips, a botanist of considerable local repute, proposed in 1825 to develop in western Brighton an 'oriental garden' inside a monstrously bulging conservatory, to be called the Athenaeum. The steam-heated conservatory would house tropical trees and plants, and the institution would include a library, a school and a museum. Its triple domes (suggesting Turkey rather than India) would be framed and linked to the seafront by Oriental Place, a new terrace which in the projected design was heavily ornamented with classical devices. In the event Phillips could not raise the funds necessary to begin the Athenaeum, but Oriental Place was eventually built under the auspices of Sir David Scott, a former Director of the East India Company.

Its architect was Amon Henry Wilds, who with his father Amon Wilds and Charles Busby was responsible for many of Brighton's most interesting terraces of this period. The pilasters of Oriental Place carry the curling fossil-shaped 'ammonite' capitals first used by George Dance,

113 The North Gate to the Royal Pavilion, Brighton

114 9 Western Terrace ('The Western Pavilion'), Brighton

◀ 112 Northgate House, Brighton

115 The projected Athenaeum and Oriental Palace, Brighton, aquatint *c.* 1825

which Amon Henry Wilds favoured as his punning trademark. In the late 1820s he designed three houses near by with oriental façades, numbers 9 and 21 Sillwood Place, opposite each other, and 9 Western Terrace, built as Wilds's own residence: it boasts in addition a small Mughal dome, and is generally known as the Western Pavilion, although its details do not closely follow those of its prototype.

Meanwhile Henry Phillips, undeterred by the failure of his Athenaeum, was planning an even larger conservatory further west in Hove, to be entitled the Antheum. This was to consist of a flattened dome of glass resting on cast-iron girders, which were sunk ten feet into the ground and anchored in brickwork. The dome was very shallow (164 feet in diameter, 65 feet high), and it referred to the Orient only in its small ogival cupola,[34] positioned on top of the dome and encircled by an observation terrace, and in its entrance, described as 'moresque'.[35] In 1833 the Antheum was built as Phillips had envisaged, and when the internal supports were removed, the dome held – for a day. The younger Wilds was once more the architect, but he had resigned (or had been dismissed) when Phillips insisted on modifications that involved removing the central iron pillar. The pillar was removed,

and before any adequate substitute could replace it, the temporary centring was taken away also; on the eve of the following day the entire roof fell in. The workmen had been celebrating inside a few hours before. The head gardener was still on the site and just managed to escape, but the disillusioned visionary Henry Phillips is reported to have gone blind ten days after the disaster. The wreckage of twisted girders lay where it had fallen for two decades, during most of which time no oriental experiments were undertaken in Brighton.

In 1837 Victoria came to the throne, and like her two predecessors she went to stay at Brighton soon after her accession. Unlike them, however, she did not appreciate the Pavilion, which she described on her first visit as 'a strange, odd, Chinese-looking thing, both inside and outside, most rooms low. I see only a morsel of the sea from one of my sitting room windows.'[36] Her mood improved, and she came to stay on four subsequent occasions, the last in February 1845. But the Pavilion and the Brighton crowds did not suit her, and in June 1850 her palace was sold to the town of Brighton for £53,000. Victoria's decision to sell the building had more to do with its lack of privacy than with any dislike of chinoiserie – she retained most of the Pavilion's

114

116 The second South Gate to the Royal Pavilion, Brighton

contents at Buckingham Palace – but her action was symbolic of mid-nineteenth-century attitudes to oriental architecture. The topographical writer Edward Brayley, who supplied a text to 'Nash's Views' at the start of Victoria's reign, clearly disliked the outward appearance of the Pavilion, preferring Repton's designs, 'which far surpass the anomalous conceptions that determined the external character of the present edifice'.[37] Brayley struggled to find words to praise the building – it was tall, unique and ingeniously ornamented, and if located on higher ground (Brayley allowed) it would doubtless impress a spectator unacquainted with classical elegance. The interiors were much more to his taste, and he dwelt lovingly on the harmony of design, the extent of the gilding, the height and the weight of the ornaments. But Brayley's scorn was aroused again by the new South Lodge, 'which has more resemblance to a gate-house prison, than to any object of architectural beauty, and is utterly unworthy of description.'[38]

After its sale in 1850, the Pavilion could not be expected to function as a centre of aristocratic fashion, and yet it remained a strong influence on Brighton's architecture. When the Town Commissioners took charge of the Pavilion estate they demolished the unpopular South Gate, but they maintained the oriental tradition by erecting two smaller domed Mughal archways forty yards to the north, with cast-iron chatris enclosing lamps, and a low iron gate in between. Although the new entrance was hardly more attractive than the old, at least it allowed more of the Pavilion to be seen.[39] 116

From the later years of the century a number of oriental allusions survive in the civic architecture of Brighton – among them the King's Road Bandstand (1884), with its flattened Islamic dome and elaborate cast-iron tracery; the semicircular arches of Madeira Drive (1895–98) at the foot of the sea-wall, which are pierced with star-shaped apertures in the manner of the stone screen of the Royal Pavilion; the elegant lampposts on the upper promenade, descendants of the Pavilion lanterns; and the lift between upper and lower levels, which is housed in a stylish little kiosk (1896), decorated with dragons and an armillary sphere on its scaled roof. Earlier in the century a design for 'Royal Zoological Gardens' at Brighton was put forward, showing spacious grounds within which the animals and birds were to be housed in some twenty-five pavilions, all in a Mughal or Chinese style or in a mixture of the two.[40] And in about 1880 Sir Albert Abdullah Sassoon built for himself in Paston Place a

117 The Sassoon Mausoleum, Brighton

118 The West Pier, Brighton, *c.* 1900

circular mausoleum with a concave roof rising to an Indian finial; the outer walls carry Mughal crenellation and scalloped arches. In this case Sir Albert was probably influenced less by the special flavour of Brighton's architecture than by the fact that the Sassoon trading empire had been based in Bombay, and his own business interests extended throughout the Near and Far East. In Brighton he entertained the Prince of Wales and the Shah of Persia, and was duly buried in his mausoleum in 1896, although his remains were later removed. The building is now put to satisfactory use as the Bombay Bar.[41]

117
118   Brighton's West Pier, built in 1863–66, played a particularly significant role in promoting the idea that elements of oriental design were appropriate in seaside architecture.[42] The West Pier was the *chef d'oeuvre* of Eusebius Birch, who in his lifetime designed no fewer than fourteen piers in England and Wales; it was also the first pier to admit oriental references in its architecture. As the next chapter will suggest, oriental architecture was unfashionable in Britain during the 1860s, and to employ it must have been a daring step on Birch's part. However, the style of the West Pier is even more generalized than that of the Pavilion. The main features of the pier as first built were two sets of four pavilions, each with arched openings, broad horizontal eaves, and gently convex roofs leading up to balustraded platforms. All but the landward pair of pavilions were given chatri-like turrets on their upper platforms. None of these forms is unambiguously Indian or Chinese in itself, but the effect is eastern without doubt. From these beginnings much followed. Most of the additions to the West Pier have made some concession to an oriental style. Subsequent piers (by Birch and by others) adopted the oriental theme, notably Brighton's own Palace Pier, built in 1891–99 from the designs of R. St George Moore. In its pavilion roofs, its railings and its series of arches in delicately-patterned ironwork, the Palace Pier is a splendid jumble of orientalia.

To this day it is considered suitable to apply a vaguely eastern style to seaside structures, although few of the twentieth-century versions have yet acquired the charm of their predecessors. Eusebius Birch must take credit for this 'seafront style', but the ultimate responsibility lies with those architects and connoisseurs of the Regency who saw the very different attributes of Chinese and Indian architecture as variants of a single pan-oriental style.

153

Chapter Eleven
Disillusion and Reaction

FOR THE FIRST QUARTER of the nineteenth century the Indian style prospered, making sporadic but confident appearances in the coastal towns of southern England, notably in the Mount Zion Baptist Chapel built at Devonport in 1823–24. The chapel was an element in an international assemblage designed by the West Country architect John Foulson, who positioned it between a Greek Doric column and a Greek Ionic house, with an Egyptian library (now Oddfellows Hall) beyond the latter. Opposite were a Greek Doric town hall and a Roman Corinthian terrace. Foulston regarded his scheme as an experiment in the interests of picturesque effect, which he confessed might not please everybody. But at least he had not committed the 'abomination' of combining different styles within the

119 Clifton Baths, Gravesend, c. 1890

same building, he wrote. Such a mixture would be 'like a monstrous union of the parts of one animal with those of another'.[1]

Unfortunately one engraving of Foulston's ambitious project shows just such a union – Decorated Gothic windows in the chapel, with Mughal pinnacles instead of crocketed finials above.[2] In his outlined view of the ensemble, however, both pinnacles and windows are Indian. But the significance of this building lies less in the detailing than in the fact that Islamic architecture could have been thought appropriate for Christian ecclesiastical purposes at all. The Chinese style never secured this degree of acceptance. Mount Zion was used for Congregationalist worship, then by the Salvation Army, and finally as a Calvinist hall, before being demolished at the beginning of the twentieth century.

The choice of Indian architecture for a bathing establishment is less surprising. Brill's seawater bath-house, which was opened on Brighton front in 1823, was circular and sported a small domed lantern; known as 'the bunion', it was distinctive without pretending to any specific oriental style.[3] But the Clifton Baths at Gravesend were full-bloodedly Mughal, with a cluster of domed towers fifty feet tall, and scalloped arches on squat columns of massive girth. The baths were erected in 1835 for a Mr Ditchburn, probably by Amon Henry Wilds who was active in Gravesend at the time.

One further building belongs to this phase of Anglo-Indian design, the lodge gateway at Dromana in county Waterford, Republic of Ireland. It was apparently built as a temporary structure to welcome Henry Villiers-Stuart (afterwards Lord Stuart de Decies) on his return with his Austrian bride from their honeymoon in 1826. Some twenty years later the gateway was rebuilt in more permanent materials, as part of a programme of improvements to Dromana House and its estate.[4] Its dome is a little attenuated, as if

120 Mount Zion Chapel and neighbouring buildings, outline engraving from John Foulston, *The Public Buildings in the West of England*, 1838

121 Lodge gateway at Dromana, Co. Waterford, Eire

it had been copied from one of the many distorted views published of the Royal Pavilion; the delicate grille-work along the parapet, on the other hand, is reminiscent of Sezincote. Minarets surround the dome, three of them replaced in 1967 by the Irish Georgian Society. The ogival windows and the indeterminate pointed shape of the main arch add a pleasantly eccentric air to the composition, which may be regarded as a unique example of the Irish-Indo-Gothic Style.

By this time elements of Indian design had appeared at Vauxhall Gardens, ever sensitive to changes in high fashion. In 1822 the Rotunda contained 'four fine views in Hindoostan, painted on the walls, as if seen through vahranda [sic] windows and doors'. Most of the supporting columns had been converted from Ionic to 'a gorgeous Indian character'. On one side of the Rotunda more Indian paintings could be seen in a recess, and on the other side 'four Hindoo columns' conducted patrons out to the Picture-room. The latest attraction stood near by, the impressively named Heptaplasiesoptron, which was a revolving display involving palm trees and twining serpents, both prominent also in the interior of Brighton's Pavilion. And over the entrance to the Saloon or Ballroom was placed 'a most magnificent effigy of the Indian Neptune, kneeling on a silver fish, with his name beneath him in the Deva-nagari character; and on either side of him, next to the Rotunda, are two splendid elephants' heads'.[5] Although the Chinese lanterns still glowed along the Cross Walk, India had conquered China at Vauxhall.

But the triumph of India was short-lived, at Vauxhall as elsewhere. Allen's plan of the gardens in 1826 shows a Chinese entrance, reflecting a renewed interest in Chinese architecture among the wealthy and fashion-conscious. For interior decoration the *beau monde* had never lost interest in Chinese and Anglo-Chinese products, despite the fact that other exotic styles were pressing rival claims:

> You'd swear Egyptians, Moors, and Turks
> Bearing good taste some deadly malice
> Had clubbed to raise a pic-nic palace . . .[6]

wrote Thomas Moore of Carlton House, whose interior design was supervised, after Henry Holland's death, by Walsh Porter. Porter's own seat at Vine Cottage, Fulham, exhibited a range of styles:

An apartment decorated with all the gaudy fineries of China, led you into a cavern, where you trembled lest you should encounter the dagger of some assassin; but, having happily passed through without accident, you were ushered in to a Turkish pavilion, which perhaps conducted you into a Grecian, &c., &c . . .[7]

In the Pavilion at Brighton the Chinese interior was interspersed with Indian motifs, particularly in the Saloon, and as late as 1842 the owner of Basildon Park in Berkshire was writing to J. B. Papworth, his architect-decorator, 'the more I think of your new Indian notion for the so-called Chinese Room, the more I like it. May you be as happy as you were in the Etruscan.'[8] The pan-oriental fashion spread to Ireland, where it was satirized in Maria Edgeworth's novel *The Absentee* (1812). For the occasion of Lady Clonbrony's ball, the suave Mr Soho, 'the first architectural upholsterer of the age', recommends in rapid succession the Turkish tent drapery, in apricot cloth or crimson velvet, with Statira canopy and seraglio ottomans; the Alhambra hangings, with porphyry columns supporting a grand dome, and 'Trebisond trellice paper'; the Chinese pagoda, created by porcelain-bordered pagoda wallpaper, josses and jars; or the Egyptian hieroglyphic paper with ibis border to match. But the last of these might not suit Lady Clonbrony, Mr Soho adds, for it was now so popular that it could be seen even in hotels.[9]

When the Napoleonic Wars were finally ended, it was decided (despite sound advice to the contrary) to make fresh overtures to the court of China. From this point the history of Anglo-Chinese relations in the nineteenth century becomes a sad recital of insult and counter-insult. In February 1816 a second British embassy was sent out, under Lord Amherst on the *Alceste*, bearing a letter from the Prince Regent which hailed the new Emperor Ch'ia Ch'ing unacceptably as 'Sir, My Brother'. On reaching the outskirts of Peking, Lord Amherst was at once required to meet the emperor, but Amherst declined on the grounds that he was tired and unsuitably dressed; whereupon the embassy was asked to leave.

If Macartney's expedition had been a failure, Amherst's was a fiasco, and there was much less compensation in the form of fresh knowledge of China. Clarke Abel, 'naturalist', composed an account of the embassy which he illustrated with some mediocre aquatints, but both his report and that of Amherst's secretary, Henry Ellis, took an understandably jaundiced view of China, and neither showed much appreciation of Chinese architecture. They duly recorded the pagodas seen on the return journey to Canton, including the Porcelain Tower at Nanking, which they had to view from a distance, since a group which set off to inspect this most famous pagoda was halted two miles away by hostile crowds. Abel wrote of 'the glittering and tawdry magnificence' of the Audience Hall at Tientsin,[10] and Ellis admitted that he was dazzled by the gilt carving which decorated the shops in the suburbs of Peking, but he felt obliged to add that 'it is extraordinary, that the profits of trade should allow of such an unproductive expenditure'.[11]

Amherst returned with nothing but a message for the Prince Regent, suggesting that the prince might continue in obedience to the Dragon Throne but need not trouble to send representatives. Yet the débâcle did not greatly damage the image of China held in the mind of the British public; indignation was expressed, but much of this was directed at the practice of sending out ineffectual and expensive embassies rather than at the Chinese themselves. During the Regency, England imported a considerable quantity of Chinese as well as Indian artefacts, and when Prince Pückler-Muskau toured England in 1826–28 he found Chinese hangings and paintings in many of the houses he visited. In London he was taken to see the Indian and Chinese curiosities on display at the East India Company Museum, where he observed the journal in which Tipu Sahib had described his dreams and their interpretations. Like many other tourists, the German prince then saw the company warehouses, 'where you may buy all sorts of Indian goods uncommon cheap, provided you ship them immediately to the Continent, in which case they pay no duty to the Government'.[12] One wholesale tea warehouse in the City, F. & R. Sparrow's at 8 Ludgate Hill, was perhaps the first urban building in England which could claim to possess Chinese façades. Designed by J. B. Papworth in 1822, it was decorated with lei-wen spirals, urns and bells, a Chinese figure in a niche at the fourth storey, and Chinese characters descending vertical panels between the orthodox late-Georgian windows.[13] According to Papworth's son and biographer, copies and imitations of the front of the building could be seen fifty years later.[14]

Among imports from the East were plants, which gave rise to 'Chinese gardens', and these in

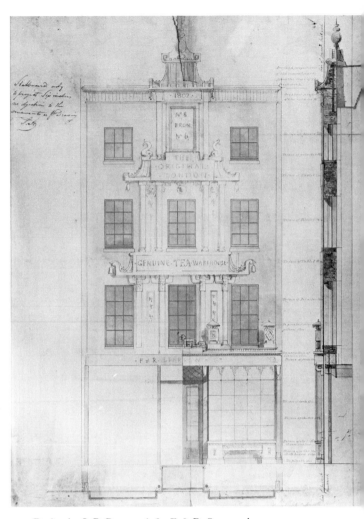

122 Design by J. B. Papworth for F. & R. Sparrow's Tea Warehouse at 8 Ludgate Hill, 1822

turn may have encouraged garden buildings in the Chinese style. At Cassiobury Park, where Humphry Repton had previously been at work, Pückler-Muskau admired the Chinese garden,

which is likewise inclosed by high trees and walls, and contains a number of vases, benches, fountains, and a third green-house – all in the genuine Chinese style. Here were beds surrounded by circles of white, blue and red sand, fantastic dwarf plants, and many dozens of large China vases placed on pedestals, thickly overgrown with trailing evergreens, and exotics. The windows of the house were painted like Chinese hangings, and convex mirrors placed in the interior, which reflected us as in a 'camera obscura'.[15]

Only five days previously, Pückler-Muskau had written with satisfaction of the Chinese garden

123 The Fishing Temple at Virginia Water, aquatint by William Daniell, *c.* 1830

and dairy at Woburn. He was less well disposed towards the Royal Pavilion when he visited Brighton a few weeks later – 'a strange Oriental Palace, which seen from the adjoining heights, with its cupolas and minarets, looks exactly like the pieces on a chess-board'.[16] But in the royal park at Virginia Water the German prince saw 'Chinese and Moorish houses executed with taste and not caricatured'. One of these would no doubt have been the Fishing Temple which King George IV had commissioned Sir Jeffry Wyatville to build in the closing months of 1825. A contemporary aquatint by William Daniell shows the pavilion on a foundation of arches at the water's edge, with smaller Chinese structures half hidden by weeping willows on each side and a covered fishing balcony running along the whole frontage. A group of Turkish tents stands a little to one side, and a Chinese boat-house a little to the other. The garden façade can be seen in more detail in a drawing by Frederick Crace. Although larger than any Anglo-Chinese pavilion built in the eighteenth century, the Fishing

Temple on Virginia Water owed more to Chambers than to Alexander in its twin hexagons and central octagon, and in its wealth of rococo detail – rows of bells, curling finials, lei-wen spirals, ornamental birds on the balcony roof and serpentine dragons draped around the three masts. The striped central roof echoed that of the Chinese Yacht formerly used by the Duke of Cumberland, great uncle of George IV and creator of Virginia Water.

The temple was begun in the winter of 1825–26, and was conceived from the first as an unusually elaborate pavilion, 'full of gilt dragons for ornaments: rather too expensive, *on dit*, considering Windsor, Buckingham House, York House & the state of the country'.[17] By August of 1826 it was clear that the cost would exceed Wyatville's estimate of £3,285; in 1828 the king was still requesting additions and alterations. Wyatville's collaborator was Frederick Crace, now greatly experienced in the design of chinoiserie, who must also have been responsible for the interior decoration, since he received much the greater share of the commission.[18] Wyatville had the less glamorous task of converting Crace's conception into a solid (or at least waterproof) structure. In this he was not altogether successful, for the pavilion was often in need of repair, and at the end of the century was replaced by a staid little Swiss Cottage. In its prime the Fishing Temple was much favoured by satirists, who could both parody the Chinese style and pun endlessly on the king's activities ('A King-Fisher', 'Hooking a Mermaid in Virgin-Water'). But the caricatures do scant justice to the sumptuous frivolity of the pavilion. Charles Greville and his companions were rowed out to the temple and its neighbouring encampment two months after the death of George IV, and were greatly impressed:

Across the water is the fishing-cottage, beautifully ornamented, with one large room and a dressing-room on each side; kitchen, offices, etc. are in a garden full of flowers, shut out from everything. Opposite the windows is moored a large boat, in which the band used to play during dinner . . .[19]

Another royal commission gave Wyatville the opportunity to design an oriental mansion himself, for Queen Adelaide's brother, the Duke of Saxe-Meiningen. The duke proposed to erect a spacious villa in his already landscaped park at Meiningen, and when the English queen came to stay with him in 1834 she recommended Wyatville as architect. Between 1836 and 1838 Wyatville sent out a variety of plans and elevations in classical, Gothic and oriental styles, of which the oriental designs are generally the latest and seemingly those regarded as most promising. Wyatville's captions distinguished between 'Dheli' [sic] and 'Hardwar' architecture, rather pretentiously in view of the fact that his oriental elevations consist of an unappealing mixture of Mughal and Chinese motifs. The Mughal elements predominate in the villa designs, while for the duke's stables Wyatville allowed a series of concave roofs to compete with a tall Mughal gateway. Neither stables nor villa was executed.[20]

While George IV's last pavilion was being built beside Virginia Water, England's last great

XII

124 'Stonehenge' and the conservatories at Alton Towers, Staffordshire, engraving from J. C. Loudon, *Encyclopaedia of Gardening*, 1828 ed.

excavated to form an Indian cave-temple appropriately inscribed, and when the 15th earl died in 1827 the first storey of a pagoda fountain (designed, like the conservatories, by Robert Abraham) had been completed. Loudon reproduced a design for this pagoda, which was to have been eighty-eight feet high, consisting of a basic stone storey and five cast-iron storeys above. From the highly ornamented roofs gas-lit lanterns would have been suspended from the mouths of assorted mythical beasts. These grotesque creatures were also expected to spout water from their eyes, nostrils, fins and tails, and from the uppermost crown of the pagoda a central jet would have shot another seventy or eighty feet into the air.[21]

Instead of this lavish creation a more modest three-storey pagoda-fountain was built, pretty enough today in its diapered paintwork and green curling roofs. Bells have replaced the proposed lanterns, and the rooflines and ring-finial suggest the example of the small pagoda engraved in the fifth plate of Chambers's *Designs*. Only the stepped stone base is immediately recognizable from Loudon's engraved design.

XIV

Of the same period but at an opposite extreme was the Chinese Gallery at Ticehurst, Sussex. On 8 December 1827 the Secretary of State was told of a private lunatic asylum at Ticehurst, 'principally calculated for the reception of patients of a superior situation in life'. Pheasantries, aviaries and extensive conservatories were at their disposal, together with the Chinese Gallery, 'which is fitted up with much taste, and affords to the invalids a secure retreat in wet weather'. A small engraving of the gallery exterior shows it to have been an elaborate exercise in late Georgian Gothic, incorporating a few decorative curls intended to suggest the Orient. Inside, the 'Chinese' elements consisted of rows of chevrons and serrations following the lines of the pointed arches, and triangular wedges at the bases and capitals of the hexagonal columns. The serrated ribs are reminiscent of the Red Drawing Room at the Royal Pavilion, but the building belongs in spirit to the tradition of Vauxhall-Gothic. The proprietor was apparently a specialist in mental illness, which is reassuring, because the bleak exoticism of the Chinese Gallery looks as if it might have aggravated his patients' condition.[22]

Not long after Pückler-Muskau's visit to Woburn, the ducal gardens received a further oriental feature in the form of a little temple in the centre of a maze, less celebrated than the

125 Unexecuted design for the pagoda at Alton Towers, Staffordshire, engraving from J. C. Loudon, *Encyclopaedia of Gardening*, 1828 ed.

landscape garden was being laid out at Alton Towers, near Cheadle in Staffordshire, the seat of the Earls of Shrewsbury. The spectacular terrain and masses of stratified sandstone were exploited to the full by Charles, 15th Earl of Shrewsbury, in a manner worthy of the eighteenth century at its most eclectic. John Claudius Loudon was there in October 1826, and although the variety of buildings was not to his taste he was clearly overwhelmed by the scale of the earl's fantasy. The garden architecture included a corkscrew fountain, a *trompe-l'oeil* cottage, a gothic prospect tower and a massive imitation of Stonehenge set on high ground, from which could be seen the seven glass domes of a long range of conservatories, oriental in impression if not in detail. The sandstone outcrops were

Chinese Dairy but equally attractive, especially since its recent restoration by Donald Insall and Company. The general account books for Woburn state that on 14 June 1833, £75 was paid to Robert Peake Nixon 'for building Chinese Temple in Pleasure Ground as agreed'.[23] The maze had now been cut down (to waist-height at the time of writing), but if it was ever intended to pose any problems at all, the hedges must have stood higher than eye-level. The visitor would not have been able to see the pavilion until, having taken the final correct turning, he was suddenly confronted with it; or perhaps he would have been aided by tantalizing glimpses of the top of its lantern. The cast-iron balustrading is a modern essay in the manner of Sir William Chambers, but the restorers have been able to reconstruct the trelliswork of the octagonal lantern on the evidence of the woodwork which remained. Although the blue and red of the glass bells seem to clash with the colouring of the pavilion itself they are the authentic colours, based on three of the original bells which the restorers discovered in Woburn Abbey.

The maze temple at Woburn was one of the last architectural products of the fashion for chinoiserie in England.[24] Until the 1830s it is possible to identify a taste (albeit a minority one) for Chinese and mock-Chinese design, such that a gentleman might erect a Chinese pavilion in his gardens without any particular affiliation to the East or any motive other than a liking for Chinese forms. But as this decade continued, and as British merchants repeatedly failed in their attempts to develop the Chinese trade, British attitudes to China as a whole began to change. The image of mild eccentricity faded, and in its place grew a belief that the Chinese were a nation of devious and cowardly prevaricators. Lord Amherst and his party had, of course, been convinced of this already; when they had finally re-embarked at Canton in January 1817, their English crew had given three cheers, prompting the embassy's chronicler to observe that 'there was an awful manliness in the sound so opposite to the discordant salutations and ridiculous ceremonies of the nation we were quitting'.[25] Something of this attitude seems to have attached itself to Chinese design, whose elaborations came to represent the 'ridiculous ceremonies' of an intractable people. And the suggestion of effeminacy, sometimes made regarding chinoiserie in the 1750s, bore a greater pejorative charge in the reigns of William IV and Victoria.

In 1834, when the East India Company's monopoly of the China trade was ended, Lord Napier was dispatched to Canton as British representative, the first of a series of unfortunate officials who were expected to mediate between the British merchants and the Chinese government. Before dying of fever, Napier aggravated the situation further by his provocative actions. Relations between the two sides deteriorated rapidly, and it became clear that the restrictions placed on European trading, particularly in the lucrative and illegal commodity of opium, would be removed only through force of arms. In Britain a considerable body of opinion was opposed to armed conflict, but the war-party was supported by stories of Chinese atrocities and insults to the British flag. In 1839, the year in which open hostilities commenced, Admiral Anson's biographer (himself a veteran of Macartney's embassy) could not resist a reference to current events:

It would be out of place here to notice (what was not *then* so generally known as *now*) the account given of the proneness to falsehood, the duplicity and knavery of the Chinese, which not only pervade every department of the government, but also, naturally enough, infect the people generally.[26]

In the following summer the town of Canton was captured by an expeditionary force of British and Indian troops, and the military weakness of the Chinese further diminished their status in British eyes. In 1842 Nanking surrendered without resistance, and the Treaty of Nanking brought the first Anglo-Chinese War to an end.

In this way the spell of the pagoda and the pavilion was finally broken, and the events of 1839–42 virtually marked the death of chinoiserie in Britain. The Porcelain Tower of Nanking, which two official embassies had failed to reach, yielded its secrets at last to an invading enemy – in fact a party of seamen attached to the British military expedition, who 'with pickaxes and hammers endeavoured to deface the walls, and remove the curiosities'.[27] Their mystique banished, pagodas could now offer only an antiquarian appeal: the Rev. G. N. Wright identified the 'cap or cupola' of the pagoda as an 'inverted nelumbium' (Chinese water-lily), and wrote provocatively of the pagoda as a variety of the Irish pillar tower. This referred to an impenetrable essay by a certain Henry O'Brien, which set out to prove that the ancient round stone towers of Ireland were 'primitive Budhist [*sic*] temples'. Wright seems to have been at least half convinced by O'Brien, but he added sensibly that 'however their [the Irish towers'] style of architecture may have been derived from the East, little reason exists for supposing that Buddhism ever prevailed in Ireland'.[28]

Another Chinese institution held sacred by eighteenth-century Englishmen, the complex of palaces of Yuan-ming yuan, was also criticized by Wright:

The mode of building possessing very few traits of permanence, on a closer examination a character of meanness, and a poverty of invention, are at once discovered; and even here, in the most luxurious and spacious of all the imperial homes, it is to the amazing number of fanciful huts and decorated sheds, rather than to their stateliness or durable pretentions, that any magnificence is ascribed.[29]

Wright still gave credit to the Chinese for their landscaped parks, but he warned that the enchantments of the Imperial Gardens at Peking (which he illustrated with an engraving after Alexander) belied the sorrows and uncertainties of life at the Imperial Court. In any case it was now recognized that the great imperial parks were not typical of Chinese gardening as a whole.

126 'Entrance to the Chinese Collection at Hyde Park Corner', frontispiece to exhibition catalogue, 1842

Extracts from the journal of James Main, a botanist who had visited Canton in 1793–94, were reproduced in the *Gardener's Magazine* of 1827. In the gardens which Main had seen, 'no *coup d'oeil* calls for admiration, no extent of undulating lawn, no lengthened vista, no depth of shadowy grove, no sky-reflecting expanse of water – nothing presents itself but a little world of insignificant intricacy'. Main ridiculed the trelliswork, the dwarf trees and the rock form-ations, finding compensation only in the neatly arranged nurseries ('the florimania is even more prevalent in China than in Europe').[30] While British travellers grew increasingly scornful of Chinese architecture and landscape gardening, the flower-gardens of China were one of the few aspects of Chinese culture to maintain their reputation.

As the war in China ended in 1842, the inhabitants of London had an opportunity – the greatest opportunity of the century – to see Chinese artefacts at first hand. It was offered by Nathan Dunn of Philadelphia, who had spent twelve years in China as a merchant and a student of Chinese life. On his return to Philadel-phia he set up in 1837 a large and successful exhibition of Chinese arts and manufactures. He was then induced to transport the exhibition to England, 'at the suggestion of many of the most influential, scientific, and learned persons of the British metropolis and kingdom'.[31] The resulting display was larger and even better attended than before: over a hundred thousand catalogues were sold at the door.

The exhibition opened in 1842 at St George's Place, Hyde Park Corner, in a hall built by Nathan Dunn for the purpose. The entrance was itself a well ornamented Chinese kiosk, 'taken 126 from a model of a summer house now in the collection', with Chinese characters over the portal signifying 'Ten Thousand Chinese Things'. Inside the hall the crowds could see a section of a Chinese temple, with three Buddhas eleven feet tall. In showcases or on pedestals were figures of Chinese from all walks of life, together with the tools of their trade. At the end of the hall was 'a perfect fac-simile of an apartment in a wealthy Chinaman's dwelling'; there was also 'an exact fac-simile of a Chinese roof' with dragons at the corners. To judge by the steel engravings in the exhibition catalogue, many others of the 'cases' consisted of rooms and shops fully furnished with trelliswork and painted decoration.

127 The Chinese Bridge, Wrest Park, Bedfordshire

In addition to the multitude of objects and specimens of natural history more than three hundred paintings were displayed, all said to be the work of Chinese artists and many of them showing interior or exterior views of Chinese buildings. A number of architectural models were also on display, representing a waterwheel, three pagodas (one, inevitably, being the 'Porcelain Pagoda' of Nanking), models of single and twin-storeyed summer-houses, and a variety of bridges. These last must have disillusioned the many visitors to whom a 'Chinese bridge' meant an insubstantial wooden structure formerly common in English landscape gardens; for the models at the Chinese Exhibition were solid, even cumbrous in design, and consisted of one, three or five stone arches without keystones. The cataloguer marvelled at the skill of the Chinese builders in laying without benefit of machinery the stone slabs, 'frequently fourteen feet long by four or five in breadth', which formed the level of their bridges.[32] An appealing example of this more substantial manner is the Chinese Bridge

built of brick and stone in 1870 at Wrest Park, where it succeeded two previous bridges of timber. 127

If an exhibition such as Nathan Dunn's had taken place before the war with China it might have created at least a temporary demand for Chinese or Anglo-Chinese products, but in the 1840s its influence was negligible. The thousands who flocked to see the art of a vanquished nation were not prepared to have anything like it at home. Perhaps also the very availability of detailed information about China deterred them. Now that an 'authentic' Chinese pavilion could be erected in Britain without any great difficulty, the fascination of Chinese architecture dwindled. When the visitors had examined the closely packed stands and read the thorough and informative catalogue, they were unable to imagine China as the mysterious fairyland that had so beguiled their grandparents.

Oriental designs were now no longer offered as models to be followed by British house-builders, and although Richard Brown's *Domestic Architec-*

128 'A Chinese Residence' from Richard Brown, *Domestic Architecture*, 1841

ture (1841) pictured a 'Persian Pavilion', a 'Chinese Residence', a 'Palatial Burmese Hall of Assembly', an 'Oriental Pavilion' and a 'Morisco-Spanish Palatial Building', each of them supported by descriptions written by recent travellers in the East, their interest was purely academic. The 'Chinese Residence' is not much less European in effect than were William Halfpenny's designs half a century before, but it is certainly more prosaic; even the bell-hung dragons are placid, and the chimney-shafts above them (represented in detail on the succeeding plate) are wholly bogus. In any case, Brown cannot have expected his readers to admire a style of which he wrote so disparagingly. 'The apartments are as deficient in proportion, as their construction is void of every rule and principle which we are apt to consider as essential to our architecture.'[33]

This was a damaging criticism, for architectural writers were increasingly concerned with maxims and slogans – Augustus Welby Pugin's contentious *True Principles of Pointed or Christian Architecture* appeared in the same year as Brown's work – and it was to the disadvantage of Chinese architecture that it seemed to lack a rationale. It was associated neither with classical authority nor with native tradition, and few were prepared to defend the peculiarities of Chinese building on utilitarian grounds. John Francis Davis, writing with the benefit of twenty years' residence at Canton, claimed that all Chinese roofs represented 'something of the catenary curve, which a rope assumes when suspended between two points'; therefore 'there is in the appearance of Chinese edifices a want of durable solidity'.[34] John Ruskin, the most ingenious propagandist of all, agreed that the form of the concave roof was intrinsically weak-looking:

The natural tendency of such an arch to dissolution by its own mere weight renders it a feature of detestable ugliness, whenever it occurs on a large scale. It is eminently characteristic of Tudor work, and it is the profile of the Chinese roof . . .[35]

129 The aviary, Dropmore, Buckinghamshire

Despite these strictures, a few oriental pavilions were admitted to Victorian gardens. The grounds of Dropmore, near Windsor, were first landscaped for Lord Grenville in the 1790s, but the remarkable range of trellised garden buildings, extending for some two hundred yards against a brick wall, probably dates from the middle of the nineteenth century. The trelliswork of the 1750s was commonly patterned in a Chinese manner, and at Dropmore too there are Chinese forms at several points, especially in the aviary, which has a skeleton of thin red-painted iron rods and a border of green glazed and pierced 'Chinese' tiles. (Pierced tiles were also adopted near by at Frogmore, in the royal dairy of 1858–59. Prince Albert played a considerable part in its design, and it is possible that the tiled ceiling of the dairy was inspired by the pierced ceiling-panels or 'heaven-wells' of China.)[36] But an equally spectacular aspect of the Dropmore pergola is not Chinese; it is a pair of lattice pavilions with Doric columns, entablature and pediment all worked in the wonderfully in-

129

appropriate material of light strips of wood. Inside, the furniture and decorations were Chinese, which with the classical portico formed another surprising combination. It is frustrating that so little is known about the origins of this small masterpiece of Victorian surrealism.

The most attractive chinoiserie of the Victorian era is to be found in the gardens at Biddulph Grange in Cheshire, whose exceptional artistry is due to two men: the proprietor James Bateman, a renowned collector of orchids and connoisseur of all exotic plants, and Edward Cooke, best known as a marine painter but also a landscape gardener and a student of geology and architecture. Cooke first came to Biddulph in 1849, and was a frequent visitor there for the next twenty years. But it was during the 1850s that he and Bateman were most active, arranging within the grounds a dozen different kinds of garden and exploiting the hilly terrain to isolate each from the others. For Ashridge, Humphry Repton had proposed (with a little cheating) 'no less than fifteen different kinds of Gardens',[37] but the

IX

gardens at Biddulph are more diverse and intricate than even Repton could have conceived.

In more than one respect the gardens at Biddulph are an embodiment of eighteenth-century ideals. The element of 'surprise', which in the parks of that century consisted of views seen unexpectedly around a corner or through a small opening, is achieved most dramatically at Biddulph, whose treasures – the Chinese Garden, Egyptian Court and the Glen in the rhododendron ground – are so carefully enclosed by natural features that the visitor has difficulty in seeing them from any other part of the grounds. If he can locate them at all it is by way of a narrow winding path, or a tunnel, or an unsuspected passage through a thick hedge. Moreover, Cooke and Bateman achieved a correspondence between architecture and vegetation that Belanger would have envied. The Chinese structures were accompanied by a great diversity of oriental plants, some recently sent back from China by Robert Fortune; and in the Egyptian Court, to complement the stone sphinxes, obelisks and idol, and entrance gateway is embedded in massive rectangular steps of clipped yew. The effect is reinforced by two free-standing yews cut into the form of pyramids.

Cooke had a talent for large-scale rockwork sculpture, which he displayed appropriately in the Chinese Garden and elsewhere, and the more novel art (perhaps inspired by Chambers's *Dissertation on Oriental Gardening*)[38] of root-sculpture. The root-garden or 'Stumpery' has now almost disappeared, but in 1856 it was described as 'a very picturesque assemblage of old roots or rugged stems and stumps of trees – chiefly the latter – piled to the height of 8 or 10 feet on either side of a winding and rapidly descending walk'.[39] This walk is one of the entrances to the Chinese Garden, known also as 'China', which can claim to be Cooke's masterpiece at Biddulph, for in addition to rockwork and stumpwork he provided a variety of eminently oriental architecture. The district is bordered by a 'Great Wall of China' with a 'Joss House' at one corner and a tower opposite. A Chinese doorway leads to a semicircular parterre on which dragons are patterned in red gravel, overlooked by a 'Chinese idol', a bull in an open kiosk. Beyond is a giant frog of stone, and a Chinese Temple giving directly on to the Chinese Waters. Opposite the temple is a Chinese bridge and zigzag railing overhung by weeping thorn.

All these features appear in a plan published by the *Gardeners' Chronicle* in 1862. The Chinese Temple is especially attractive, with its patterned apertures and indented rooflines; Cooke, formerly an official draughtsman of Egyptian antiquities at the British Museum, is likely to have taken his designs from a specific source, but this has not yet come to light. However, both Edward Kemp in the *Gardeners' Chronicle* and the Biddulph sale catalogue of 1871[40] refer to the 'willow-pattern' effect of the Chinese Garden, and the view from its threshold still recalls that design. The positioning of the zigzag fencing beside the bridge is especially close to the familiar scene which has appeared on English dinner-tables for two centuries.

When Edward Kemp first reviewed the grounds at Biddulph he wrote scornfully of the gardens to be found in 'China', with their 'puny fort', 'quaint covered bridge' and other 'exaggerated strainings after picturesqueness'. He was therefore unimpressed by the architectural aspects of Bateman's garden, although he admired his ability to raise Chinese and Japanese plants (one species looked 'as ragged and dwarf as even a Chinese could require').[41] But when Kemp returned to Biddulph in 1862 he showed a greater appreciation of the Chinese buildings, now fully complete, and of all the architectural decorations which he judged appropriate and, above all, 'free from an affectation of fineness or finish. There is a roughness and a masculine character about them which should always belong to garden ornaments . . .'[42] – an observation which fundamentally distinguishes the attitudes current in the 1860s from those which prevailed a hundred years earlier.

The reputation of the Chinese reached its nadir in 1860, after internal conflict had weakened the government still further. By this time the British had exacted many of the concessions they had sought, but treaties had been broken and a British expeditionary force was again in China, under the command of the 8th Earl of Elgin. In October 1860 the French and English plundered Yuan-ming yuan, and to forestall resistance by delivering a final blow to the Chinese court, Lord Elgin had the gardens and their palaces burnt.

In the following month[43] *Punch* depicted the earl sternly confronting a cowering Chinese with cannon-balls, under the caption of 'New Elgin Marbles' – words which were perhaps more

IX

130 'The Dancing Platform at Cremorne Gardens', oil painting by Phoebus Levin, 1864

ironical than the cartoonist intended. For while neither the 7th earl's removal of the Parthenon sculptures nor the 8th earl's destruction of the Summer Palace was entirely without justification, it is nevertheless remarkable that father and son should each have been responsible for desecrating the cherished symbol of a great civilization.

On his return from China, the quartermaster of the British expeditionary force, Lt-Col. Wolseley, published an account of his experiences. Although in some respects a sensitive observer, he could find little to admire in Chinese architecture. He wrote that the whole army had been disappointed by Peking, which they had been led to imagine as little short of paradise. In general, he considered that 'both in landscape gardening and building, the Chinaman loses sight of grand or imposing effects, in his endeavours to load everything with ornament; he forgets the fine in his search after the curious. In their thirst after decoration, and in their inherent

love for minute embellishment, the artists and architects of China have failed ...' Colonel Wolseley believed that the grotto at Cremorne Pleasure Gardens in Chelsea, with its 'diminitive representations of mountains and rustic scenery', was a fair specimen of what was considered beautiful by the Chinese.[44]

Pleasure gardens were among the few public places in Victorian England in which Chinese architecture was still thought to be appropriate. The entertainments at Cremorne Gardens began in 1846, and although they never drew the fashionable company that had gathered at Vauxhall and Ranelagh in their prime, the pleasure-gardens at Cremorne operated in much the same tradition for thirty years. In the southwest corner of the gardens was the dancing platform, and a three-storey pagoda of cast-iron stood in its centre. The orchestra played in the second stage, above the dancers but below the double upswept roofs. The surviving views of the pagoda[45] do not suggest that its designer took 130 much trouble to provide authentically Chinese detail, but this hardly mattered; the *Illustrated London News* claimed in 1857 that the place was 'many times gayer than Vauxhall on its most brilliant nights'.[46]

Another cast-iron pagoda, similar to the upper two storeys of the structure at Cremorne, stands in the water garden at Cliveden in Buckinghamshire. It is better described as an open hexagonal pavilion, whose lower roof is supported by six columns painted in strips to simulate fluting, while a grimacing serpent is impaled on a spike above the upper roof. The lower roof seems to have been patterned in gold on a dark green ground, and birds and flowers were painted on its underside. The pagoda was constructed for the Paris Exhibition of 1867 and transferred from there to Bagatelle, where it was bought by the first Lord Astor and moved again in the 1890s to Cliveden.[47] It is pleasantly situated on a small island amidst dwarf maples and other oriental plants; in such surroundings one can almost overlook the ponderousness of the iron pillars and the balustrade.

During the earlier part of Queen Victoria's reign Indian architecture was even less fashionable than Chinese. Ruskin saw it as the product of idolatrous religion, and thus inevitably degraded; he believed also that the ogival form of the Islamic dome was in itself undignified, and he thought it no accident that the same form appeared in the turrets of 'corrupt' Tudor Gothic. (Ruskin found other reasons to admire the ogival domes of St Mark's in Venice.) As a twenty-year-old undergraduate his imagination had been captured by descriptions of the cave-temples at Salsette and Elephanta, which formed the subject of his successful entry for the Newdigate Prize for Poetry in 1839 – a tepid melodrama concerning the wild 'Mithratic rites' of frenzied devotees, who in the last few lines deserted the dark path of idolatry and embraced Christianity. But in his subsequent writings he was hostile to Indian art of all kinds, and after the Sepoys' Revolt of 1857 he repeatedly associated Indian art and architecture with barbarism and cruelty.[48]

But it is probable that the Sepoys' Revolt, like the Opium Wars, did no more than confirm an attitude to oriental architecture that was already prevalent in England. Well before 1857 the monuments of India had lost much of their appeal for British architects. In 1841 Richard Brown acknowledged that the Taj Mahal was richly decorated and splendid in its way; 'but,

after all, how poor, how mean, are all the associations connected with it! It is a monument of the boundless exactions of a beauty's vanity, of the yielding folly of a proud voluptuous slave-governed sensualist, for such was Sha-jehan.'[49]

In the later years of the century, however, there were many individuals for whom 'the associations' of Indian architecture were not in the least poor or mean, and who valued it as a reminder of colonial glory. Such people were concerned not with imaginative adaptations of Indian styles, but with recreating a small portion of the Indian empire on English soil. A famous example is the Durbar Room constructed in 1890 at the Empress of India's own residence of Osborne House, where Bhai Ram Singh and John Lockwood Kipling (father of Rudyard Kipling) were responsible for the elaborate low-relief plasterwork of the walls, hung with trophies and memorials of the queen's dominion of India. Indian columns flank the fireplace, and only the heavy late-Victorian ceiling defies the attempt to carry out a faithful reproduction of Indian design. Another Durbar room can be seen at Hastings Museum: it was designed by two natives of the Punjab, who were brought to England in 1885, and in 1886 it was shown in the Colonial Industrial Exhibition at South Kensington. After the exhibition Lord Brassey, formerly husband of the traveller Anna Brassey and one of the exhibition's commissioners, transferred it to his museum at 24 Park Lane; in 1919 his son presented the structure and its contents to the town of Hastings.

The viceroy who proclaimed Queen Victoria Empress of India in 1877 was the Earl of Lytton, who also hoped to house his collection in a suitably Indian environment when he returned to England. A museum for this purpose was to be built at Knebworth in Hertfordshire, based on designs which H. C. Cole had copied with great precision from monuments in India; the interior, too, was to be decorated with designs taken from Indian paintings and bas-reliefs, whose various origins Cole carefully listed. His drawings are preserved at Knebworth House, but the earl died before his conception could be realized.

The exiled Maharajah Duleep Singh was more fortunate. Queen Victoria had taken to the 'poor fallen Indian Prince' who had lost his kingdom to the British, especially since he appeared to her 'a Christian and completely European (rather more English) in his habits and feelings'.[50] But when in 1857 the Maharajah was

slow to condemn the Sepoys' Revolt, the queen continued to defend him; did he not possess, 'with all his amiability and gentleness, an *Eastern nature?*'[51] He was allowed to live at Elveden Hall in Suffolk, which was converted in 1863–70 to represent both the European and the eastern aspects of Duleep Singh's character: its exterior was Italianate, its interior elaborately Indian in the outline of its columns and arches but Victorian in the patterning of the stucco, inlaid marble and tiled floor.[52] The architect was John Norton, a specialist in Gothic architecture. In 1893 Lord Iveagh bought the estate and enlarged the house, adding an opulent Indian hall.

Peterson's Tower, near Sway in Hampshire, is another case of architectural nostalgia on the part of a retired dignitary, but it is altogether less orthodox. Andrew Peterson, formerly judge to the High Court of Calcutta, built himself a mausoleum tower 218 feet high to demonstrate the efficacy of Portland cement. For six years, from 1879 to 1885, he employed six labourers who built up the tower in thirteen stages, pouring concrete into frames from the inside.[53] The tower is square, with a domed hexagonal turret on the top and a spiral staircase inside lit by lancet windows. Despite three sets of cornices projecting from the tower, the total effect is only just recognizable as Indian.

All these structures commemorated personal connections with India, but for civic purposes Indian architecture was unacceptable. Although Turkish baths might be dressed in Turkish trappings – a vivid specimen was built at Cookridge Street, Leeds, by Cuthbert Brodrick in 1867[54] – to borrow Indian motifs for an institution so dignified as the India Office was another matter. One of the two architects concerned with the design of the new building in Whitehall was Matthew Digby Wyatt, Surveyor to the East India Company and a man who had already shown himself sympathetic to the arts of India. Yet the choice of designs for the new India Office did not involve an Indian style; after Gilbert Scott's Gothic and Byzantine proposals had each been rejected, in 1861 his Italianate design prevailed, even in the ceremonial 'Durbar Court'. References to India were restricted to sculptured reliefs of incidents between Englishmen and Indians, statues of 'Anglo-Indian Worthies' and the inscribed names of Indian rivers and cities.[55]

It is clear that, well before the middle of the nineteenth century, British architects had lost the capacity to be inspired by Chinese or Indian modes of building. Both were associated with the extravagance of George IV, and to some extent also with unwelcome events in China and India themselves. But in the latter half of the century a third source of oriental design presented itself. On 8 July 1853 Commodore Matthew Perry of Virginia arrived at the coast of Japan, from which the Tokugawa Shoguns had managed to exclude all but a handful of foreigners for two centuries. Others followed, Yokohama was established as a trading post, and in the 1860s Japanese prints and porcelain were beginning to impress 'aesthetic' circles in Britain. The architects Eden Nesfield and Richard Norman Shaw adopted Japanese spirals and roundels (or 'pies') as a motif which they applied to plaster or stone surfaces, while Dante Rossetti employed the same device to decorate his picture-frames.[56] A less easily demonstrated but probably more fundamental Japanese influence on this group of designers may be seen in their bold handling of asymmetry and their exploitation of blank space: it has been suggested[57] that the irregular arrangement of wall and windows in E. W. Godwin's first design for Whistler's White House in Chelsea derived more than a little from that architect's enthusiasm for Japanese art. In the 1870s Japanese elements became integrated into the vocabulary of 'Queen Anne'; conversely, when Thomas Jeckyll designed a three-tiered Japanese pavilion of wrought and cast-iron for the Philadelphia Centennial Exhibition of 1876, he encircled it with a railing of 'aesthetic' sunflowers standing shoulder to shoulder around the base of the pavilion.[58]

However, the spirit of aesthetic Japanese design in 1870 was far removed from that which animated the chinoiserie of 1750. To Nesfield, Shaw and Godwin, 'Japanese' represented relaxed simplicity, unfussy but carefully calculated ornament, and a reaction against High Victorian elaboration. Whereas the Halfpennys had assimilated Chinese to Gothic, the new generation of designers associated Japanese with Gothic – but austere English domestic Gothic, not the riot of crockets and finials which the early Georgians envisaged. A visitor to the Japanese display at the London International Exhibition of 1862 epitomized the new taste in a casual remark: 'English Gothic is small as our landscape is small', this visitor proposed in a letter to a friend; 'it is sweet, picturesque, homely, farmyardish, *Japanese* . . .'[59]

◀ 132 The Indian hall at Elveden Hall, Suffolk

133 'Chinese Pavilion, Labyrinth Gardens, Pagoda . . ., built in Philadelphia 1823', watercolour by D. J. Kennedy

Chapter Twelve
Oriental Experiments in North America

IN NORTH AMERICA the landscape garden was never adopted with the enthusiasm and reckless expenditure that characterized the *jardins anglo-chinois* of Europe. 'Landscape-Gardening is practised in the United States on a comparatively limited scale,' observed J. C. Loudon, 'because, in a country where all men have equal rights, and where every man, however humble, has a house and garden of his own, it is not likely that there should be many large parks.' Garden architecture was relatively neglected, and oriental pavilions were scarce. No doubt in the formative years of the United States they were thought altogether too frivolous, and perhaps there was some justice in Loudon's suggestion that 'in every new country, the useful departments are more generally cultivated than the ornamental'.[1]

Oriental architecture reached North America by the longer route – via Europe, and particularly Britain, rather than through direct contact across the Pacific. The few recorded examples are therefore doubly curious, for both English and American elements can often be seen in combination with those of the Far East. Some vestiges of eighteenth-century chinoiserie survive, but scarcely amount to a fashion; nor was there an 'Indian Revival' in the English sense. Instead, a number of individual structures present themselves, some of them associated with public entertainment but otherwise unconnected with one another.

The taste for chinoiserie seems to have crossed the Atlantic surprisingly swiftly in the middle of the eighteenth century: there is a 'Chinese Room' at Gunston Hall in Fairfax County, Virginia, built in 1758, and the Miles Brewton house in Charleston (1769) contains some original rococo-Chinese decoration.[2] Preceding Gunston Hall was the James Reid house in Charleston, described in an advertisement as 'new built ... after the Chinese taste'. The advertisement was published in the *South Carolina Gazette* on 1 April 1757, too early to have been

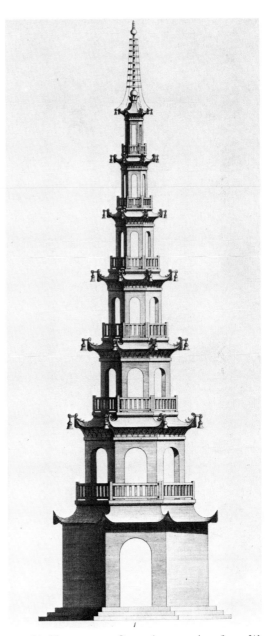

134 'A Tower near Canton', engraving from W. Chambers, *Designs of Chinese Buildings*, 1757

173

influenced by the *Designs of Chinese Buildings* published by Sir William Chambers in the following month. And although Britain was the primary source of architectural chinoiserie, Chinese artefacts were imported directly into North America before the nineteenth century. Andreas Everardus van Braam Houchgeest, employed in 1758 as a supercargo by the Dutch East India Company and later Dutch Consul at Charleston, built himself a house to contain the collection of Chinese furniture, ornaments and servants which he had accumulated. An engraving of 1800[3] depicting his 'China Retreat' in Bucks County, Pennsylvania, portrays it as an orthodox timber-framed mansion of two storeys; it does not, however, show the small bell-hung pagoda that stood for a few years on the centre of the roof.

The only tangible remnants of the American taste for Chinese architecture are wooden fretwork railings. A good example can be seen in Fairmount Park, Philadelphia, curving around the balcony of Lemon Hill,[4] and of several external and internal balustrades designed by Thomas Jefferson the most notable is the continuous wooden lattice-rail which runs above the Tuscan colonnades of the University of Virginia, Charlottesville, built to Jefferson's specifications in 1817–25. Jefferson intended the university buildings to be instructive, illustrating the types of classical architecture, so that each of the ten pavilions linked by the colonnades was built after a different model in the Doric, Ionic or Corinthian mode. His Chinese railings are even more varied, exhibiting a dozen different fretwork patterns. Jefferson was scornful of contemporary English architecture, and had no English scruples about combining Chinese with classical, for his railings not only run along a classical entablature but pass directly through the pavilion porticoes. It is a notion that would have surprised Palladio, but among the trees of the long court the balustrade is entirely successful, adding a touch of Virginian sparkle to the neoclassical severity of Jefferson's composition.[5]

Two years after the arrival of the first students at the University of Virginia, the Pagoda and Labyrinth Garden in Philadelphia were opened to the public. This pagoda was contemporary with that of Alton Towers, one of the last built in England, and like it the Philadelphia structure was inspired by Sir William Chambers – in particular by 'a Tower near Canton' engraved in Chambers's *Designs* of seventy years before. The

building beside the seven-storey pagoda was also purportedly Chinese, and the square blocks supporting concave roofs at each end were possibly suggested by the Pavilion at Brighton. The architect of both buildings was William Strickland, who later designed a church in the Egyptian style at Nashville.[6]

Brighton's Royal Pavilion was the avowed source of the most spectacular of all American-oriental structures, which was built for the greatest of all showmen, P. T. Barnum. In 1846 Barnum felt ready, after many successful promotions, to settle down in Connecticut with his family 'in comparative tranquillity', as he imagined. But in typical fashion he built himself a house at Bridgeport close to the New York and New Haven railroad, and the style of his residence was calculated to act as a permanent advertisement for the novelty and extravagance of Barnum's enterprises. He described the genesis of his home in his autobiography:

Visiting Brighton, I was greatly pleased with the Pavilion erected by George IV. It was the only specimen of Oriental architecture in England, and had not been introduced into America. I concluded to adopt it, and engaged a London architect to furnish me with a set of drawings in the style of the Pavilion, differing sufficiently to be adapted to the spot of ground selected for my homestead.[7]

If there was a London architect involved, his identity is unknown, but Leopold Eidlitz of New York claimed, no doubt justifiably, to have supplied the drawings through an agency.[8] In any case, Barnum's mansion was built as he had specified, reminiscent of Brighton but 'differing sufficiently' without any doubt. While Barnum toured the United States with General Tom Thumb, a three-storey block with two-storey wings was constructed for him, crowned by a large central dome and several subsidiary domes. The plan of the building has nothing in common with the Royal Pavilion, but many of the details must have come from Nash's palace, their finer points eroded in the course of their transatlantic crossing – minarets, triangular crenellation, scallop-arched windows, apertures in the domes at their broadest diameter, and at each side small upswept 'Chinese' roofs above conservatories. The lower storey and the centre of the storey above were protected by perforated screens again derived from the Pavilion at Brighton. Barnum's house was thus doubly removed from the Orient, but he christened it 'Iranistan',

135

133

134

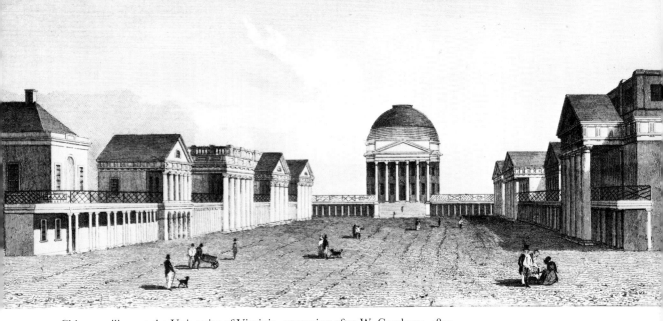

135 Chinese railings at the University of Virginia, engraving after W. Goodacre, 1831

explaining that this meant '"Eastern Country Place", or, more poetically, "Oriental Villa"'.[9]

The thousand guests who attended Barnum's house-warming in November 1848 would have found the tradition of George IV maintained in the Chinese Library, which was appointed with Chinese landscapes and furniture.[10] (His study was lined with a brocade of orange satin, perhaps a version of Mr Soho's 'apricot cloth'.) Engravings of Iranistan show that the stables and outbuildings were also domed and decorated with eastern motifs, and the pointed iron railings and gateway to the grounds continued the theme. One of the garden buildings presumably housed the rare poultry which Barnum acquired; elk and reindeer grazed on the lawns. Barnum's parade of exoticism was not in vain, for an engraving of Iranistan which he had printed on his notepaper induced Jenny Lind to give a concert-tour in the United States under Barnum's management – or so the celebrated singer told him.[11] On the other hand, such ostentation was bound to evoke criticism. Andrew Jackson Downing, the designer of Picturesque villas and cottages, took a prim view:

So far as an admiration of foreign style in architecture arises from the mere love of novelty, it is poor and contemptible; so far as it arises from an admiration of truthful beauty of form or expression, it is noble and praiseworthy. A villa in the style of a Persian palace (of which there is an example lately erected in Connecticut), with its oriental domes and minarets, equally unmeaning and unsuited to our life or climate, is an example of the former; as an English cottage, with its beautiful home-expression and its thorough comfort and utility, evinced in steep roofs to shed the snow, is of the latter.[12]

In the boldness of its conception Iranistan is comparable with Fonthill Abbey and the original Hafod, and like them it had a short life and a dramatic end. When Barnum became bankrupt at the end of 1855, the house was taken over by his creditors, but in the words of his biographer 'they found it impossible to sell the weird residence',[13] and Barnum was allowed the use of it. Then in December 1857 the greatly under-insured building was destroyed by fire, less than a decade after its completion.

Despite his caustic reference to Iranistan, Downing was not wholly averse to oriental notions in American architecture. His collaborator Alexander Davis designed villas in several oriental idioms,[14] while some of the columned verandahs in Downing's own designs for country houses display brackets at the column-heads which could well be regarded as

136 'Cottage Residence of Nathan Dunn, Esq., Mount Holly, N.J.',
engraving from A. J. Downing, *Landscape Gardening*, 1841

Chinese, and are similar to those illustrated in the
128 'Chinese Residence' of Richard Brown's *Domestic
Architecture*.[15] Downing also depicted in his
136 *Landscape Gardening* the residence of Nathan
Dunn,[16] the wealthy sinophile who was to set up
his Chinese Exhibition in London. Dunn's house
was designed by John Notman of Philadelphia; it
was described as 'semi-oriental', fairly enough
since the curious pinnacles and serrations were
not specifically Chinese, although the disposition
of the façade is again reminiscent of Brown's
imaginary Chinese Residence.

If the sight of Iranistan amazed the passengers
who were carried along the railroad to New
Haven, they would have been still more aston-
ished on their arrival at the terminus, where a
137 grandiose station was erected in the same year as
Barnum's mansion. Its highly eclectic architecture was the work of Henry Austin, who designed
an arcade 328 feet long with a double roof above
the centre and tall towers at each end. The
arcades and central roofs are ambiguous, but the
outer towers leave little doubt that an oriental
reference was intended: one approximated to the
shape of an Indian *stupa*, the other shaded the
faces of its clock with drooping hoods, and
halfway up each was a broad projecting parapet.
Downing might justify his own use of projecting
roofs in the southern states on the grounds that
they provided shade in a hot climate,[17] but no such
claim could be made for the New Haven

parapets, which were unashamedly decorative.
The balance of arcades and roofs in Austin's
design has something in common with Daniell's
view of the palace in the fort of Allahabad,[18]
which Repton had exploited in his designs for the
Pavilion at Brighton. But Austin had none of
Repton's inhibitions over homogeneity of style;
clearly he sought an unprecedented combination
of forms suitable for the new genre of railway
architecture. Unfortunately his building was
superseded in 1874.

Whereas British architects had regarded
Gothic as the closest relation to Chinese and
Indian styles, in North America it seems that
oriental designs were assimilated most often to
Italianate. The New Haven railroad station is a
case in point, and another is Samuel Sloan's
'Design for an Oriental Villa', whose overall
proportions, arcade and deep eaves are 'orienta-
lized' only by the addition of horseshoe arches in
the window-casings and an onion-domed box
placed absurdly above.[19] In a second volume
Sloan put forward a more wholehearted and
exciting 'Oriental Villa', octagonal and of three   138
storeys, the third comprising a cylindrical
lantern which supported the flattened Islamic
dome.[20] It was an elaborate design, incorporating a variety of European and oriental motifs,
and the interior (indicated in Sloan's sectional
view) was to be ornamented with corresponding
opulence.

137 'New Haven Railroad Station', engraving from *Gleason's Pictorial*, 1851

138 'Design for an Oriental Villa', pl. LXIII from Samuel Sloan, *The Model Architect*, vol. II, 1852

139 Longwood, Natchez, Mississippi

Sloan must have put forward this design without much hope of its ever being realized, but in a few years his enterprise was rewarded by a commission from Dr Haller Nutt, a cotton-planter who had visited Egypt. Sloan built a mansion for Nutt near Natchez beside the Mississippi, basing the structure on his second oriental design and adding two storeys to the original three. Longwood, as the house is called, has an interesting plan: the central rotunda is surrounded by four rooms of twenty-four feet by eighteen, and these are themselves encircled by four more rectangular rooms centred on the junctions of the inner series. These outer rooms are linked by verandahs and an entrance porch. Longwood provided Sloan with the opening

139

design of his *Homestead Architecture* of 1861. Unfortunately the building was not complete when, at the outbreak of the Civil War, the Northern workmen left the site. In 1864 Nutt died, but Longwood (known also as Nutt's Folly) has survived to be appreciated by tourists on the 'Natchez Pilgrimage'.[21]

Shortly after the publication of Sloan's *Model Architect*, which contained designs for several small kiosks as well as his villa projects, two architects used an octagonal ground-plan similar to Sloan's for the New York Crystal Palace which housed the World's Fair of 1853–54.[22] George Carstensen and Charles Gildemeister's octagon consisted of a cross-shaped building of broad intersecting corridors with lower halls filling in

140

the four triangular spaces between the arms. A large dome was placed above the point of the corridors' intersection. The whole was constructed of glass on an iron framework, like its London prototype of 1851. Once again the forms of the architecture were largely inspired by the royal estate at Brighton, but in this instance it was Porden's Stables rather than Nash's Pavilion that furnished most of the architects' ideas – the obtuse angles between the long façades, the minarets marking the junctions, the large ray-patterned windows (situated above rather than beside the principal façades of the American building), and the shape of the central dome. Only the little patterned perforations around the dome appear to have been derived from the Royal Pavilion itself.

From the Trianon de Porcelaine onwards, oriental buildings in Europe and North America seem to have been particularly vulnerable to changes in fashion, rotting timbers or disastrous accidents. At least as many delightful 'Chinese' or 'Indian' structures have been cut off in their youth as have survived to the present time. Each of the two bulky transatlantic offspring of the Royal Pavilion estate was destroyed by fire – Iranistan in 1857, and the New York Crystal Palace in 1858. Even the Royal Pavilion itself, the most exuberant and brilliant combination of oriental styles, only narrowly escaped demolition in 1850 and destruction by petrol bomb in 1976. May it continue to evade the fate which has overtaken so many deviants from the sober norms of western architecture.

140 'The New York Crystal Palace', frontispiece to G. J. B. Carstensen & C. Gildemeister, *The New York Crystal Palace*, 1854

Notes

Chapter One

1 Rev. Samuel Purchas, *Purchas his Pilgrimage* (1613), IV, xi. The 1614 edition has 'Xamdu'. In Coleridge's *Preface* of 1816, in which the poet recalls the circumstances of his dream, he misquotes from memory the passage in Purchas: 'Here the Khan Kubla commanded a palace to be built, and a stately garden thereunto. And thus ten miles of fertile ground were inclosed with a wall.' 'Stately garden' would have been still less apt than 'stately pleasure-dome', particularly in the context of 'that deep romantic chasm . . . A savage place!'
   Coleridge also knew *Purchas his Pilgrimes* (4 vols., 1625), a much larger compilation, in which the two buildings seen by Marco Polo are described as 'a marvellous and artificiall Palace of Marble . . . 'a royall House on pillars gilded and varnished . . .' (1906 ed., vol. 11, p. 231).

2 *The Travels of Marco Polo*, tr. William Marsden, ed. Thomas Wright (1854), pp. 153–54. Marsden's translation (1818) is from the Italian of Giovanni Battista Ramusio (1559), who gives the fullest account of this pavilion. John Frampton's translation (1975) from Santaella's Sicilian version is briefer but contains the essential points: 'In the middest of these Meddowes is a great house . . . compassed about with greate Canes, that be gilded and covered with Canes that be varnished . . . It is tyed with above 200 cordes of silke, after the manner of tentes, or pavilions' (*The Most Noble and famous Travels of Marco Polo*, ed. N. M. Penzer, 1929, p. 60).

3 *Travels* (1854), pp. 177–80.

4 *The Texts and Versions of John de Plano Carpini and William de Rubruquis*, ed. C. R. Beazley (Hakluyt Soc., 1903), p. 109.

5 *Ibid.*, p. 118.

6 *Hakluytus Posthumus; or, Purchas his Pilgrimes* (Hakluyt Soc., 1905–07), vol. 11, pp. 118, 364. Concerning the authorship of Mandeville's *Travels*, three main possibilities emerge: (a) that Sir John Mandeville wrote the book, but adopted the name Jean de Bourgogne for most of his life; (b) that Jean de Bourgogne was the author, but used 'Sir John Mandeville' as his *nom de*

plume; or (c) that the author was Jean d'Outremeuse, an undoubtedly historical figure who almost certainly translated the *Travels* from French into Latin, and who himself attested the truth of (a). See Malcolm Letts, *Sir John Mandeville* (1949).

7 *Cathay and the Way Thither*, ed. Sir H. Yule and H. Cordier (Hakluyt Soc. 1913–16), vol. 2, pp. 218–22.

8 *The Travels of Sir John Mandeville*, ed. A. W. Pollard from the Cotton MS (1900, reprint 1964), p. 205.

9 The theory of direct Indian influence was first put forward by Albrecht Haupt, *Die Baukunst der Renaissance in Portugal* (1890), and followed by Joan Evans, who states categorically (*Pattern*, 1931, vol. 2, p. 59) that 'the tower of Belém owes its balconies and ribbed cupolas to the palace of Udaipur'. W. C. Watson (*Portuguese Architecture*, 1908) opposed this view, and drew attention to parallels with contemporary Spanish design. The most authoritative advocate of Moorish influence is Reinaldo dos Santos (e.g. in *L'Art Portugais*, Paris, 1953). Raul da Costa-Tôrres (*Arquitectura dos Descobrimentos*, Braga, 1943) claimed that the Manueline style and the 'Jesuit-Baroque' which succeeded it derived from Chinese structures, possibly seen on imported textiles or porcelain designs. Unfortunately this notion has practically no evidence to support it.

10 See D. Lach, *Asia in the Making of Europe*, vol. II (1970), pp. 165 ff.

11 Joan Evans, *Pattern* (1931), vol. 2, p. 59.

Chapter Two

1 See D. Lach, *Asia in the Making of Europe*, vol. I, bk I (1965), p. 183.

2 Juan Gonzalez de Mendoza, *The Historie of the great and mightie kingdome of China . . .*, tr. R. Parke (1588), pp. 16–17.

3 *Hakluytus Posthumus; or, Purchas his Pilgrimes* (1905–07), vol. 10, p. 192.

4 *Ibid.*, vol. 12, pp. 95, 116.

5 F. M. Pinto, *His Travels in the Kingdoms of Ethiopia, China, Tartaria*, tr. H. Cogan (1653), p. 136.

6 *The Letters of Dorothy Osborne to William Temple*, ed. G. C. Moore Smith (1928), letter 59, p. 148.

7 Alvarez Semedo, *The History of That*

Great and Renowned Monarchy of China . . . (1655), p. 15.

8 Jan Nieuhof, *An Embassy . . .* (1669), p. 165.

9 *Ibid.*, pp. 225, 226.

10 *Ibid.*, pp. 128–29.

11 *Ibid.*, pp. 62, 110.

12 *Ibid.*, p. 81.

13 Translated from Félibien des Avaux, *Déscription sommaire du Chateau de Versailles* (1674), pp. 108–09. Excerpts are quoted in Robert Danis, *La Première Maison Royale de Trianon 1670–1687* (1926), which includes engravings and an 'Essai de Restitution' of the Trianon de Porcelaine.

14 Louis le Comte, *Memoirs and Observations . . . made in a late Journey through the Empire of China* (English translation 1699), pp. 58–60.

15 *Ibid.*, pp. 77–78.

16 In 1674 it was stated that 'le Trianon de Versailles avoit fait naistre à tous les Particuliers le desir d'en avoir; que presque tous les grand Seigneurs qui avoient des Maisons de Campagne en avoient fait bastir dans le Parc . . .' (*Mercure Galant*, 1674, vol. 4, p. 111; quoted in Eleanor von Erdberg, *Chinese Influence on European Garden Structures*, 1936, p. 61). Whether these garden buildings were in any way oriental is not recorded.

17 Johann Bernard Fischer von Erlach, *A Plan of Civil and Historical Architecture . . .*, translated by Thomas Lediard (1730), bk III, pl. 14.

18 Emmanuel Héré de Corny, *Receuil des Plans, Elévations et Coupes . . . des Chateaux Jardins . . .* [1753].

19 'It is a pity, that at that time the book by the Englishman Chambers was not known here, otherwise Büring could have been better informed about the real architecture of the Chinese. As far as is known, they do put pagodas and idols in their temples, but never on the roofs' (Heinrich L. Manger, *Baugeschichte von Potsdam* (1789), p. 237, translated in E. von Erdberg, *op. cit.*, p. 83).

20 See E. von Erdberg, *ibid.*, pp. 75, 159.

21 *Ibid.*, pp. 73–74, 178–79.

22 See Bo Gyllensvärd, 'The Chinese Pavilion at Drottningholm', in *The Westward Influence of the Chinese Arts from the 14th to the 18th Century*, ed. W. Watson, *Colloquia on Art and Archaeology*

in Asia; no. 3 (1972), pp. 52ff.; also Ake Setterwall *et al.*, *The Chinese Pavilion at Drottningholm* (1977); and Osvald Sirén, *China and the Gardens of Europe* (1950), pp. 171ff.

Chapter Three

1 In the following paragraphs I have relied heavily on Osvald Sirén's splendid book *The Gardens of China* (New York, 1949), among whose assets are photographs of what remained of the great Chinese gardens in the 1920s and 1930s.
2 Quoted in O. Sirén, *ibid.*, p. 71.
3 *Ibid.*, p. 18.
4 *Ibid.*, p. 36.
5 See Osvald Sirén, *The Imperial Palaces of Peking*, 3 vols. (1928). A more recent photograph of the few remaining ruins can be seen in M. and C. Beurdeley, *Giuseppe Castiglione*, trans. M. Bullock (1972).
6 This and the following quotations are taken from *The Works of Sir William Temple, Bart* (2 vols., 1740), vol. I, pp. 175–86.
7 Sir Nikolaus Pevsner, 'The Genesis of the Picturesque', *Architectural Review*, XCVI (1944), reprinted in Pevsner, *Studies in Art, Architecture and Design* (1968), vol. I, p. 82.
8 Sir Nikolaus Pevsner and S. Lang ('A Note on Sharawaggi', *Architectural Review*, CVI (1949), reprinted in Pevsner, *Studies in Art, Architecture and Design* (1968), vol. I, pp. 102–07) believe that 'travellers cannot have been very helpful'. Moreover they take the surprising view that the printed sources 'contain little about gardens and what they say seems curiously standardized, non-committal and sometimes even embarrassed' (p. 104). In support of this conclusion they quote passages from Matteo Ricci, Johann Greuber and Jan Nieuhof, none of which, it is true, are particularly startling. But they do not quote Nieuhof's remarks on the Imperial Gardens at Peking, which are more lively and observant, nor even Marco Polo's description of those gardens. Indeed, in *Purchas his Pilgrimes* – an obvious potential source for Temple which Pevsner and Lang do not mention – the general attitude of travellers towards oriental gardens is one of appreciation. And on that subject the travel-books 'substitute fantasy for truth' (p. 104) relatively seldom.
9 *Ibid.*, pp. 103–04.
10 Letter of 14 February 1713, written probably by Samuel Molyneux: Civic

Records Office, Southampton, D/M 1/3.
11 See especially *The Spectator*, nos. 414 and 415 (25 and 26 June 1712) quoted here.
12 Stephen Switzer, *Ichnographia Rustica* (1718), III, p. 82.
13 Letter from Sir Thomas Robinson to Lord Carlisle, 23 Dec. 1734: *Historical Manuscripts Commission*, vol. 15, appendix 6 (1897), pp. 142–43.
14 This and the following quotations are taken from *The Memoirs of Father Ripa*, tr. F. Prandi (1844), pp. 54 ff.
15 *Memoirs*, p. 62.
16 Rudolf Wittkower, *Palladio and English Palladianism* (1974), pp. 185–88.
17 *Memoirs*, p. 73.
18 *Ibid.*, pp. 183–84.
19 Joseph Spence, *Observations, Anecdotes, and Characters of Books and Men* (ed. J.M. Osborn, 1966), vol. 2, p. 647. Shortly afterwards Spence advised that lights should prevail over shades, 'to give the whole a joyous air rather than a melancholy one. In this again the Chinese seem very much to exceed our pleasure-ground makers. They have scarce any such thing as close or thick groves in any of their near views: they fling them all on some of the hills at a distance'. The Burlington album, which Spence may have seen, now contains only thirty-four engravings.
20 J.-D. Attiret, *A Particular Account of the Emperor of China's Gardens near Pekin*, tr. 'Sir Harry Beaumont' [Joseph Spence] (1752), pp. 9–15.

Chapter Four

1 A drawing dated 21 Sep. 1702 of Durdans House, near Epsom (Bodleian Library: Gough Maps 30, fol. 63), shows a covered seat with diagonal latticework, emerging from a wooded hillside; but on this evidence alone, it can hardly be described as Chinese.
2 MS (uncatalogued) in the Huntington Library, San Marino, California, p. 16. I am grateful to Mr George Clarke of Stowe School for his generous assistance in tracing the vicissitudes of the Chinese House.
3 British Museum Add. MSS 22, 926: 'Some Observations made in a Journey, begun June the 7th, and finish'd July the 9th. 1742.', pp. 126–33.
4 *The Gentleman's Magazine*, XII (1742), p. 435.
5 The very informative notes to 'The Triumphs of Nature' in *The Gentleman's Magazine* of 1742 (pp. 324, 380–82, 435–36) were reprinted verbatim in *A Description of the Gardens of Lord Viscount Cobham at Stow in Buckinghamshire*, 'sold

by B. Seeley, Writing-master', published in 1744 and subsequently. The appendix to the third (1742) edition of Defoe's *Tour through . . . Great Britain*, vol. 3, p. 281, seems to have extracted its few basic facts about the Chinese House from the notes in *The Gentleman's Magazine*. Other accounts are contained in a letter from the Marchioness Grey of 5 July 1748, Bedfordshire County Record Office, L30/9a/1, p. 171; and [Rev. William Gilpin], *Dialogue upon the Gardens* (1748), pp. 26–28.
6 In the same year Seeley's engraving was inaccurately reproduced in George Bickham's *The Beauties of Stow*, in which the roof of the Chinese House is made to appear concave and the corners of the windows are squared off. Moreover Bickham portrayed the Palladian Bridge and the Chinese House together on the same plate, thereby giving rise to the belief that the Chinese House was situated beside the Palladian Bridge, which still crosses the Octagon Lake near the lake's eastern extremity. In all subsequent editions of Bickham's book (from 1753 onwards) the Palladian Bridge is depicted alone, and no further mention is made of the Chinese House.
7 'The law courts in Westminster Hall, the Chinese Gothic house at Esher, and the Choir Screen in the Cathedral at Gloucester; none of these are now remaining to disparage his [Kent's] fame.' (Note by J. Dallaway in Horace Walpole, *Anecdotes of Painting*, ed. R. Wornum (1849), vol. 3, p. 779).
8 Letter of 20 May 1751, *Travels thro' England of Dr. Richard Pococke*, Camden Soc. (1888), vol. I, p. 165.
9 *The Diary of John Evelyn*, ed. E.S. de Beer (1955), vol. 3, pp. 373–74.
10 *Ibid.*, vol. 4, p. 288.
11 *Ibid.*, vol. 5, pp. 428–29. See also vol. 2, p. 53; vol. 3, pp. 425–26; vol. 4, p. 99; vol. 5, p. 147.
12 John Stalker and George Parker, *A Treatise on Japanning and Varnishing* (1688), final page of preface.
13 [W. Shakespeare], *The Fairy-Queen* (1692), p. 48.
14 S. Lang, 'The Genesis of the Landscape Garden', in *The Picturesque Garden and its Influence outside the British Isles*, ed. Sir N. Pevsner (1974), illustrates two stage sets, by Inigo Jones and Filippo Juvarra, which bear a resemblance to garden temples at Stowe and Stourhead respectively. She also points out that several of the leaders of the landscape garden movement, such as Vanbrugh, Pope, Addison and Burlington, had strong links with the stage.

15 A. B. Granville, *St. Petersburgh*, 2nd ed. (1829), vol. 2, p. 477.

16 Du Halde, *A Description of the Empire of China and Chinese-Tartary . . .* (1741), vol. 2, p. 278.

17 *Ibid.*, p. 326.

18 See p. 45.

19 *The Diary of Samuel Pepys*, ed. R. Latham and W. Matthews, vol. 9 (1976), pp. 17–18, 22.

20 *Ibid.*, p. 18n. The Latin version of Nieuhof's work, *Legatio Batavica . . .*, was also published in 1668.

21 W. and J. Halfpenny, *Rural Architecture in the Chinese Taste* (1752), pp. 1–2.

22 Philip Yorke (2nd Earl of Hardwicke), 'Journal of What I Observed Most Remarkable in a Tour to the North', in J. Godber, 'The Marchioness Grey of Wrest Park', *Bedfordshire Historical Record Society*, vol. 47 (1968), p. 132.

23 Vyner MSS 5565 (288/1), Leeds Archive Dept.

24 Yorke, *op. cit.*, p. 150.

25 Staffordshire County Record Office, D260/M/F/4/21 (Hatherton Papers). I am grateful to Mr W..T.C. Walker for this reference.

26 See *The History of Ripon*, printed and sold by W. Farrer, 2nd ed. (1806), p. 220; and E.W. Brayley and J. Britton, *The Beauties of England and Wales*, vol. 16 (1812), p. 693.

27 Thomas Pennant, *The Journey from Chester to London* (Dublin, 1783), pp. 70–71.

28 Letter of Jemima Marchioness Grey, quoted in J. Godber, *op. cit.*, p. 137. See also Lady Grey's letter of 4 Nov. 1748: Bedfordshire County Record Office, D.D.L. 30/9a/2, p. 3.

29 Letter of Elizabeth Anson, 14 Nov. 1752: Staffordshire County Record Office D 615, P (S) 1/1.

30 Eileen Harris, 'Thomas Wright: Architect of Rococo Gardens', *Country Life*, 2, Sept. 1971, p. 614.

31 The latest view of the pagoda is by Moses Griffith (N.T. Guide no. 70), which one would expect – in the light of Griffith's association with Thomas Pennant – to have been executed about 1780. But Christopher Hussey has quoted a carpenter's bill of 1772, for 'repairing some of the remains of the pagoda. £1 4s.' (*Country Life*, 22 Apr. 1954, p. 1222). This bill can no longer be traced at Staffordshire County Record Office.

32 Walpole to John Chute, 4 Aug. 1753, *The Yale Edition of Horace Walpole's Correspondence*, ed. W.S. Lewis, vol. 35, p. 74.

33 See W. Hawkes, 'Miller's Work at Wroxton', *Cake and Cockhorse* (Banbury History Soc., 1969), iv, pp. 99–106; and J. Godber, *op. cit.*, p. 139, where two of the Chinese pavilions are shown to have been built by August 1748.

34 T. Smollett, *Humphrey Clinker* (1967 ed.), pp. 123–24.

35 *A Sketch of the Spring Gardens, Vaux-Hall*, printed for G. Woodfall n.d., [*c.* 1755], p. 19.

36 R. Morris, *Architectural Remembrancer* (1751), pp. 7–8 and pl. 47.

37 *The Gentleman's Magazine*, XII (Aug. 1742), p. 419.

38 William Halfpenny, *New Designs for Chinese Temples* (1750), pl. 2.

39 T. Smollett, *Humphry Clinker* (1967 ed.), p. 120.

40 H. Repton, *An Enquiry into the Changes of Taste in Landscape Gardening* (1806), p. 139.

41 W. Marshall, *On Planting and Rural Ornament*, 1796, p. 319.

Chapter Five

1 Walpole to Sir Horace Mann, 2 Aug. 1750, *Correspondence*, vol. 20, p. 166. The editor notes some sketches which 'may be jottings for improvements at Mistley'.

2 Walpole to Mann, 25 Feb. 1750, *ibid.*, p. 127.

3 'A Description of the Villa of Mr Horace Walpole', in *The Works of Horace Walpole* (1798), vol. 2, p. 432, records the design.

4 Walpole to Mann, 12 June 1753, *Correspondence*, vol. 20, p. 382. By 1760 two other neighbours of Walpole displayed chinoiserie interiors: see *A Short Account of the Principal Seats and Gardens in and about Twickenham* (1760), pp. 38–45.

5 *The World*, XV, 22 March 1753.

6 W. Hogarth, *The Analysis of Beauty* (1753), p. 45.

7 Walpole to Chute, *Correspondence*, vol. 35, p. 74. Publication of *The Analysis of Beauty* was advertised in 1752; Walpole may have read it in draft form. Elsewhere in the *Analysis* Hogarth condemned Chinese painting and sculp as exhibiting for the most part 'a mean taste'. 'The whole nation in these matters seems to have but one eye' (p. xix).

8 *Letters on the English Nation*, vol. II, letter LVI, pp. 261–62.

9 *The Connoisseur*, vol. 2, no. 73 (19 June 1955), p. 338.

10 *Ibid.*, no. 65 (24 Apr. 1755), p. 387.

11 *Travels thro. England*, vol. II, pp. 258–61. A few months earlier Pococke saw a small garden building which has been described as Chinese on account of the deep overhang of its roof (M.R. Gloag, *A Book of English Gardens* (1906), pp. 119–21 and illustration). But Pococke writes simply of a lake 'with a summer house built in it' (*Travels*, vol. 2, p. 244). We can sympathize with his reluctance to see this pavilion as oriental, since its heavy rectangular door and windows appear to have been entirely English and typical of the mid-eighteenth century. The tradition that the Beckett pavilion was not only 'Chinese' but designed by Inigo Jones is hard to take seriously.

12 W. and J. Halfpenny, *New Designs for Chinese Temples* (1750), p. 8, pl. XXVII.

13 Robert Lloyd, 'The Cit's Country Box', *The Connoisseur* 135 (26 Aug. 1756).

14 R. Morris, *Rural Architecture* (1750), Preface.

15 R. Morris, *The Architectural Remembrancer* (1751), pls. 26 and 15, pp. xiii, 10–11.

16 J.-B. Du Halde, *A General History of China*, vol. 2, p. 160.

17 W. Hogarth, *The Analysis of Beauty* (1753), pp. xix, 45.

18 *The Ladies Amusement* (n.d.), p. 4.

19 Richard Pococke noted several Chinese features when he visited Bateman's estate in August 1754: '. . . a Chinese alcove seat, near which there is a Chinese covered bridge to an island, and another uncovered bridge beyond it to another island . . . At one corner of this meadow is the farm house, with a small garden in parterre and a greenhouse; this is in the Chinese taste; in the room below they commonly breakfast in summer, above is the library and within it a museum' (*Travels thro. England*, vol. II, pp. 64–65).

20 Walpole to George Montagu, 24 Sep. 1762, *Correspondence*, vol. 10, p. 43.

21 Walpole to the Earl of Strafford, 13 June 1781, *ibid.*, vol. 35, p. 359.

22 Letter of Lady Gregory of 5 July 1748, Bedfordshire County Record Office, L30/9a/1, pp. 165–71.

23 Letter to Lady Gregory of 25 July 1760, *ibid.*, L30/9a/3, p. 47.

24 Letter of Lady Gregory of 4 Sep. 1748, *ibid.*, L30/9a/2, p. 3.

25 *Ibid.*, L33/125–26. The design is dated 25 Aug 1765.

26 Letter from Elizabeth Anson to Jemima Grey of 20 Aug. [1750], *ibid.*, L30/9/3, p. 24: 'Captain Brett being now here, I design to have some Conversation with him about the Galley.'

27 Quoted by Joyce Godber, *Bedfordshire Historical Record Society*, 47 (1968), p. 68.

The Chinese pavilion at Wrest has been tentatively attributed to Chambers (J. Harris, *Sir William Chambers*, p. 254) on the basis of a letter of 18 May 1767 from Philip Yorke (now the 2nd Earl of Hardwicke) asking Chambers to 'settle with him'. The Marchioness's letter of 1761 demonstrates that the pavilion was built at a rather earlier date than had been suspected, but this does not rule out the possibility of Chambers's authorship.

28 See Mark Girouard, 'Living in a Folly', *Country Life*, 6 Nov. 1958, pp. 1040–01.

29 Letter of 21 August 1816, *John Constable's Correspondence*, ed. R. B. Beckett (1962–68), vol. 2, p. 196.

30 Arthur Young, *A Six-Months Tour through the North of England* (1770), vol. I, pp. 29–30.

31 *Passages from the Diaries of Mrs Phillip Lybbe Powys*, ed. E. J. Climenson (1899), pp. 114–15 (entry for 16 Aug. 1766). The interior is described in *Windsor and its Environs* (1768), p. 88, which mentions a third room, used as a kitchen.

32 See Bellamy Gardner, 'Duke William's Chinese Yacht', *Connoisseur*, Mar. 1948, pp. 22–25. Richard Pococke observed the 'Chinese ship., amongst other craft, in August 1754 (*Travels through England*, vol. II, p. 63).

33 *Travels through England*, vol. II, entry for 2 July 1754.

34 *Passages from the Diaries of Mrs Philip Lybbe Powys*, p. 170 (entry for Aug. 1776).

35 A comparable but more obviously Chinese 'Umbrello'd Seat' is illustrated in a pattern-book of the late 1750s by Charles Over (*Ornamental Architecture in the Gothic, Chinese and Modern Taste*, pl. 8), where it is described as 'one of the most agreeable Decorations yet known, for its affording a Shade when extended, and being on occasion easily contracted or removed'.

36 British Museum Add. MSS 6767, 'Tour into Nottingham-shire, Wilt-shire . . . by James Essex, F.S.A.' On the title page is pencilled 'read Dec. 1803/N.B. Not much in it. T.K.' [Thomas Kerrich].

37 A. Kircher, *Antiquities of China*, bound with J. Nieuhof, *An Embassy to China* (1669), p. 98.

38 J.-B. Du Halde, *The General History of China* (1736), vol. 1, p. 25, and see vol. 2, p. 158.

39 See J. Throsby, *Select Views in Leicester-shire*, vol. I, p. 313.

40 A drawing of the Painshill tent, by F. M. Piper, is in the Swedish Academy of Art, Stockholm. It has been suggested that the Painshill tent was moved to Stourhead, but this is most unlikely, since Piper visited Stourhead in 1779, and a French visitor enjoyed the cushions of the Turkish Tent at Painshill in 1787 (J. de Cambry, *De Londres et ses Environs*, 1788, pp. 134, 141). For the Vauxhall tent see *The Gentleman's Magazine*, 1765, p. 354; for the Bellevue tent see John Ferrar, *A View of Ancient and Modern Dublin . . . to which is added a Tour to Bellevue in the County of Wicklow* (1796), pp. 109, 111.

41 See O. Sirén, *China and the Gardens of Europe* (1950), pp. 179–98.

42 See *The Greville Memoirs 1814–1860*, ed. L. Strachey and R. Fulford (1938), vol. 2, p. 30.

Chapter Six

1 J. Fleming, *Robert Adam and his Circle* (1962), p. 359: letter of 14 Sep. 1756.

2 James Boswell, *Life of Johnson* (1953), p. 1211.

3 See a letter from John Chambers to William Chambers, 3 July 1756 (R.A. Correspondence), regretting that he had 'no designs of Chinese houses'.

4 The Sans Souci design is reproduced in J. Harris, *Sir William Chambers*, pl. 42.

5 Letter from Thomas Brand of The Hoo, Hertfordshire, to Chambers, 1 July 1764 (R.I.B.A.), quoted by J. Harris, *ibid.*, p. 211.

6 B. Bartlett, *Manduessedum Romanorum* (1791), p. 139. The model appears in *Designs*, pl. 4, no. 2.

7 Duchy of Cornwall Office, Frederick, Prince of Wales, vol. 17 (1748–49).

8 *Journal of the Walpole Society*, vol. 30 (1955), Vertue Notebooks VI, p. 153 (12 Oct. 1750).

9 W. Chambers, *Plans . . . of the Gardens and Buildings at Kew* (1763), p. 4.

10 J. Harris, 'Exoticism at Kew', *Apollo* (1963), pp. 103–08, and *Sir William Chambers* (1970), pp. 33–34.

11 J. A. Rouquet, *The Present State of the Arts in England* (1755), p. 61.

12 'Preparing the Chineys Temple to be moved': Duchy of Cornwall Office, Kew accounts, vol. 42, 25 Sep. 1758.

13 A. Young, *A Six-Months Tour through the North of England* (1770), I, pp. 297–98; repeated almost verbatim in W. Watts, *Seats of the Nobility and Gentry* (1779–86), text to pl. V.

14 *Plans . . . of Kew*, p. 4.

15 See J. Harris, *Sir William Chambers*, pp. 34–35 and pls. 24 and 25.

16 *Plans . . . of Kew*, p. 5.

17 W. Chambers, *Designs of Chinese Buildings*, p. 5n., quoting from Du Halde's *Description of . . . China*.

18 *Plans . . . of Kew*, p. 5, quoting from Nieuhof's *Embassy*.

19 Rev. Richard Woodyeare, in *Wiltshire Archaeological and Natural History Magazine*, X (1867), p. 84. See also Pococke, *Travels thro. England*, vol. II, p. 58 (entry for Aug. 1754).

20 J. Hanway, *A Journal of Eight Days' Journey*, I (1757), p. 198; quoted in J. Harris, *Sir William Chambers*, p. 196.

21 Letter of 23 Nov. 1772, B. M. Add. MSS 41134, pp. 13–14; quoted by J. Harris, *ibid.*

22 W. Chambers, *Designs of Chinese Buildings* (1757), pp. 14–19.

23 E. Burke, *A Philosophical Enquiry into our Ideas of the Sublime and the Beautiful*, ed. J. T. Boulton (1958), pp. 57ff.

24 T. Whately, *Observations on Modern Gardening* (1770), p. 107.

25 W. Chambers, *A Dissertation on Oriental Gardening* (1772), p. 37.

26 *Monthly Review*, XLVII (Aug. 1772), p. 139.

27 *London Magazine*, XLI (June 1772), p. 287.

28 Letter to W. Mason, 25 May 1772: *Correspondence*, vol. 28, p. 34.

29 R.C. Bald, 'Sir William Chambers and the Chinese Garden', *Journal of the History of Ideas*, XI, no. 3 (June 1950), p. 300.

30 W. Mason, *An Heroic Epistle to Sir William Chambers* (1773), p. 13.

31 *A Dissertation*, 2nd ed. (1773), pp. 115–16.

32 *Ibid.*, p. 131.

33 Letter bound in a copy of *A Dissertation on Oriental Gardening* (2nd ed., 1773), College of Architecture, Cornell University; reprinted as Appendix XIII of J. Harris, *Sir William Chambers*, pp. 192–93.

Chapter Seven

1 D . . ., M. [Antoine Nicolas Dézallier d'Argenville], *Voyage Pittoresque des Environs de Paris*, 3rd (enlarged) ed. (1768), p. 5.

2 Translated from the Prince de Ligne, *Coup d'oeil sur Beloeil*, ed. E. de Ganay (1922), p. 175.

3 M.-A. Laugier, *Essai sur l'Architecture* (2nd ed., 1755), p. 258.

4 *Ibid.*, p. 241. For Laugier's attitude to gardening see Wolfgang Herrman, *Laugier and Eighteenth-century Theory* (1962), pp. 141 ff.

5 Walpole to Rev. William Mason, 6 Sep. 1775, *Correspondence*, vol. 28, p. 220.

6 Walpole to Mason, 10 Sep. 1775, *ibid.*, p. 222.

7 Walpole, 'The History of the Modern Taste in Gardening', ed. I. Chase, in *Horace Walpole: Gardenist* (1943), pp. 21–22.

8 *Ibid.*, p. 23.

9 *Mémoires Concernant l'Histoire, les Sciences, les Arts, Moeurs, Usages des Chinois*, Par les Missionaires de Pe-Kin, VIII (1782), p. 326; quoted in Harris, *Sir William Chambers*, p. 161n.

10 Prince de Ligne, *ibid.*, pp. 105–06.

11 *Ibid.*, p. 213.

12 *Ibid.*, pp. 55–56, 242, 257.

13 For this and the following quotation see L. Carmontelle, *Jardin de Monceau, près de Paris . . .* (1779), Prospectus. For a contemporary British opinion of Monceau see Thomas Blaikie, *Diary of a Scotch Gardener*, ed. F. Birrell (1931), pp. 178 ff.

14 Letter from Napoleon to Gaudin, 5 Mar. 1807, cited in Robert Hénard, *Les Jardins et les Squares de Paris* (1911), p. 118.

15 W. Robinson, *The Parks and Gardens of Paris* (2nd ed., 1878), p. 42.

16 See 'Jardins en France 1760–1820', exhibition catalogue, Caisse Nationale des Monuments Historiques et des Sites, Paris (1977), pp. 59 ff.

17 J. C. Krafft, *Plans des Plus Beaux Jardins Pittoresques . . .* (1809), vol. 2, *cahier* 1, pl. 4, and J. C. Krafft, *Recueil d'Architecture Civile* (1812), pl. 36.

18 A. Young, *Travels during the Years 1787, 1788 and 1789 (in) . . . France* (1792), p. 69.

19 For further information concerning the Désert de Retz see O. Choppin de Janvry, 'Désert de Retz', *L'Oeil*, Sep. 1967, pp. 30–41, 80; and 'Jardins en France 1760–1820'.

20 Translated from A. de Laborde, *Nouveaux Jardins de la France et ses Anciens Chateaux* (1808), pp. 149–50.

21 The 'saut du Niagara' is illustrated and described in 'Jardins en France 1760–1820', pp. 163–65.

22 H. de Balzac, *La Physiologie du Mariage*, in *La Comédie Humaine*, ed. P. Citron, vol. 7 (1966), p. 408.

23 Illustrated in 'Jardins en France 1760–1820', p. 25.

24 Illustrated in O. Choppin de Janvry, *Le Pavillon Chinois de Cassan* (1975), pp. 2–3.

25 See Monique Mosser, '*Monsieur de Marigny et les jardins, projects inédits pour Menars*', B.S.H.A.F. (1972).

26 Text to Le Rouge's first *cahier*, in the Bibliothèque Nationale, Paris; quoted in O. Sirén, *China and the Gardens of Europe*, pp. 107–10.

27 J.-C. Krafft, *Plans* (1809), vol. I, *cahier* 6, pl. 45.

28 *Ibid.*, *cahier* 9, pl. 68.

29 Quoted in 'Jardins en France 1760–1820', p. 141.

30 G. Le Rouge, *Détails des nouveaux jardins à la mode*, *cahier* XVIII (1782), p. 30.

31 See Anna Zador, 'The English Garden in Hungary' in *The Picturesque Garden and its Influence outside the British Isles*, ed. Sir N. Pevsner (1974).

32 For this and subsequent references to Polish garden buildings see Brian Knox, 'The Arrival of the English Landscape Garden in Poland and Bohemia', in *The Picturesque Garden and its Influence outside the British Isles* (1974).

33 Rev. William Coxe, *Travels into Poland, Russia, Sweden and Denmark* (3 vols., 1784–90), vol. I, pp. 175–81.

34 *Ibid.*, vol. I, p. 287.

35 Letter from Catherine II to Voltaire, 25 June 1772, quoted in G. H. Hamilton, *The Art and Architecture of Russia* (1954), p. 218.

36 See V. and A. Kennett, *The Palaces of Leningrad* (1973), pp. 138–39; Maurice Craig, 'The Palace of Tsarskoe Selo', *Country Life* (20 Jan. 1966), pp. 108–12; and Isobel Rae, *Charles Cameron* (1971), p. 92.

37 Jan Nieuhof, *An Embassy . . .* (1669), p. 62.

38 See Edward Croft-Murray, 'The Palazzina Cinese at Palermo', *Country Life* (10 Oct. 1947), pp. 724–25; and Claude Arthaud, *Dream Palaces* (1973), pp. 301 ff.

Chapter Eight

1 However, a Scotsman, John Bell of Antermony, had served as physician to the Russian embassy to Peking of 1720–21, and published his *Travels* in 1763. See John Bell, *A Journey from St. Petersburg to Pekin 1719–22*, ed. J. L. Stevenson (1965).

2 *Autobiographical Memoir of Sir John Barrow, Bart.* (1847), p. 49.

3 Alexander did not accompany the delegation to the Great Wall and to Jehol, but redrew sketches made on this expedition by Parish, for the engraver's use. A 'View of Gehol' after Parish and Alexander was published in Barrow, *Travels in China* (1804), opp. p. 128.

4 *An Embassy to China, Lord Macartney's Journal*, ed. J. L. Cranmer-Byng (1962), p. 127; quoted also in John Barrow, *Some Account of . . . the Earl of Macartney* (2 vols., 1807), vol. 2, p. 266.

5 *Ibid.*, p. 126; Barrow, *Some Account*, p. 264.

6 *Ibid.*, p. 133. Macartney added that the closest approximation to Chambers's description which he had seen was a mock-town at one of the Empress of Russia's palaces – presumably at Tsarskoe Selo.

7 *Ibid.*, pp. 197–99; quoted also in Barrow, *Some Account*, pp. 374–77, in Clarke Abel, *Narrative of a Journey in the Interior of China* (1818), pp. 196–97n., and in G.N. Wright, *China in a Series of Views . . .* (4 vols., 1843), vol. 1, pp. 50–51.

8 *Ibid.*, p. 272. However, Macartney was surprisingly reticent about the celebrated gardens at Yuan-ming yuan, which had been described by Attiret and more recently illustrated in Georges Le Rouge's *Détails des nouveaux jardins anglo-chinois*. Macartney referred tantalizingly to 'several hundreds of pavilions scattered through the grounds and all connected together by close arbours, by passages apparently cut through stupendous rocks, or by fairyland galleries', but then declared himself incapable of describing so impressive a scene (*Journal*, pp. 95–96). Sir John Barrow, *An Autobiographical Memoir* (1847), p. 49.

10 For a more detailed discussion of the furniture of Carlton House see Dorothy Stroud, *Henry Holland* (1966), pp. 77ff.

11 See Dorothy Stroud, *ibid.*, p. 80 and pls. 48, 53.

12 I am grateful to Mr Henry Joyce, formerly curator at Woburn, for this information.

13 *A Tour in England, Ireland and France, in the years 1826, 1827, 1828 & 1829 . . .* by A German Prince [Pückler-Muskau], revised ed. (1940), pp. 37–38.

14 Windsor, R.A. 33513.

15 J. de Cambry, *De Londres et ses Environs* (1788), p. 13.

16 'Antony Pasquin' [John Williams], *The New Brighton Guide*, 6th ed. (1796), p. 16n.

17 *Nash's Illustrations of Her Majesty's Palace at Brighton* (2nd ed.), ed. E. W. Brayley (1838), p. 2.

18 Windsor, R.A. 33528.

19 R.P. Knight, *The Landscape, A Didactic Poem* (1794), lines 216–21 and 228–31. Knight continued to pour scorn on Chambers's *Dissertation* in *An Analytical Inquiry into the Principles of Taste*, 4th ed.(1808), pp. 384–85.

20 Quoted in H.A.N. Brockman, *The Caliph of Fonthill* (1956), p. 25.

21 The pagoda is visible in a painting dated (by Colt Hoare) 1753, reproduced in John Harris, 'Fonthill, Wiltshire, I: Alderman Beckford's Houses',

Country Life, Nov. 24 1966, pp. 1370–04.

22 For these quotations I have relied on Boyd Alexander, *England's Wealthiest Son* (1962), pp. 12, 45, 85.

23 *The Journal of William Beckford in Portugal and Spain 1787–1788*, ed. Boyd Alexander (1954), pp. 112, 128–29.

24 [William Beckford], *Recollections of an Excursion to the Monasteries of Alcobaça and Batalha* (1835), pp. 136–37.

25 *Journal*, pp. 194, 175.

Chapter Nine

1 Garcia da Orta, *Colloquies on the Simples and Drugs of India*, translated by Sir C. Markham (1913), p. 446.

2 Samuel Purchas, *Purchas his Pilgrimes* (1625), vol. 4, p. 439.

3 *Ibid.*, vol. 4, p. 440.

4 *Ibid.*, vol. 9, p. 32.

5 John Pinkerton, *A General Collection of the Best and most Interesting Voyages . . .* (1811), vol. 8, p. 173.

6 Pierre Sonnerat, *A Voyage to the East Indies and China*, translated by F. Magnus (1788), vol. I, p. 123.

7 *Asiatick Researches*, I (1788), p. 411.

8 Sir J. Reynolds, *Discourses on Art*, ed. R. R. Wark (1959), p. 242 (Discourse of 11 Dec. 1786).

9 A copy of the *Dissertation*, and the two known stipple engravings, were exhibited in June 1977 by Hartnoll & Eyre Ltd, to whose expert knowledge I am indebted.

10 *A Dissertation on the Prototypes of Architecture . . .* (1787), p. 4.

11 W. Hodges, *Select Views in India* (1785–88), text to pl. 19.

12 See E. W. Brayley, *Londiniana* (1829), vol. I, p. 92; and Dorothy Stroud, *George Dance, Architect 1741–1825* (1971), pp. 170–71. Elsewhere (*Country Life*, 2 April 1964, p. 771) the same writer has suggested that Dance was primarily influenced by Hodges's pl. 19, 'View of a Mosque at Chunar Gur'. Sir Nikolaus Pevsner's *London*, I (3rd ed., p. 191) seems to doubt the Indian element in the Guildhall façade.

13 Farington's *Diary*, 25 March 1804; quoted in D. Stroud, *George Dance*, p. 198.

14 Letter postmarked 22 Dec. 1806, quoted in William Knight, *Memorials of Coleorton* (1887), vol. I, p. 189.

15 T. and W. Daniell, *A Picturesque Voyage to India by the Way of China* (1810), text accompanying pl. 39.

16 T. and W. Daniell, *Oriental Scenery*, pt. I, XI, dated Jan. 1796.

17 Text accompanying W. Daniell's engravings of the Melchet Park temple.

See also the *European Magazine* (1802), pp. 448–49.

18 Rev. A. Gay, quoted in Sir Charles Lawson, *The Private Life of Warren Hastings* (1905), p. 249.

19 Quoted in Evan Cotton, 'The Hindu Temple at Melchet Park', *Bengal Past and Present*, XL (Oct.–Dec. 1930), p. 77.

20 *Ibid.*

21 *Ambulator*, 5th ed. (1793), p. 210.

22 Walter W. Druett, *The Stanmores of Harrow Weald* (1938), p. 192.

23 James Malton, *An Essay on British Gothic Architecture* (1798), p. 10.

24 Thomas Hope, *Household Furniture and Interior Design* (1807), text to pl. VI.

25 *Ibid.*, pl. X and text.

26 H. Repton, *Designs for the Pavillon at Brighton* (1808), v.

27 Royal Archives (Privy Purse Miscellany).

28 *Designs for the Pavillon*, vi.

29 MS copy of *Designs for the Pavillon*, Royal Library, Windsor. E.W. Brayley's introduction to the second edition of Nash's *Views* also states that Repton received his 'command' in 1805, and that he 'had already been employed in improving the grounds at Brighton' (*Illustrations of Her Majesty's Palace at Brighton*, 1838, p. 2).

30 *Designs for the Pavillon*, vn.

31 R.I.B.A. Drawings Collection, Cat. H. Repton J5/15.

32 *Ibid.*, Cat. T. Daniell, Sezincote 10 Letter 3.

33 Letter of 11 July 1845, in *The Letters of Robert Browning and Elizabeth Barrett Barrett 1845–46*, ed. Elvan Kintner (1969), vol. I, p. 119.

34 Watercolours of Hope End by Phillip Ballard and Arabella Barrett respectively are reproduced in *Diary by E.B.B.*, ed. P. Kelley and R. Hudson (Athens, Ohio, 1969), and in *The Barretts at Hope End*, ed. E. Berridge (1974). Two photographs of the house in about 1860 are reproduced by Sandra Blutman, 'Hope End, Herefordshire', *Country Life*, 19 Sep. 716.

35 George Moulton-Barrett wrote to Robert Browning in 1889 that 'the architect was I believe Wyatt, but am not sure' (*Diary by E.B.B.*, p. xiv). However there is no further reason to associate any of the Wyatt family with Hope End.

36 *Diary by E.B.B.*, p. 328 (Sale Catalogue p. 4).

37 *Ibid.*, p. 167 (letter of 24 Oct. 1831).

38 *Ibid.*, p. xv.

39 *Ibid.*, p. 327.

40 In a sketchbook in the collection of the

Royal Pavilion, Art Gallery & Museums, Brighton. A very similar conservatory design, attributed to J.A. Repton, is in the R.I.B.A. Drawings Collection (Cat. J.A. Repton [9]).

41 George Wightwick, *The Palace of Architecture* (1840), p. 35.

42 Quoted in W. Feaver, *John Martin* (1975), p. 44. For a more detailed study of Martin's sources see Norah Monckton, 'Architectural Backgrounds in the Pictures of John Martin', *Architectural Review*, civ (1948), pp. 81–84. In the light of the mixed ancestry of 'Belshazzar's Feast', there is an additional justice in Charles Lamb's criticism of that painting as nothing but a scene of alarm at dinner in the Royal Pavilion ('The Last Essays of Elia', *Life, Letters and Writings of Charles Lamb*, ed. P. Fitzgerald (1876), vol. 4, pp. 91–94).

43 J. Gandy, 'On the Philosophy of Architecture', *Magazine of the Fine Arts* (1821), p. 292.

44 J. Farington, *Diary*, quoted in Dorothy Stroud, *George Dance*, p. 181. Farington suggested that Dance might discuss this question in his forthcoming lectures as Professor of Architecture at the Royal Academy, but the lectures never took place.

45 W. Hodges, *A Dissertation . . .*, p. 2.

46 R. Lugar, *Architectural Sketches for cottages, rural dwellings, and villas . . .* (1805; reprinted in 1815 and 1823), pls. 32, 36 and 37.

47 E. Aikin, *Designs for Villas and other Rural Buildings* (1808; reprinted 1835), pp. 14–20; pls. 11–13, 23–24.

48 H. Repton, *Designs for the Pavillon at Brighton* (1808), vi.

49 *Ibid.*, v–viii, pp. 29–30.

50 *Ibid.*, p. 30.

Chapter Ten

1 John Byng (Lord Torrington), *A Toure into Sussex* (1788), in *The Torrington Diaries*, ed. C. Bruyn Andrews (1934), vol. I, p. 371.

2 Royal Academy, 1797, no. 1136 (p. 30).

3 Joseph Farington, *The Farington Diary*, ed. J. Grieg (1922–28), vol. 3, p. 7: entry for 30 Sep. 1904.

4 Design in Chester Record Office, reproduced in *Country Life*, 11 Feb. 1971, p. 305, fig. 4.

5 *The Farington Diary*, vol. 2, p. 270: entry for 20 July 1804. In 1808–11 F. J. Belanger constructed an innovatory iron dome to replace the burnt-out wooden structure.

6 Quoted by E.W. Brayley, *Illustrations of*

Her Majesty's Palace at Brighton (1838), p. 16 n.

7 *Ibid.*, p. 17.

8 One of these, the western elevation, was exhibited at the Royal Academy in 1806 (no. 803).

9 W. Alexander, *The Costume of China* (1805), text to 'South Gate of the City of Ting-Hai'.

10 E.W. Brayley (apparently quoting a letter from William Porden to his daughter), *Illustrations of Her Majesty's Palace at Brighton* (1838), p. 16n.

11 H. Repton, *Designs for the Pavillon at Brighton* (1808), vn.

12 *Ibid.*, p. 41.

13 *Works of T.L. Peacock* (1924–34), I, p. 30.

14 *An Enquiry into the Changes of Taste in the Landscape Garden (1806)*, p. 136n; *Observations on the Theory and Practice of Landscape Gardening* (1803), p. 130 & n. See also *Observations*, p. 151.

15 W. Daniell after J. Wales, 'Viswakarma, External View' (*Oriental Scenery*, book 4, no. 22; published 1 June 1803). In place of the solid square pedestal Repton created a fluted, heavily tapered column.

16 For the differences between the handwritten and the printed versions see Patrick Conner, 'Unexecuted Designs for the Royal Pavilion at Brighton', *Apollo* (Mar. 1978), pp. 192–99.

17 J. C. Loudon (ed.), *The Landscape Gardening and Landscape Architecture of the late Humphry Repton, Esq.* (1840), p. 19.

18 Letter from Repton to the Prince Regent, bound into MS of the *Designs*, the Royal Library, Windsor; quoted in full in C. Musgrave, *The Royal Pavilion* (1959), p. 58.

19 *Life at Fonthill 1807–1822*, ed. Boyd Alexander (1957), p. 133.

20 *Ibid.*, p. 137.

21 *Diary*, 18 Sep. 1813.

22 R. Elsam, *An Essay on Rural Architecture* (1803), p. 16. Hafod Abbey was largely burnt down in 1807, but rebuilt by Johnes: the dome can be clearly seen in a photograph reproduced in *Country Life*, 24 Apr. 1958, p. 888. In the summer of 1959 the ruins of Hafod were completely demolished.

23 J. Elmes, *Metropolitan Improvements* (1829), p. 48. A subdued version of the Sussex Place cupolas exists at Southborough Lodge in Surrey, also designed by Nash.

24 *The Gentleman's Magazine*, Aug. 1814, pp. 182–83.

25 *Ibid.* The bridge was taken down in 1820, 'to the great inconvenience of the inhabitants of Westminster' (*The Orig-*

inal Picture of London, ed. J. Britton [1828], p. 160).

26 J. Nash, draft preface to 'Views of the Royal Pavilion', MS in Royal Archives: quoted in full in C. Musgrave, *The Royal Pavilion* (2nd ed., 1959), pp. 62–64.

27 See for example Batty Langley, *Gothic Architecture Improved . . .* (1747), p. 39.

28 Samuel Lewis, *A Topographical Dictionary of England*, 5th ed. (1842), vol. I, p. 372; J. A. Erredge, *History of Brighthelmstone* (1862), p. 269.

29 These references to the Pavilion are quoted more fully in C. Musgrave, *Life In Brighton* (1970), pp. 162–63.

30 J. Farington, *Diary*, 9 Sep. 1818.

31 Lord Chamberlain's office records: quoted in Musgrave, *op. cit.*, p. 158.

32 C. Musgrave, *The Royal Pavilion*, appendix I, p. 160.

33 Letter of Sir William Knighton to Robert Gray, Keeper of the Privy Purse, 21 Nov. 1822, quoted in Musgrave, *ibid.* p. 75.

34 The upper part of the Antheum can be seen in 'Mason's Panoramic View of Brighton'.

35 Henry C. Porter, *The History of Hove* (1897), p. 141. The best modern account of the Antheum is to be found in A. Dale, *Fashionable Brighton 1820–1860* (1971), pp. 154–55; Porter's book contains two versions which conflict somewhat (pp. 18, 141). See also the *Brighton Gazette*, 5 Sep. 1833, p. 3, which claims that the Antheum had the largest dome in the world.

36 Quoted in E. Longford, *Victoria R.I.* (1964), pp. 76–77.

37 E. W. Brayley, *Illustrations of Her Majesty's Palace at Brighton* (1838), p. 3.

38 *Ibid.*, p. 15.

39 See J. A. Erredge, *History of Brighthelmstone* (1862), p. 277.

40 Undated lithograph of *c.* 1840 in Brighton Art Gallery, stating 'Matthew Wyatt the younger' to be the architect.

41 See Cecil Roth, *The Sassoon Dynasty* (1941), p. 166, and Stanley Jackson, *The Sassoons* (1968).

42 For this observation I am indebted to Antony Dale's chapter on pier architecture in Simon H. Adamson, *Seaside Piers* (1977).

Chapter Eleven

1 J. Foulston, *The Public Buildings erected in the West of England . . .* (1838), p. 3.

2 See *Devonshire Illustrated* (1829).

3 See Clifford Musgrave, *Life in Brighton* (1970), p. 202 and pl. opp. p. 128.

4 See Mark Bence-Jones, *Burke's Guide to*

Country Houses, vol. I: Ireland (1978), pp. 108–09; and Brian de Breffny and Rosemary ffolliott, *The Houses of Ireland* (1975), pp. 190–01.

5 *A Brief Historical and Descriptive Account of the Royal Gardens, Vauxhall*, published by the proprietors (1822), pp. 15–20.

6 *The Twopenny Post-bag* [1813], letter VIII.

7 R. Ackermann, *Repository of Arts*, 1st series, III (1810), p. 393.

8 Wyatt Papworth, *J. B. Papworth, Architect to the King of Wurtemburg* (1879), p. 91: letter from James Morrison of 20 July 1842.

9 M. Edgeworth, *Castle Rackrent and The Absentee* (Everyman Library, 1960), pp. 94–95.

10 C. Abel, *A Narrative of a Journey in the Interior of China . . . in 1816 and 1817* (1818), p. 158.

11 H. Ellis, *A Journal of the Proceedings of the Late Embassy to China* (1818), vol. 1, p. 267).

12 Ed. E. M. Butler, *A Regency Visitor, The English Tour of Prince Pückler-Muskau described in his Letters 1826–28* (1957), p. 290 (14 Jan. 1828).

13 R.I.B.A. Drawings Cat., Papworth [88] 1–4, and see W. Papworth, *John B. Papworth, Architect to the King of Wurtemburg* (1879), pp. 67–68. Papworth also designed a Chinese aviary for William Leaf at Park Hill, Streatham, in the 1830s (R.I.B.A. Cat. [185] 94).

14 W. Papworth, *ibid.*, p. 67.

15 *A Regency Visitor*, pp. 116–17 (26 Dec. 1826).

16 *Ibid.*, p. 159 (8 Feb. 1827).

17 Elizabeth Vassall, Baroness Holland, *Elizabeth, Lady Holland to her Son 1821–1845*, ed. the Earl of Ilchester (1946), p. 47.

18 A summary of the bills in the Public Record Office (Works 1/13–16) is given in D. Linstrum, *Sir Jeffry Wyatville: Architect to the King* (1973), p. 200–02.

19 *The Greville Memoirs 1814–1860*, ed. L. Strachey and R. Fulford (1938), vol. 2, p. 30 (entry for 20 Aug. 1830).

20 Wyatville's designs are in the R.I.B.A. Drawings Collection (Cat. Sir Jeffry Wyatville 25/1–36); see also Linstrum pp. 213–16.

21 J. C. Loudon, *An Encyclopaedia of Gardening* (1860 ed., pp. 256–63). J. B. Papworth may have been associated with the early stages of the pagoda: see W. Papworth, *John B. Papworth* (1879), p. 47. The so-called Chinese Temple at Alton consists of three diminishing hexagonal storeys, but is otherwise Gothic.

22 See T. W. Horsfield, *The History, Anti-*

quities & *Topography of the County of Sussex* (1835), vol. I, p. 590 & n.

23 Bedfordshire County Record Office R. 5/1127.

24 An unambitious open Chinese kiosk at Cheshunt Cottage near Enfield is illustrated in the *Gardeners' Magazine* for Dec. 1839 (p. 651). It stood on a mound formed by the excavation of a pond, and was accompanied by Chinese vases and rockwork. Cheshunt Cottage was the residence of William Harrison, who was his own landscape gardener (p. 635).

25 H. Ellis, *Journal*, vol. 2, p. 420–21.

26 Sir John Barrow, *The Life of George Lord Anson* (1839), p. 72.

27 G. N. Wright, *China, in a Series of Views* (1843), vol. 2, p. 34. In the following decade the Porcelain Tower was destroyed by the Taipings. 'It must have been a noble building,' wrote a British soldier who visited the site in 1860, 'as the pieces of broken porcelain, now scattered about, testify to the beauty of the materials used in its construction.' (Lt-Col. G. J. Wolseley, *Narrative of the War with China in 1860* (1862), p. 358).

28 *Ibid.*, p. 32, and see H. O'Brien, *The Round Towers of Ireland*, 2nd ed. (1834), p. 4.

29 *Ibid.*, vol. 3, p. 8.

30 *Gardeners' Magazine*, 2 (1827), pp. 136–39. For another critical view of Chinese gardens see J. F. Davis, *The Chinese* (1836), vol. 1, pp. 367–68; a collection of opinions on Chinese gardening is contained in J. C. Loudon, *An Encyclopaedia of Gardening* (1828) etc.).

31 William B. Langdon, *A Descriptive Catalogue of the Chinese Collection . . .* (1842), ix.

32 *Ibid.*, p. 68.

33 R. Brown, *Domestic Architecture* (1841), p. 295 n.

34 J. F. Davis, *The Chinese* (1836), vol. 2. p. 320.

35 J. Ruskin, *The Stones of Venice*, vol. I (1851), in *Complete Works*, ed. E. T. Cook and A. Wedderburn (1903–12), vol. 9, pp. 161–62.

36 See Winslow Ames, *Prince Albert and Victorian Taste* (1968), p. 110.

37 H. and J. A. Repton, *Fragments on the Theory and Practice of Landscape-Gardening* (1816), pp. 139 ff. Repton includes in his list 'connecting interior walks' and 'connecting exterior walks'.

38 Chambers's reference to the Chinese art of arranging 'decayed trees, pollards and dead stumps, of picturesque forms' is noted by Peter Hayden, 'Edward Cooke at Biddulph Grange', *Garden History*, VI, no. 1 (Spring 1978), p. 30.

39 Edward Kemp, *Gardeners' Chronicle*, 6 Dec. 1856, p. 807.

40 Edward Kemp, *ibid.*; sale catalogue of July 1871 reprinted in *Garden History*, IV, no. 1 (Spring 1978), pp. 33–41.

41 Edward Kemp, *ibid.*

42 Edward Kemp, *Gardeners' Chronicle* (1862), p. 719. Other articles illustrating the gardens at Biddulph are to be found in *Country Life*, vol. 17 (1905), pp. 18–28, and in *The Garden*, vol. 102, pt 5 (May 1977), pp. 193–96.

43 *Punch*, 24 Nov. 1860.

44 G. J. Wolseley, *Narrative of the war with China in 1860* (1862), pp. 233–37, 280, 305–06.

45 An engraving appeared in the *Illustrated London News*, 30 May 1857, p. 515; and Phoebus Levin's oil painting of the Dancing Platform in 1864 is in the Museum of London (*Catalogue*, 1970, p. 128).

46 *Ibid.*, p. 516.

47 I am grateful to Mr. C.R. St. Q. Wall of the National Trust for this information.

48 For 'Salsette and Elephanta' see *Works*, vol. 2, pp. 90–100; for Ruskin's criticism of the ogee see *Works*, vol. 9, p. 162; for his many derogatory references to Indian art see the index volume (*Works*, vol. 39).

49 R. Brown, *Domestic Architecture* (1841), p. 298.

50 Memorandum from Queen Victoria of 15 Dec. 1856, in *The Letters of Queen Victoria*, ed. A. C. Benson and Viscount Esher (1908), vol. 3, p. 219.

51 Letter of 23 Sep. 1857 to the Earl of Clarendon, *ibid.*, p. 248.

52 Details of Elveden's interior design are illustrated in the *Architect*, vol. 5 (Mar. 1871), opp. p. 147.

53 See R. W. F. Potter, *Hampshire Harvest* (1977), pp. 141–42.

54 See D. Linstrum, 'Architecture of Cuthbert Brodrick', *Country Life*, 1 June 1967, pp. 1379–81.

55 See Lavinia Handley-Read, 'Legacy of a Vanished Empire', *Country Life*, 9 July 1970, pp. 110–12.

56 See Mark Girouard, 'A Young Arin Kent', *Country Life*, 30 Aug. 1973, pp. 554–58, and *The Victorian Country House* (1971), pp. 48, 138, 145.

57 See Mark Girouard, *Sweetness and Light* (1977), pp. 179ff.

58 The pavilion (built by Barnard, Bishop and Barnard of Norwich) was re-erected at the Paris Exhibition of 1878, and shown in exhibitions at Vienna, Buenos Aires and London, before being bought for £500 by Norwich Corporation; it stood in Chapel Field Gardens, Norwich, until it was dis-

mantled in 1949. See also Elizabeth Aslin, *The Aesthetic Movement* (1969), ch. 4.

59 Letter of Warrington Taylor in the Fitzwilliam Museum, quoted by Mark Girouard, *Sweetness and Light*, p. 15.

Chapter Twelve

1 J. C. Loudon, *An Encyclopaedia of Gardening* (enlarged ed., 1835), p. 401.

2 For this and several of the following observations I am indebted to Clay Lancaster, 'Oriental Forms in American Architecture 1800–1870', *Art Bulletin*, XXXIX (1947), pp. 183 ff.

3 See William Birch, *The City of Philadelphia* (1800).

4 See John Cornforth, 'Fairmount Park, Philadelphia – II', *Country Life*, 18 Jan. 1973, pp. 150–53.

5 See Marcus Binney, 'University of Virginia I & II', *Country Life*, 12 and 19 Jan. 1978, pp. 74–77 and 142–45.

6 H. D. Eberlein and C. Hubbard, *Portrait of a Colonial City, Philadelphia* (1939), p. 432, quoted in C. Lancaster, *op. cit.*

7 *The Autobiography of P.T. Barnum* (1855), p. 403.

8 Montgomery Schuyler, 'A Great American Architect: Leopold Eidlitz', *Architectural Record*, vol. 24, no. 3 (Sep. 1908), p. 169.

9 *Autobiography*, p. 403.

10 See M.R. Werner, *P.T. Barnum* (1923), p. 106.

11 *Ibid.*, p. 117.

12 A. J. Downing, *The Architecture of Country Houses* (1853), p. 27.

13 M.R. Werner, p. 231.

14 See Clay Lancaster, *op. cit.* p. 187.

15 See for example A. J. Downing, *The Architecture of Country Houses* (1861), pp. 119, 312–13; R. Brown, *Domestic Architecture* (1841), pl. XLIII.

16 A. J. Downing, *Landscape Gardening* (1841), p. 346.

17 A. J. Downing, *The Architecture of Country Houses* (1861), p. 312.

18 T. and W. Daniell, *Oriental Scenery*, pt. I, no. VIII (1795).

19 S. Sloan, *The Model Architect* (1852), vol. I, pls. LXXII-LXXIII.

20 *Ibid.*, vol. 2, pls. LXIII-LXVI.

21 Longwood was given in 1970 to the Pilgrimage Garden Club of Natchez, and is designated a National Historic Landmark; it is advertised as 'the largest octagonal house remaining in America'.

22 See G. J. B. Carstensen and C. Gildemeister, *The New York Crystal Palace* (1854).

Bibliography

Place of publication is London unless stated otherwise

ABEL, CLARKE, *A Narrative of a Journey in the Interior of China . . . in 1816 and 1817*, 1818.

ACKERMANN, RUDOLPH (publisher), *Historical Sketches of Moscow*, 1813.

The Repository of Arts, Literature, Commerce, Manufactures, Fashions, and Politics, 1st series, 14 vols., 1809–15.

ACLOQUE, GUY, and JOHN CORNFORTH, 'The Eternal Gothic of Eaton', I, *Country Life*, 11 Feb. 1971, pp. 304–07.

AIKIN, EDMUND, *Designs for Villas and other Rural Buildings*, 1808; reprinted 1835.

ALEXANDER, BOYD, *England's Wealthiest Son. A study of William Beckford*, 1962.

ALEXANDER, WILLIAM. *The Costume of China*, 1805.

AMES, WINSLOW, *Prince Albert and Victorian Taste*, 1968.

ANONYMOUS, 'Some Observations made in a Journey, begun June the 7th, and finish'd July the 9th. 1742', British Museum Add. MSS 22, 926.

APPLETON, WILLIAM W., *A Cycle of Cathay*, New York, 1951.

ARTHAUD, CLAUDE, *Dream Palaces*, 1973.

Asiatick Researches, 20 vols., Asiatic Society of Bengal, Calcutta, 1788–1839.

ASLIN, ELIZABETH, *The Aesthetic Movement*, 1969.

ATTIRET, JEAN-DENIS, *A Particular Account of the Emperor of China's Gardens near Pekin*, tr. 'Sir Harry Beaumont' [Joseph Spence], 1752.

BALD, R.C. 'Sir William Chambers and the Chinese Garden', *Journal of the History of Ideas*, XI, no. 3 (June 1950).

BALTRUSAITIS, JURGIS, *Le Moyen Age fantastique*, Paris, 1955.

Jardins et Pays d'illusion, Paris, 1957.

BALZAC, HONORÉ DE, *La Physiologie du Mariage*, in *La Comédie Humaine*, ed. P. CITRON, 7 vols., 1966, vol. 7.

BARNUM, PHINEAS TAYLOR, *The Autobiography of P. T. Barnum*, 1855.

BARRETT, ELIZABETH BARRETT (later Browning), *The Letters of Robert Browning and Elizabeth Barrett Barrett 1845–46*, ed. Elvan Kintner, Cambridge, Mass., 2 vols., 1969.

Diary by E.B.B., ed. P. Kelley and R. Hudson, Athens, Ohio, 1969.

The Barretts of Hope End: the Early Diary of Elizabeth Barrett Browning, 1974.

BARROW, SIR JOHN, *Travels in China*, 1804.

Some Account of . . . the Earl of Macartney, 2 vols., 1807.

The Life of George Lord Anson, 1939.

Autobiographical Memoir of Sir John Barrow, Bart., 1847.

BARTLETT, B., *Manduessedum Romanorum*, 1791.

BECKFORD, WILLIAM, *Vathek*, 1786–87; 1971.

Recollections of an Excursion to the Monasteries of Alcobaça and Batalha, 1835; ed. Boyd Alexander, 1972.

The Journal of William Beckford in Portugal and Spain 1787–1788, ed. Boyd Alexander, 1954.

Life at Fonthill 1807–1822, ed. Boyd Alexander, 1957.

BELEVITCH-STANKEVITCH, H., *Le Gout Chinois en France au temps de Louis XIV*, Paris, 1910.

BELL, JOHN, *A Journey from St. Petersburg to Pekin 1719–22*, ed. J. L. Stevenson, Edinburgh, 1965.

BENCE-JONES, MARK, *Burke's Guide to Country Houses*, vol. I: Ireland, 1978.

BETJEMAN, SIR JOHN, 'Sezincote, Moreton-in-Marsh, Gloucestershire', *Architectural Review*, May 1931, pp. 161–66.

BEURDELEY, MICHEL AND CECILE, *Giuseppe Castiglione, a Jesuit Painter at the Court of the Chinese Emperors*, tr. M. Bullock, 1972.

BICKHAM, GEORGE (the younger), *The Beauties of Stow*, 1750.

BINNEY, MARCUS, 'University of Virginia I & II', *Country Life*, 12 and 19 Jan. 1978, pp. 74–77 and 142–45.

BIRCH, WILLIAM, *The City of Philadelphia*, 1800.

BLAGDON, FRANCIS, *A Brief History of Ancient and Modern India*, 1808.

BLAIKIE, THOMAS, *Diary of a Scotch Gardner at the French Court at the end of the Eighteenth Century . . .*, ed. F. Birrell, 1931.

BLUTMAN, SANDRA, 'Hope End, Herefordshire', *Country Life*, 19 Sep. 1968, pp. 715–17.

BOSWELL, JAMES (the elder), *Boswell's Life of Johnson*, Oxford, 1953.

BOYD, ANDREW, *Chinese Architecture and Town Planning 1500 B.C.–A.D. 1911*, 1962.

BRAYLEY, EDWARD W., *Londiniana; or, reminiscences of the British metropolis*, 1828 [1829].

(ed.), *Nash's Illustrations of Her Majesty's Palace at Brighton*, 2nd printing of the plates, 1838.

BRAYLEY, EDWARD W., and JOHN BRITTON, *The Beauties of England and Wales*. 18 vols., 1801–16.

BREFFNY, BRIAN DE, and ROSEMARY FFOLLIOTT, *The Houses of Ireland*, 1975.

BRITTON, JOHN (ed.), *The Original Picture of London* [1828].

BROCKMAN, H.A.N. *The Caliph of Fonthill*, 1956.

BROWN, RICHARD, *Domestic Architecture*, 1841.

BURKE, EDMUND, *A Philosophical Enquiry into the Origin of our Ideas of the Sublime and the Beautiful*, 1757; ed. J.T. Boulton, 1958.

BYNG, JOHN, VISCOUNT TORRINGTON, *The Torrington Diaries*, ed. C. Bruyn Andrews, 4 vols., 1934.

CAMBRY, JACQUES DE, *De Londres et ses Environs*, 1788.

CARMONTELLE, LOUIS DE, *Jardin de Monceau, près de Paris . . .*, 1779.

CARPINI, JOHN DE PLANO, *The Texts and Versions of John de Plano Carpini and William de Rubruquis*, ed. C.R. Beazley, Hakluyt Soc., 1903.

CARSTENENSEN, G. J. B., and C. GILDEMEISTER, *The New York Crystal Palace*, New York 1854.

CHAMBERS, SIR WILLIAM, *Designs of Chinese Buildings, Furniture, Dresses, Machines and Utensils . . .*, 1757.

A Dissertation on Oriental Gardening, 1772.

Plans, elevations, Sections and Perspective Views of The Gardens And Buildings At Kew in Surry, 1763.

CHOPPIN DE JANVRY, Olivier, 'Desert de Retz', *L'Oeil*, Sep. 1767, pp. 30–41, 80, and B.S.H.A.F., 1970.

Le Pavillon Chinois de Cassan, l'Isle-Adam, (pamphlet), La Revue Française, 1975.

CLARK., H. F. 'Eighteenth-Century Elysiums', *Journal of the Warburg and Courtauld Institutes*, 6, 1943, pp. 165–89.

COLLIS, MAURICE, *The Great Within*, 1941.

The Grand Peregrination . . . The life and adventures of Fernão Mendes Pinto, 1949.

COLVIN, HOWARD, *A Biographical Dictionary of British Architects, 1600–1840*, revised ed., 1978.

CONSTABLE, JOHN, *John Constable's Correspondence*, ed. R. B. Beckett, 6 vols., 1962–68.

COOPER, NICHOLAS, 'Indian Architecture in England, 1780–1830', *Apollo*, Aug. 1970, pp. 124–33.

CORDIER, HENRI, *La Chine en France au XVIIe siecle*, Paris, 1910.

CORNFORTH, JOHN, 'Fairmount Park, Philadelphia – II', *Country Life*, 18 Jan. 1973, pp. 150–53.

COSTA-TÔRRES, Raúl da, *Arquitectura dos descobrimentos e o renascimento iberico*, Braga, 1943.

COTTON, EVAN, 'The Hindu Temple at Melchet Park', *Bengal Past and Present*, XL (Oct.–Dec. 1930), pp. 71–78.

COXE, REV. WILLIAM, *Travels into Poland, Russia, Sweden and Denmark*, 3 vols., 1784–90.

CRAIG, MAURICE, 'The Palaces of Tsarskoe Selo', *Country Life*, 20 Jan. 1966, pp. 108–12.

CRANMER-BYNG, J.L. (ed.), *An Embassy to China, Lord Macartney's Journal*, 1962.

CROFT-MURRAY, EDWARD, 'The Palazzina Cinese at Palermo', *Country Life*, 10 Oct. 1947, pp. 724–25.

Decorative Painting in England 1537–1837, 2 vols., 1962 and 1970.

CROOK, JOSEPH MORDAUNT, *The Greek Revival: Neoclassical Attitudes in British Architecture 1760–1870*, 1972.

DALE, ANTONY, *James Wyatt*, Oxford, 1956.

Fashionable Brighton 1820–1860, 1967.

'The Architecture of Amusement', in Simon H. Adamson, *Seaside Piers*, 1977.

DANIELL, THOMAS AND WILLIAM, *Oriental Scenery*, 6 vols., 1795–1808.

A Picturesque Voyage to India by the Way of China, 1810.

DANIS, ROBERT, *La Première Maison Royale de Trianon, 1670–1687*, Paris, 1926.

DAVIS, JOHN FRANCIS, *The Chinese: a general description of the Empire of China and its inhabitants*, 2 vols., 1836.

DAVIS, TERENCE, *John Nash, The Prince Regent's Architect*, 1966; revised ed., Newton Abbot, 1973.

DECKER, PAUL, *Chinese Architecture Civil and Ornamental*, 1759.

DEFOE, DANIEL, *A Tour thro' the Whole Island of Great Britain . . .*, 3 vols., 1724–27; 3rd ed., 1742.

DÉZALLIER D'ARGENVILLE, ANTOINE NICOLAS, *Voyage Pittoresque des Environs de Paris*, 1755; 3rd (enlarged) ed., 1768.

DOWNING, ANDREW JACKSON, *Landscape Gardening*, 1841.

The Architecture of Country Houses, 1861.

DRUETT, WALTER W., *The Stanmores of Harrow Weald through the Ages*, 1938.

DU HALDE, JEAN-BAPTISTE, *Description . . . de la Chine*, Paris, 1735.

The General History of China, tr. R. Brookes, 4 vols., 1736.

A Description of the Empire of China and Chinese-Tartary . . ., 2 vols, 1741.

EBERLEIN, H. D., and C. HUBBARD, *Portrait of a Colonial City, Philadelphia*, 1939.

EDGEWORTH, MARIA, *The Absentee*, 1812; *Castle Rackrent and The Absentee*, 1960.

EDWARDS, R., and MATTHEW DARLY, *A New Book of Chinese Designs*, 1754.

ELLIS, HENRY, *A Journal of the Proceedings of the Late Embassy to China*, 1818.

ELMES, JAMES, *Metropolitan Improvements*, 1829.

ELSAM, RICHARD, *An Essay on Rural Architecture*, 1803.

ERDDBERG, ELEANOR VON, *Chinese Influence on European Garden Structures*, Cambridge, Mass., 1936.

ERREDGE, J.A. *History of Brighthelmstone*, 1862.

ESSEX, JAMES, 'Tour into Nottinghamshire, Wiltshire . . .', British Museum Add. MSS 6767.

EVANS, JOAN, *Pattern. A study of ornament in Western Europe from 1180 to 1900*, 2 vols., Oxford, 1931.

EVELYN, JOHN, *The Diary of John Evelyn*, ed. E.S. de Beer, 6 vols., Oxford, 1955.

FARINGTON, JAMES, *The Farington Diary*, ed. J. Grieg, 8 vols., 1922–28, and typescript of complete MSS in British Museum Print Room.

FARRER, WILLIAM, *The History of Ripon*, 2nd ed., 1806.

FEAVER, WILLIAM, *John Martin*, Oxford, 1975.

FÉLIBIEN DES AVAUX, JEAN FRANÇOIS, *Déscription sommaire du Chateau de Versailles*, Paris, 1674.

FERRAR, JOHN, *A View of Ancient and Modern Dublin . . . to which is added a Tour to Bellevue in the County of Wicklow*, 1796.

FISCHER VON ERLACH, JOHN BERNARD, *A Plan of Civil and Historical Architecture . . .*, trans. Thomas Lediard, 1730.

FLEMING, JOHN, *Robert Adam and his Circle in Edinburgh and Rome*, 1962, reprinted 1978.

FOULSTON, JOHN, *The Public Buildings erected in the West of England . . .*, 1838.

GALLET, MICHEL, *Paris Domestic Architecture of the Eighteenth Century*, 1972.

GANDY, JOSEPH, 'On the Philosophy of Architecture', *Magazine of the Fine Arts*, 1821, p. 292.

GARDNER, BELLAMY, 'Duke William's Chinese Yacht', *Connoisseur*, Mar. 1948, pp. 22–25.

[GILPIN, REV WILLIAM], *A Dialogue upon the Gardens of the Right Honourable the Lord Viscount Cobham*, 1748.

GIROUARD, MARK, 'Living in a Folly, *Country Life*, 6 Nov. 1956, pp. 1040–01.

The Victorian Country House, Oxford, 1971.

'A Young Architect in Kent', *Country Life*, 30 Aug. 1973, pp. 554–58.

Sweetness and Light, The 'Queen Anne' Movement 1860–1900, Oxford, 1977.

GLOAG, M. R., *A Book of English Gardens*, 1906.

GRANVILLE, AUGUSTUS BOZZI, *St Petersburgh. A journal of travels . . .*, 2 vols., 1828; 2nd (enlarged) ed., 1829.

GREVILLE, CHARLES C. F., *The Greville Memoirs 1814–1860*, ed. L. Strachey and R. Fulford, 8 vols., 1938.

GREY, JEMIMA, 'The Marchioness Grey of Wrest Park', ed. Joyce Godber, *Bedfordshire Historical Record Society*, vol. 47, 1968.

HAKLUYT, RICHARD, *The Principall Navigations, Voiages and Discoveries of the English nation, made by Sea or ouer Land*, 1598.

The Principal Navigations Voyages Traffiques & Discoveries of the English Nation, 12 vols., Hakluyt Soc., Glasgow, 1903–05.

HALFPENNY, WILLIAM, *Rural Architecture in the Chinese Taste*, 4 pts (comprising *New Designs for Chinese Temples . . . Bridges . . . Doors . . . Gates*, the last three parts in collaboration with John Halfpenny), 1750–52.

HALFPENNY, WILLIAM AND JOHN, *Chinese and Gothic Architecture Properly Ornamented*, 1752.

The Country Gentleman's pocket companion and builder's assistant, 1753.

HALFPENNY, WILLIAM AND JOHN, ROBERT MORRIS, AND TIMOTHY LIGHTOLER, *The Modern Builder's Assistant*, 1757.

HAMILTON, GEORGE H. *The Art and Architecture of Russia*, Harmondsworth, 1954.

HANDLEY-READ, LAVINIA, 'Legacy of a Vanished Empire', *Country Life*, 9 July 1970, pp. 110–12.

HANWAY, JONAS, *A Journal of Eight Days Journey from Portsmouth to Kingston-upon-Thames . . .*, 2 vols., 1757.

HARRIS, EILEEN, 'Thomas Wright' I–III, *Country Life*, 1971, pp. 492–95, 546–50, 612–15.

'Burke and Chambers on the Sublime

and Beautiful', in *Essays in the History of Architecture presented to Rudolf Wittkower*, e. Fraser, Hibberd and Lewine, 1967.

HARRIS, JOHN, 'Exoticism at Kew', *Apollo*, Aug. 1963, pp. 103–08.

'Fonthill, Wiltshire, I: Alderman Beckford's Houses', *Country Life*, 24 Nov. 1966, pp. 1370–74.

'English Country House Guides, 1740–1840', in *Concerning Architecture*, ed. J. Summerson, Harmondsworth, 1968.

Sir William Chambers. Knight of the Polar Star, 1970.

'Painter of Rococo Gardens: Thomas Robins the Elder', *Country Life*, 7 Sep. 1972, pp. 551–54.

HAUPT, ALBRECHT, *Die Baukunst der Renaissance in Portugal. . .* 2 Bde, FRANKFURT, 1890, 1895.

HAWKES, W. 'Miller's Work at Wroxton', *Cake and Cockhorse*, Banbury History Society, 1969 (iv), pp. 99–106.

HAYDEN, PETER, 'Edward Cooke at Biddulph Grange', *Garden History*, VI, no. 1, Spring 1978.

HÉNARD, ROBERT, *Les Jardins et Les Squares de Paris*, 1911.

HÉRÉ DE CORNY, Emmanuel, *Recueil des Plans, Elévations et Coupes . . . des Chateaux Jardins . . .* 1753.

HERRMAN, WOLFGANG, *Laugier and Eighteenth Century Theory*, 1962.

HIBBERT, CHRISTOPHER, *The Dragon Wakes*, 1970.

HIRSCHFELD, C. C. L., *Théorie de l'art des Jardins*, 6 vols., Leipzig, 1779–85.

HODGES, WILLIAM, *Select Views in India drawn on the spot, in the years 1780, 1781, 1782, and 1783*, n.d. (plates published 1785–88).

A Dissertation on the Prototypes of Architecture, Hindoo, Moorish and Gothic, 1787.

Travels in India During the years 1780, 1781, 1782 and 1783, 1793.

HOGARTH, WILLIAM, *The Analysis of Beauty*, 1753.

The Analysis of Beauty. With the rejected passages from the manuscript drafts and autobiographical notes, ed. Joseph Burke, Oxford, 1955.

HONOUR, HUGH, *Chinoiserie: The Vision of Cathay*, 1961.

HOPE, THOMAS, *Household Furniture and Interior Design executed from Designs by Thomas Hope*, 1807; Reprinted, 1970.

HORSFIELD, THOMAS WALKER, *The History, Antiquities and Topography of the County of Sussex*, 2 vols., 1835.

HUDSON, GEOFFREY F., *Europe and China. A survey of their relations from the earliest times to 1800 . . .*, 1931.

HUSSEY, CHRISTOPHER, 'Sezincote, Gloucestershire', I–II, *Country Life*, 1939, pp. 502–06, 528–32.

'Shugborough, Staffordshire', I–III, *Country Life* 1954, pp. 510–13, 590–93, 676–79.

JACKSON, STANLEY, *The Sassoons*, 1968.

'JARDINS EN FRANCE 1760–1820', exhibition catalogue, Caisse Nationale des Monuments Historiques et des Sites, Paris, 1977.

KENNETT, VICTOR AND AUDREY, *The Palaces of Leningrad*, 1973.

KIRCHER, ATHANASIUS, *A. Kircheri China monumentis . . .*, Amsterdam, 1667.

Special remarks taken at large out of A. Kircher's Antiquities of China, printed with Jan Nieuhof, *An Embassy to . . . China*, tr. J. Ogilby, 1669.

KNIGHT, RICHARD PAYNE, *The Landscape, A Didactic poem*, 1794.

An Analytical Inquiry into the Principles of Taste, 4th ed., 1808.

KNIGHT, WILLIAM, *Memorials of Coleorton*, 2 vols., 1887.

KRAFFT, JOHANN-CARL, *Plans des Plus Beaux Jardins Pittoresques de France, d'Angleterre et d'Allemagne . . .*, 2 vols., Paris, 1809, 1810.

Recueil d'Architecture Civile, Paris, 1812.

LABORDE, ALEXANDRE, L. J. DE *Nouveaux Jardins de la France et ses Anciens Chateaux*, 1808.

LACH, DONALD F., *Asia in the making of Europe*, 2 vols., Chicago and London, 1965 and 1970.

LAMB, CHARLES, 'The Last Essays of Elia', in *The Life, Letters and Writings of Charles Lamb*, ed. P. Fitzgerald, 1876, vol. 4.

LANCASTER, CLAY, 'Oriental Forms in American Architecture 1800–1870', *Art Bulletin*, XXXIX, 1947, pp. 183 ff.

LANG, S., 'The Genesis of the Landscape Garden', in *The Picturesque Garden and its Influence outside the British Isles*, ed. Sir N. Pevsner, Dumbarton Oaks, 1974.

LANGDON, WILLIAM B., *A Descriptive Catalogue of the Chinese Collection . . .*, 1842.

LANGLEY, BATTY, *Gothic Architecture Improved . . .*, 1747.

LAUGIER, MARC ANTOINE, *Essai sur l'Architecture*, Paris, 1753; 2nd ed., 1755.

LAWSON, SIR CHARLES A., *The Private Life of Warren Hastings*, 2nd ed., 1905.

LE COMTE, LOUIS DANIEL, *Memoirs and Observations . . . made in a late Journey through the Empire of China*, 1699.

LE ROUGE, GEORGES, *Détails des nouveaux jardins à la mode* (some volumes entitled *Jardins Anglo-Chinois*, etc.), 21 vols., Paris, 1774–89.

LETTS, MALCOLM, *Sir John Mandeville: the man and his book*, 1949.

LEWIS, SAMUEL, *A Topographical Dictionary of England*, 4 vols., 1831; 5th ed., 1842.

LIGHTOLER, TIMOTHY, *The Gentlemen and Farmer's Architect*, 1762.

LIGNE, PRINCE CHARLES J. E. DE, *Coup d'oeil sur Beloeil . . .*, ed. E. de Ganay, Paris, 1922.

LINSCHOTEN, JAN HUYGEN VAN, *Itinerario. Voyage ofte Schipvaert van Jan Huygen van Linschoten . . .*, Amsterdam, 1596.

The Voyage of J. H. van Linschoten to the East Indies (English translation of 1598), ed. A.C. Burrell and P.A. Tiele, 2 vols., Hakluyt Soc., 1885.

LINSTRUM, DEREK, 'Architecture of Cuthbert Brodrick', *Country Life*, 1 June 1967, pp. 1379–81.

Sir Jeffry Wyatville: Architect to the King, Oxford, 1973.

LONGFORD, ELIZABETH, *Victoria R. I.*, 1964.

LOUDON, JOHN CLAUDIUS, *An Encyclopedia of Gardening*, 1822; enlarged eds., 1828, 1835 and 1850.

LOVEJOY, A.C., 'The Chinese Origin of a Romanticism', in *Essays in the History of Ideas*, Baltimore, 1948, pp. 99–135.

LUGAR, ROBERT, *Architectural Sketches for cottages, rural dwellings, and villas . . .*, 1805; reprinted in 1815 and 1823.

MALINS, EDWARD, AND THE KNIGHT OF GLIN, *Lost Demesnes. Irish Landscape Gardening 1660–1845*, 1976.

MALTON, JAMES, *An Essay on British Gothic Architecture*, 1798.

MANDEVILLE, SIR JOHN, *The Travels of Sir John Mandeville. The version of the Cotton Manuscript in modern spelling*, ed. A.W. Pollard from the Cotton MS, 1900, reprint 1964.

Mandeville's Travels. Texts and Translations, ed. Malcolm Letts, Hakluyt Soc., 1953.

MANGER, HEINRICH L., *Baugeschichte von Potsdam*, 1789.

MARSHALL, WILLIAM, *On Planting and Rural Ornament*, 1796.

MASON, WILLIAM, *An Heroic Epistle to Sir William Chambers*, 1773.

Mémoires Concernant l'Histoire, les Sciences, les Arts, les Moeurs, les Usages, etc., des Chinois, Par les Missionaires de Pe-Kin, 15 vols., Paris, 1776–91.

MENDOZA, JUAN GONZALEZ DE, *The Historie of the great and mightie kingdome of China . . .*, tr. Richard Parke, 1588.

MITTER, PARTHA, *Much Maligned Monsters. A History of European Reactions to Indian Art*, Oxford, 1977.

MONCKTON, NORAH, 'Architectural Backgrounds in the Pictures of John Martin', *Architectural Review*, CIV, 1948, pp. 81–84.

MONTANUS, ARNOLDUS, *Atlas Japannensis*, tr. J. Ogilby, 1670.

Atlas Chinensis, tr. J. Ogilby, 1671.

MORRIS, R., *Rural Architecture*, 1750.

The Architectural Remembrancer, 1751.

MOSSER, MONIQUE, *Monsieur Marigny et ses jardins, projets inédits pour Menars*, B.S.H.A.F., 1972.

MUSGRAVE, CLIFFORD, *The Royal Pavilion, an Episode in the Romantic*, 2nd (revised) ed., 1959.

Life in Brighton, 1970.

NIEUHOF, JAN, *An Embassy from the East-India Company of the United Provinces to the Grand Tartar Cham Emperour of China . . .*, tr. J. Ogilby, 1669.

NORTON, PAUL F., 'Daylesford: S.P. Cockerell's Residence for Warren Hastings', *Journal of the Society of Architectural Historians*, XXII, Oct. 1963, pp. 127–29.

O'BRIEN, HENRY, *The Round Towers of Ireland*, 2nd ed., 1834.

ORME, WILLIAM, *Twenty Four Views of Hindostan*, 1808.

ORTA, GARCIA DA, *Colloquies on the Simples and Drugs of India*, tr. Sir C. Markham, 1913.

OSBORNE, DOROTHY, *The Letters of Dorothy Osborne to William Temple*, ed. G. C. Moore-Smith, Oxford, 1928.

OVER, CHARLES, *Ornamental Architecture in the Gothic, Chinese, and Modern Taste*, n.d., [*c.* 1758].

PAPWORTH, WYATT, *J. B. Papworth, Architect to the King of Wurtemburg*, 1879.

PASCAL, GEORGES, *Histoire du Chateau de Bagatelle*, Paris, 1921.

PASQUIN, ANTHONY [John Williams], *The New Brighton Guide*, 6th ed., 1796.

PEACOCK, THOMAS LOVE, *Headlong Hall* (1815), in *The Works of T. L. Peacock* (Halliford Edition), 10 vols., 1924–34, vol. I.

PENNANT, THOMAS, *The Journey from Chester to London*, 1782; Dublin, 1783.

Views of Hindostan, 1798.

PEPYS, SAMUEL, *The Diary of Samuel Pepys*, ed. R. Latham and W. Matthews, 11 vols., 1970–.

PEVSNER, SIR NIKOLAUS, 'The Genesis of the Picturesque', *Architectural Review*, XCVI, 1944; reprinted in N. Pevsner, *Studies in Art, Architecture and Design*, 1968, vol. I, pp. 78–101.

London, I, 'Buildings of England' series, 3rd ed., (revised by Bridget Cherry), Harmondsworth, 1973.

(with S. Lang) 'A Note on Sharawaggi', *Architectural Review*, CVI, 1949; reprinted in N. Pevsner, *Studies in Art, Architecture and Design*, 1968, vol. I, pp. 102–07.

PEVSNER, SIR NIKOLAUS (ed.), *The Picturesque Garden and its Influence outside the British Isles*, Dumbarton Oaks, 1974.

PILLEMENT, JEAN, *The Ladies Amusement; or, whole Art of Japanning made easy*, n.d. [*c.* 1765].

PINKERTON, JOHN, *A General Collection of the Best and Most Interesting Voyages . . .*, 17 vols., 1808–14.

PINTO, FERNÃO MENDES, *His Travels in the Kingdoms of Ethiopia, China, Tartaria*, tr. Henry Cogan, 1653.

POCOCKE, BISHOP RICHARD, *Travels thro' England of Dr. Richard Pococke*, ed. James Joel Cartwright, 2 vols., Camden Society, 1888 and 1889.

POLO, MARCO, *The Travels of Marco Polo*, tr. William Marsden, ed. Thomas Wright, 1854.

The Most Noble and famous Travels of Marco Polo, tr. John Frampton, ed. N. M. Penzer, 1929.

PORTER, HENRY C., *The History of Hove*, 1897.

POTTER, ROBERT W. F., *A Hampshire Harvest: A Traveller's Notebook*, 1977.

POWYS, MRS PHILLIP LYBBE, *Passages from the Diaries of Mrs Phillip Lybbe Powys*, ed. E. J. Climenson, 1899.

PÜCKLER-MUSKAU, PRINCE HERMANN L. H. VON, *A Tour in England, Ireland and France, in the Years 1826, 1827, 1828 & 1829 . . . by a German Prince*, tr. Sarah Austin, 1832; revised ed., Zurich, 1940.

A Regency Visitor, The English Tour of Prince Pückler-Muskau described in his Letters 1826–28, ed. E.M. Butler, 1957.

PUGIN, AUGUSTUS WELBY NORTHMORE, *The True Principles of Pointed or Christian Architecture*, 1841.

PURCHAS, SAMUEL THE ELDER, *Purchas his Pilgrimage*, 1613.

Purchas his Pilgrimes, 4 vols., 1625.

Hakluytus Posthumus; or, Purchas his Pilgrimes, 20 vols., Hakluyt Soc., Glasgow, 1905–07.

RAE, ISOBEL, *Charles Cameron*, 1971.

REICHWEIN, ADOLF, *China and Europe: intellectual and artistic contacts in the eighteenth century*, tr. J. C. Powell, 1925 (reissued 1968).

REPTON, HUMPHRY, *Observations on the Theory and Practice of Landscape Gardening*, 1803.

An Enquiry into the Changes of Taste in Landscape Gardening, 1806.

Designs for the Pavillon at Brighton, 1808.

Fragments on the Theory and Practice of Landscape-Gardening, 1816.

The Landscape Gardening and Landscape Architecture of the late Humphry Repton, Esq., ed. J. C. Loudon, 1840.

REYNOLDS, SIR JOSHUA, *Discourses on Art*, ed. R. R. Wark, 1959; New Haven, 1975.

RIPA, MATTEO, *The Memoirs of Father Ripa*, tr. Fortunato Prandi, 1844.

ROBINSON, WILLIAM, *The Parks and Gardens of Paris*, 2nd ed., 1878.

ROTH, CECIL, *The Sassoon Dynasty*, 1941.

ROUQUET, JEAN ANDRÉ, *The Present State of the Arts in England*, 1755.

ROWAN, ALISTAIR, *Garden Buildings*, R.I.B.A. Drawings Series, 1968.

ROYAL INSTITUTE OF BRITISH ARCHITECTS, *Catalogue of the Drawings Collection of the R.I.B.A.*, 1968.

RUBRUQUIS, WILLIAM DE, *The Texts and Versions of John de Plano Carpini and William de Rubruquis*, ed. C.R. Beazley, Hakluyt Soc., 1903.

RUSKIN, JOHN, *The Stones of Venice*, in *The Complete Works of John Ruskin*, ed. E.T. Cook and A. Wedderburn, 39 vols., 1903–12, vols. 9–11.

SANTOS, REINALDO DOS, *L'Art Portuguais*, Paris, 1953.

SCHUYLER, MONTGOMERY, 'A Great American Architect: Leopold Eidlitz', *Architectural Record*, 24, no. 3, Sep. 1908.

[SEELEY, BENTON], *A Description of the Garden of Lord Viscount Cobham at Stow in Buckinghamshire*, 1744.

SEMEDO, ALVAREZ, *The History of that great and renowned Monarchy of China*, 1655.

SETTERWALL, AKE, *et al.*, *The Chinese Pavilion at Drottningholm*, Malmö, 1977.

[SHAKESPEARE, WILLIAM], *The Fairy-Queen: an Opera. Represented at the Queen's-Theatre by Their Majesties Servants*, 1692.

SHEBBEARE, JOHN, *Letters on the English Nation*, 1756.

SHERATON, THOMAS, *The Cabinet maker and Upholsterer's Drawing Book and Repository*, 1793; ed. Joseph Aronson, 1973.

SIRÉN, OSVALD, *The Imperial Palaces of Peking*, 3 vols., G. van Oest, Paris and Brussels, 1928.

Gardens of China, New York, 1949.

China and Gardens of Europe of the Eighteenth Century, New York, 1950.

SLOAN, SAMUEL, *The Model Architect*, 2 vols., 1852.

SMOLLETT, TOBIAS, *The Expedition of Humphry Clinker*, 1771; Harmondsworth, 1967.

SONNERAT, PIERRE, *A Voyage to the East Indies and China . . . between the years 1774 and 1781 . . .*, tr. F. Magnus, 3 vols., Calcutta, 1788, 1789.

SPENCE, JOSEPH, *Observations, Anecdotes, and Characters of Books and Men*, ed. J. M. Osborn, 2 vols., Oxford, 1966.

STALKER, JOHN, AND GEORGE PARKER, *A Treatise on Japanning and Varnishing*, 1688.

STAUNTON, SIR GEORGE L., *An Authentic Account of an Embassy from the King of Great Britain to the Emperor of China*, 2 vols., 1797.

STROUD, DOROTHY, *Humphry Repton*, 1962.

'The Novelty of the Guildhall Façade', *Country Life*, 2 Apr. 1964, pp. 770–71.

Henry Holland, 1966.

George Dance, Architect, 1741–1825, 1971.

STUEBE, ISABEL, 'William Hodges and Warren Hastings: A study in eighteenth-century patronage', *Burlington Magazine*, CXV, Oct. 1973, pp. 659–66.

SULLIVAN, RICHARD, J., *Observations made during a Tour through Parts of England, Scotland, and Wales, in a Series of Letters*, 1780; reprinted with alterations in William F. Mayor, *The British Tourists*, 6 vols., 1798–1810, vol. 3.

SUMMERSON, SIR JOHN, 'The Vision of J. M. Gandy', in *Heavenly Mansions*, 1949.

John Nash, revised ed., 1949.

SUTTON, THOMAS, *The Daniells: Artists and Travellers*, 1954.

SWITZER, STEPHEN, *Ichnographia Rustica*, 1718.

TEMPLE, SIR WILLIAM, *The Works of Sir William Temple, Bart*, 2 vols., 1740.

THROSBY, JOHN, *Select Views in Leicestershire . . .*, 2 vols., 1790–92.

[TWICKENHAM], *A Short Account of the Principal Seats and Gardens in and about Twickenham*, 1760.

VASSALL, ELIZABETH, BARONESS HOLLAND, *Elizabeth, Lady Holland to her Son 1821–1845*, ed. Earl of Ilchester, 1946.

[VAUXHALL GARDENS], *A Sketch of the Spring Gardens, Vaux-Hall*, printed for G. Woodfall, n.d. [*c.* 1755].

A Brief Historical and Descriptive Account of the Royal Gardens, Vauxhall, published by the proprietors, 1822.

VICTORIA, QUEEN, *The Letters of Queen Victoria*, ed. A.C. Benson and Viscount Esher, 3 vols., 1908.

WALPOLE, HORACE, *Anecdotes of Painting in England*, ed. R.N. Wornum, 3 vols., 1849.

'The History of the Modern Taste in Gardening', in I. Chase, *Horace Walpole: Gardenist*, Princeton, 1943.

The Works of Horatio Walpole, 9 vols., 1798–1825.

The Yale Edition of Horace Walpole's Correspondence, ed. W. S. Lewis, 39 vols., New Haven, 1937–74.

WARD-JACKSON, PETER, *English Furniture Designers of the Eighteenth Century*, Victoria and Albert Museum, 1958.

WATELET, CLAUDE HENRI, *Essai sur les Jardins*, Paris, 1774.

WATKIN, DAVID, *Thomas Hope 1769–1831 and the Neo-classical Idea*, 1968.

WATSON, WALTER CRUM, *Portuguese Architecture*, 1908.

WATSON, WILLIAM (ed.), *Colloquia on Art and Archaeology in Asia*, no. 3, 1972.

WEINHARDT, CARL J., JNR, 'The Indian Taste', *Metropolitan Museum of Art Bulletin*, n.s. XVI, Mar. 1958, pp. 208–16.

WERNER, MORRIS R., *P. T. Barnum*, 1923.

WHATELY, THOMAS, *Observations on Modern Gardening*, 1770.

WIGHTWICK, GEORGE, *The Palace of Architecture*, 1840.

Windsor and its Environs, 1768.

WITTKOWER, RUDOLF, *Palladio and English Palladianism*, 1974.

WOLSELEY, LT-COL. G. J., *Narrative of the War at China in 1860*, 1862.

WRIGHT, REV. GEORGE N., *China in a Series of Views . . .*, 4 vols., 1843.

WRIGHTE, WILLIAM, *Grotesque Architecture, or, Rural Amusement*, 1767.

YORKE, PHILIP (2nd Earl of Hardwicke), 'Journal of What I Observed Most Remarkable in a Tour to the North', in J. Godber, 'The Marchioness Grey of Wrest Park', *Bedfordshire Historical Record Society*, vol. 47, 1968.

YOUNG, ARTHUR, *A Six-Months Tour through the North of England*, 4 vols., 1770.

Travels during the Years 1787, 1788 and 1789 (in) . . . France, 1792.

YULE, SIR HENRY, AND HENRI CORDIER, *Cathay and the Way Thither*, 4 vols., Hakluyt Soc., 1913–16.

List of Illustrations

69 Henry Holland's design for a Chinese façade at the Royal Pavilion, 1801. Reproduced by gracious permission of Her Majesty the Queen.

70 Henry Holland's designs for buildings on the royal estate at Brighton, 1802. Royal Pavilion, Art Gallery and Museums, Brighton.

71 and 72 Alternative styles of gardening. Engravings by Thomas Hearne from Richard Payne Knight, *The Landscape, a Didactic Poem*, 1794.

73 Indian architecture as portrayed in Jan Huygen van Linschoten, *Itinerario . . .*, 1596.

74 'View of the Musjid at Jionpoor'. Engraving from W. Hodges, *Select Views in India*, 1785–88. India Office Library, London.

75 The Guildhall, London. Photo the author.

76 George Dance's executed design for the eastern gateway, Stratton Park, Hampshire. Reproduced by permission of the Trustees of Sir John Soane's Museum, London. Photo courtesy of the Courtauld Institute of Art.

77 'The Temple at Melchet Park'. Aquatint drawn and engraved by W. Daniell, 1802. India Office Library, London.

78 'An Ancient Hindoo Temple, in the Fort of Rotas, Bahar'. Aquatint from T. & W. Daniell, *Oriental Scenery*, 1795–1808, 1st series. Brighton Reference Library.

79 The Indian Room. Engraving from Thomas Hope, *Household Furniture and Interior Design*, 1807. British Architectural Library, RIBA, London.

80 Gate of the Lahl Baug, Faizabad. Aquatint from T. & W. Daniell, *Oriental Scenery*, 1795–1808, 4th series. Brighton Reference Library.

81 South front and garden, Sezincote, Gloucestershire. Aquatint drawn and engraved by John Martin, 1817. Royal Pavilion, Art Gallery and Museums, Brighton.

82 The bridge, Sezincote, Gloucestershire. Aquatint drawn and engraved by John Martin, 1817. Royal Pavilion, Art Gallery and Museums, Brighton.

83 The temple pool, Sezincote, Gloucestershire. Aquatint drawn and engraved by John Martin. Royal Pavilion, Art Gallery and Museums, Brighton.

84 Farm buildings, Sezincote, Gloucestershire. Aquatint drawn and engraved by John Martin, 1817. Royal Pavilion, Art Gallery and Museums, Brighton.

85 Cottage at Lower Swell, Gloucestershire. Photo National Monuments Record, London.

86 The stable block, Hope End, Hereford and Worcester. Photo Country Life.

87 Design for a conservatory by G. S. Repton. Royal Pavilion, Art Gallery and Museums, Brighton.

88 'Belshazzar's Feast'. Mezzotint by John Martin after his painting of 1820. Reproduced by courtesy of the Trustees of the British Museum.

89 Design for 'a large Villa or Mansion' in the Indian style. From Edmund Aikin, *Designs for Villas and other Rural Buildings*, 1808.

90 'Hindoo columns'. Aquatint from H. Repton, *Designs for the Pavillon at Brighton*, 1808. Royal Pavilion, Art Gallery and Museums, Brighton.

91 Unexecuted design by William Porden for Eaton Hall, Cheshire, 1804. Chester Public Library.

92 The Jami' Masjid at Delhi. Aquatint from T. & W. Daniell, *Oriental Scenery*, 1795–1808, 1st series. Royal Pavilion, Art Gallery and Museums, Brighton.

93 'Interior of the Stables at Brighton'. Engraving from John Nash, *Views of the Royal Pavilion*, 1826. Royal Pavilion, Art Gallery and Museums, Brighton.

94 'The Royal Stables at Brighton'. Engraving, 1806. Royal Pavilion, Art Gallery and Museums, Brighton.

95 Design for a Royal Pavilion (east front) in the Chinese style by William Porden, *c*. 1805. Royal Pavilion, Art Gallery and Museums, Brighton.

96 Design for a Royal Pavilion (west front) in the Chinese style by William Porden, *c*. 1805. Royal Pavilion, Art Gallery and Museums, Brighton.

97 'A Front View of the Hall of Audience in the Palace of Yuen-min-yuen.' Engraving after W. Alexander, 1797. Brighton Reference Library.

98 Design for a Royal Pavilion in the Chinese style by William Porden, *c*. 1805. Royal Pavilion, Art Gallery and Museums, Brighton.

99 Design for the west front of the Royal Pavilion, as seen from the Stables. Aquatint from H. Repton, *Designs for the Pavillon at Brighton*, 1808. Royal Pavilion, Art Gallery and Museums, Brighton.

100 Design for the garden pool and gateway of the Royal Pavilion estate. Aquatint from H. Repton, *Designs for the Pavillon at Brighton*, 1808. Royal Pavilion Art Gallery and Museums, Brighton.

101 'View of the Palace in the Fort of Allahabad'. Aquatint from T. & W. Daniell, *Oriental Scenery*, 1795–1808, 1st series. Brighton Reference Library.

102 Design for a Pheasantry at the Royal Pavilion. Aquatint from H. Repton, *Designs for the Pavillon at Brighton*, 1808. Royal Pavilion, Art Gallery and Museums, Brighton.

103 'Hindoo Temples at Bindrabund on the River Jumna'. Aquatint from T. & W. Daniell, *Oriental Scenery*, 1795–1808, 1st series. Brighton Reference Library.

104 Design for an Aviary at the Royal Pavilion. Aquatint from H. Repton, *Designs for the Pavillon at Brighton*, 1808. Royal Pavilion, Art Gallery and Museums, Brighton.

105 'View from the Proposed Private Apartment'. Aquatint from H. Repton, *Designs for the Pavillon at Brighton*, 1808. Royal Pavilion, Art Gallery and Museums, Brighton.

106 The Pagoda in St James's Park. Etching published in 1814 by James Whittle and Richard Laurie. Photo reproduced by kind permission of Sotheby Parke Bernet & Co., London.

107 'The Corridor of the Royal Pavilion at Brighton'. Aquatint after A. C. Pugin, from John Nash, *Views of the Royal Pavilion*,

Index

Page numbers in *italics* refer to illustrations in black and white.
Roman numerals refer to colour plates between pages 32 and 41.